PUBLICATIONS OF THE BUREAU OF BUSINESS
AND ECONOMIC RESEARCH
UNIVERSITY OF CALIFORNIA, LOS ANGELES

Previously published in this series:

THE NATURE OF COMPETITION IN GASOLINE DISTRIBUTION AT
THE RETAIL LEVEL
by Ralph Cassady, Jr., and Wylie L. Jones (1951)

THE PACIFIC COAST MARITIME SHIPPING INDUSTRY, 1930–1948
VOLUME I: AN ECONOMIC PROFILE
by Wytze Gorter and George H. Hildebrand (1952)

THE ROLE OF MERGERS IN THE GROWTH OF LARGE FIRMS
by J. Fred Weston (1953)

THE PACIFIC COAST MARITIME SHIPPING INDUSTRY, 1930–1948
VOLUME II: AN ANALYSIS OF PERFORMANCE
by Wytze Gorter and George H. Hildebrand (1954)

THE MEXICAN PETROLEUM INDUSTRY, 1930–1958
by J. Richard Powell (1956)

THE PERSECUTION OF HUGUENOTS AND FRENCH ECONOMIC
DEVELOPMENT, 1680–1720
by Warren C. Scoville (1960)

"DISGUISED UNEMPLOYMENT" IN UNDERDEVELOPED AREAS
by Yong Sam Cho (1963)

THE DEVELOPMENT OF
THE SPANISH TEXTILE INDUSTRY,
1750-1800

PUBLICATIONS OF THE
BUREAU OF BUSINESS AND ECONOMIC RESEARCH
UNIVERSITY OF CALIFORNIA, LOS ANGELES

THE DEVELOPMENT
OF THE SPANISH
TEXTILE INDUSTRY,
1750-1800

BY

James Clayburn La Force, Jr.

UNIVERSITY OF CALIFORNIA PRESS

BERKELEY AND LOS ANGELES

1965

UNIVERSITY OF CALIFORNIA PRESS
BERKELEY AND LOS ANGELES

CAMBRIDGE UNIVERSITY PRESS
LONDON, ENGLAND

PRINTED IN THE UNITED STATES OF AMERICA

To
BARBARA, JESSICA, and ALLISON

The opinions expressed in this study are those of the author. The functions of the Bureau of Business and Economic Research are confined to facilitating the prosecution of independent scholarly research by members of the faculty.

Preface

Inspiration for this study emerged out of stimulating discussions in Professor Warren C. Scoville's seminar in European Economic History at the University of California, Los Angeles, during the fall of 1958. Although my proposal originally called for an investigation into the industrial growth of Spain during the last half of the eighteenth century, a few months in the Spanish archives convinced me that a focus on the textile industry of that period would prove more manageable for an initial project.

Directing my research to this narrower province, I became increasingly aware that the textile industry had been the center of a concerted drive by the kings of Spain to induce industrial expansion. Here was an early attempt by a government to marshal the resources of its land and expedite economic progress. Out of this effort evolved a comprehensive program, embracing nearly all aspects of Spain's commercial and industrial life. But critical errors of omission and commission weakened the usefulness of the king's efforts, and the consequent developments fell short of expectations.

It is not my wish to impute from this research a "correct" policy for the underdeveloped nations of our day. Rather, my purpose is merely to add another study of a government's endeavor to promote growth to other investigations already in existence. From this larger sample other economists may make generalizations regarding the efficacy of alternative programs of economic development.

The completion of this volume owes much to many persons who have generously given their time, counsel, criticism, and other assistance during the various stages of research and writing. To Warren C. Scoville I shall forever be indebted. My decision to specialize in economic history stemmed primarily from the stimulating, satisfying classes and discussions that I have had with him. Furthermore, it was at his urging that I initially became interested in the Iberian Peninsula's past as a dissertation topic. He later assisted in arranging financial assistance for a year's research in Spain, gave strong encouragement during those hectic, sometimes bewildering, first months in the Spanish archives, and followed my progress with interest and solicitude at all times while I remained in Europe. When time came to read the various drafts of the chapters, Professor Scoville found time to criticize and edit my words without delay or complaint. Although I found his aid invaluable and appreciated his efforts at the time, only now do I fully realize, and thus more completely prize, the extent of his sacrifice. Other members of the Department of Economics at the University of California, Los Angeles, also read the manuscript at various stages and offered constructive criticism—to Professors Dudley F. Pegrum and Robert Baldwin I offer my thanks.

Archivists, librarians, and other employees of the National History Archives at Madrid, the Archives of the Secretary of the Hacienda at Madrid, the General Archives of Simancas, the Archives of the College of the Greater Art of Silk at Valencia, the Archives of the City of Barcelona, the Archives of the Kingdom of Aragon, the National Library at Madrid, and the Municipal Library at Barcelona likewise generously fostered my efforts. Antonio Matilla Tascón, Director of the Archives of the Secretary of the Hacienda, and José Serra Roselló, of the Archives of the City of Barcelona, were especially helpful at all times. Luis Chapa and Vicente Ruiz, president and secretary, respectively, of the College of the Greater Art of Silk at Valencia, graciously permitted me to inspect the records of their organization. I should also like to thank the personnel of the Interlibrary Loan Section of the library at the University of California, Los Angeles, for their patient, continuing, and efficient aid in obtaining numerous rare books.

Although I have never personally met Professor Earl J. Hamilton, I am well acquainted with his many articles and monumental volumes on Spanish economic history. My debt to him and his works is enormous. Professor Hamilton's insights into the past of Spain, the depth of his research in Spanish banking and monetary history, and his extensive bibliography all proved invaluable aids. Perhaps of equal importance, he left a splendid legacy in Spain for all scholars to follow; Spanish archivists still speak with awe and respect of the intensity, duration, and fruitfulness of his labors in the archives and libraries.

I am grateful to three academic journals for their permission to reproduce wholly or partially the following:

1. *Journal of Economic History* for "Royal Textile Factories in Spain, 1700–1800."
2. *Technology and Culture* for "Technological Diffusion in the 18th Century: The Spanish Textile Industry."
3. *Explorations in Entrepreneurial History* for "Royal Joint Stock Companies in Spain, 1700–1800."

To the Social Science Research Council I offer my sincere gratitude for two Research Training Fellowships, which made possible a year's research in Spain and another year's labor in this country. My thanks also go to the Bureau of Business and Economic Research, University of California, Los Angeles, for its generous assistance in preparing the manuscript for publication. Its director, Ralph Cassady, Jr., and its administrative assistant, Miss Patricia Hay, have cheerfully and liberally given their time and valuable counsel. To them I shall forever be indebted. I likewise thank Mrs. Teresa Joseph and Mr. Robert Aubey for their efficient editorial assistance.

Without the unceasing devotion, encouragement, and resoluteness of my wife, Barbara Lea La Force, through several austere years, this volume would never have been completed, let alone begun. And the constant support and encouragement of my mother and father likewise eased the task of completing this project.

Contents

Table of Equivalents

Money	Equivalent
Vellon real	About 20 United States cents in 1792
Maravedis	34 equaled a vellon real
Escudo	37 vellon reals and 22 maravedis
Doubloon	2 escudos
Ducat	375 maravedis
Vellon peso	15 vellon reals and 2 maravedis

Weights and measures	
Arroba	25 pounds
Fanega	55 liters
Vara	About 33 inches
League	About 4.4 miles

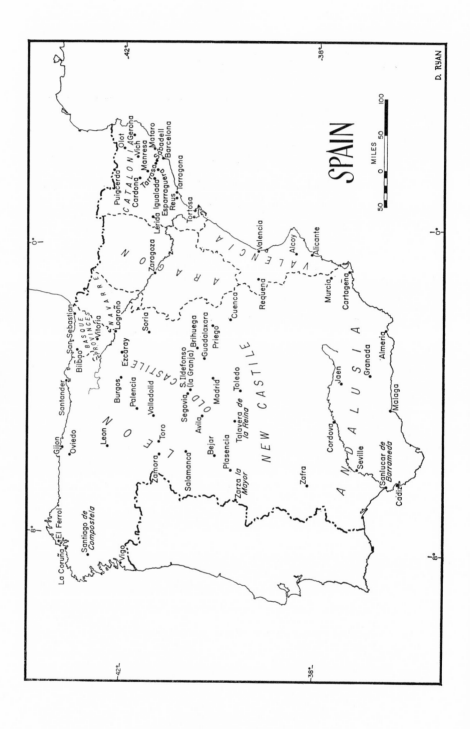

SPAIN

MILES

D. RYAN

I

Introduction

From its inception during the Stone Age to the present, the manufacture of textiles has been in the vanguard of economic change. This was especially true during the last half of the eighteenth century. For these years witnessed a marked increase in the output of cloth, particularly of cotton fabrics in England, and prophesied revolutionary growth for the future. It was a time of rapid advances in technology, of the establishment of true factories, and of the introduction of large-scale production. Many writers have suggested that Spain experienced comparably swift industrialization during those fifty years as she responded to economic policies of the Bourbon kings and to other favorable circumstances.[1] This economic surge supposedly reëstablished her textile industry to its once renowned position.

Spain's power, prestige, and wealth had reached their zenith earlier during the reigns of Charles I and Philip II. Vast areas of the earth's surface were under her command, gold and silver enriched her treasury, and her industry flourished, nurtured by a populous colonial market. Suddenly all of this began to slip away. Nothing that Philip III, Philip IV, or Charles II did in the seventeenth century could halt a disastrous loss of power, prestige, and wealth. Seldom has so powerful a nation experienced so great, so ruinous, and so humiliating a decline in a period of only one hundred years.

Her fortunes lay crumpled about her on November 1, 1700, when Charles II died without an heir, thus ending the Hapsburg dynasty in Spain. Selected as the first Bourbon king to reign south

---

[1] For examples, see: Earl J. Hamilton, *War and Prices in Spain, 1651–1800* (Cambridge, Massachusetts, 1947), pp. 220–225; Richard Herr, *The Eighteenth Century Revolution in Spain* (Princeton, New Jersey, 1958), pp. 134–147; Manuel Colmeiro y Penido, *Historia de la Economía Política en España*, 2 vols. (Madrid, 1863), II, 221; Antonio Joseph Cavanilles, *Observaciones sobre la Historia Natural, Geografía, Agricultura, Población y Frutos del Reyno de Valencia*, 2 vols. (Madrid, 1795), I, 24.

of the Pyrenees, Philip of Anjou was confronted with a dejected, destitute nation. Industry and commerce stood by helplessly as foreigners supplied Spain's domestic and colonial markets, an empty royal treasury futilely sought revenue from withered sources, the army and navy no longer provided adequate defense, and a shrinking population bore gloomy witness to her misery.

Having learned well the ways of his famous grandfather, Louis XIV, and accepting the counsel of French ministers, Philip V introduced a fresh approach to government in Spain—enlightened royal absolutism. In the economic sphere this meant adoption of aggressive, all-encompassing mercantilistic policies similar to those perfected earlier in France by Colbert. The new king launched his own reforms and programs for industrial and commercial revival, spurning many of the economic policies of his predecessors but accepting their wish for a favorable balance of trade. Building upon this groundwork, his successors assumed ever greater roles in directing economic activity and culminated their efforts with dazzling and far-reaching programs during the years 1750 to 1800. A thriving domestic industry, reasoned the kings, would reduce imports, increase exports, and reverse Spain's unfavorable balance of trade.

Serious obstacles, however, threatened their plans. Spain lacked modern technology, skilled workers, capital, and efficient transportation facilities. Her adversaries possessed these requisites and thus held a competitive advantage. To remove the many imposing drawbacks would require a degree of skill, energy, and optimism heretofore absent in Spain. Philip and his successors sought to provide the missing elements. Here was a time when government could assist an economy by importing technology, improving transportation facilities, reducing taxes, removing barriers to the mobility of capital and labor, and shielding industry from foreign competition during its infancy.

Though leather goods, paper, glass, porcelain, and crystal, among other items, received considerable attention from the royal economic programs, textiles enjoyed first priority. One of the means employed to promote the cloth industry were royal factories. All four Bourbons of the eighteenth century constructed, owned, and operated textile manufactories for the purpose of implanting the production of fine fabrics in Castile and Leon and of training skilled artisans for Spanish industry.[2] Some of these institutions were large, self-contained mills, others were small, quasi factories;

---

[2] See chapter iii.

inefficiency hounded them all, and had it not been for constant subsidies from the royal treasury they would have quickly disappeared. Yet they lived on, some for decades, flooding Spain with fine textiles and competing vigorously with private manufacturers for markets on the peninsula and in the colonies.

Royal joint-stock companies were another tool of industrial development. Chartered by kings, domestic companies first appeared about mid-century and, as their principal missions, organized textile production and sold their merchandise in foreign markets.[3] Litigation, bankruptcies, dishonesty, and civil disruption littered their short histories.

Both royal factories and royal joint-stock companies found it necessary to import foreign artisans when staffing their producing units. As the eighteenth century progressed, this search for skills and technology heightened and became an integral part of royal economic programs.[4] Upon the successful recruitment of foreigners rested much of Spain's hopes for industrial growth, for not only had she lost a significant portion of her finer skills and knowledge during the disastrous seventeenth century, but other nations had continued to improve theirs. Kings now tried to retrieve that lost ground with a massive program to capture the skills and knowledge of other nations.

Once in Spain, however, foreign artisans clashed with craft guilds, those entrenched relics of medieval origin. Even Spanish artisans found it difficult, often impossible, to enter certain trades or to migrate from one city to another and then take up their occupations again. Guild rules also closely regulated the activities of members: volume of output, quality of products, and methods of production were rigidly controlled. Energetically attacked by kings and challenged by rapidly changing economic conditions during the years 1750 to 1800, this monopoly power slowly disintegrated.[5]

Still another roadblock obstructed the industry in 1750. Many regressive excise taxes smothered basic commodities and productive resources, pyramiding through each transaction from the first to the last. Kings came to the aid of the textile industry when they exempted producers and merchants from many imposts and reformed the tax system.[6] Colonial commerce likewise suffered from a confusion of duties and controls. A plethora of levies and pro-

[3] See chapter iv.
[4] See chapter v.
[5] See chapter vi.
[6] See chapter vii.

hibitions on the shipment of commodities, intermixed with other severe restrictions of trade, curbed entry into the American market. By consciously manipulating these duties and embargoes and by easing the limitations on colonial trade, kings sought to benefit domestic manufacturers of textiles.[7]

While the development programs of kings directly aided the production of cloth, the ideas of the Enlightenment stirred the imagination of Spain's best minds and thereby indirectly promoted this industry. Scholarly works from France rushed into the peninsula, and printing presses turned out an increasing flow of books and newspapers. In them, writers sought the answer to the economic ills of Spain, kindling a national debate. Whether proponents of government control or of free trade, they all explained Spain's weaknesses and suggested cures. The last half of the eighteenth century saw this discussion at its height.[8] These intellectuals were not content, however, with merely writing about their country's dilemma; they created institutions to promote industry. The economic societies were thus born.[9] Over fifty of these private organizations, among other activities, translated and published foreign books, encouraged new methods of production, introduced new processes and products, and supervised instruction in many fields of thought and activity.

Although these societies contributed materially to education and training after 1750, kings did much more. The government created trade schools for spinning, dyeing, design, printing on cloth, and similar tasks. Dominated by scholasticism and apathetic to important new ideas, higher education underwent substantial changes as Charles III and Charles IV launched reforms during the last third of the century.[10]

The ambitious royal programs for economic progress collided with other institutions standing in the way. The Catholic Church lost as a result. After 1753 Spanish kings could appoint Church officials and tax Church lands; Charles III expelled the Jesuits from Spanish dominions in 1767; and over the last half of the century kings gradually nullified the power of the Inquisition. Land tenure and the Mesta (sheepherders' guild) also felt the reforming zeal of Spain's vigorous leadership after 1750.[11]

New ideas and dedicated men thus made the years 1750 to 1800

---

[7] See chapter viii.
[8] See chapter ix.
[9] *Ibid.*
[10] *Ibid.*
[11] *Ibid.*

memorable ones; the output of goods and services rose and added more luster to this half-century. Responding to royal inducements and other favorable influences, production of paper, porcelain, crystal, glass, leather goods, and coal, among other items, ascended during the last half of the eighteenth century.[12] But it was in textiles that expanding production catches the eye most quickly. Output of linens grew moderately as did woolen output; silks expanded impressively and cottons raced skyward. Geographical specialization marked this growth. Linen production, a household industry, increased in the provinces of Burgos, Catalonia, Galicia, Salamanca, Soria, and Valencia; the greatest expansion in woolen manufacturing occurred in the provinces of Valencia, Guadalaxara, and Catalonia. Catalonia and particularly Valencia enjoyed the bulk of the rise in silk output; the cotton industry became centered exclusively in Catalonia.[13]

Except for its remarkable development in Catalonia and Valencia, the textile industry responded disappointingly. Part of the blame for this uneven pattern of growth must rest with the royal programs themselves. Kings often lost sight of market forces and overemphasized engineering or technical considerations. They obtained Europe's finest artisans, they imported delicate machinery that spun fine thread and wove fine cloth, they built large, sophisticated factories that produced superfine and fine woolens, silks, and cottons, and they imposed rules to enforce the manufacture of high quality textiles. Yet they overlooked the economic fact that consumers in Spanish markets demanded mainly common fabrics. Even when selling their superfine and fine cloth from royal factories, kings ignored the market and set prices at which the quantity demanded fell far short of equaling the quantity supplied.

Not all royal programs neglected market forces. To increase labor mobility, to permit production on a larger scale, and to allow use of new techniques, kings reduced the power of guilds. They removed many tax inequities, though their efforts were

---

[12] Ángel Ruiz y Pablo, *Historia de la Real Junta Particular de Comercio de Barcelona, 1758–1847* (Barcelona, 1919), p. 121; Jaime Carrera y Pujal, *Historia de la Economía Española*, 5 vols. (Barcelona, 1943–1947), IV, 107, 132–135; Jaime Carrera y Pujal, *Historia Política y Económica de Cataluña, Siglos XVI al XVIII*, 4 vols. (Barcelona, 1946–1947), IV, 187; Antonio Perez Rioja, "La Protección del Libro Bajo Carlos III: Dos Reales Cédulas de 1778 y otra de 1780," *Revista de Archivos, Bibliotecas y Museos*, LIX, nos. 1–3 (1953), 248–249; Eugenio Larruga y Boneta, *Memorias Políticas y Económicas sobre los Frutos, Comercio, Fábricas y Minas de España*, 45 vols. (Madrid, 1787–1800), I, 48; Archivo del Ministerio de Hacienda [hereafter cited as AMH], *Colección de Órdenes Generales de Rentas*, XXI, 474–478; José Canga Argüelles, *Diccionario de Hacienda*, 2 vols. (Madrid, 1833–1834), I, 190.

[13] See chapter ii.

tardy and feeble. And kings tried to direct market forces to Spain's advantage by manipulating tariffs and by imposing import and export prohibitions.

Ignorance of market forces, nevertheless, undermined the royal struggles to awaken industry. It was partly for this reason that production in Castile and Leon, recipient of the lion's share of government aid, slumbered through the century. Catalonia and Valencia, though slighted by most royal developmental programs, experienced remarkable expansion of industry. Textile manufacturers in these latter two regions, protected by general tariff walls and import-export prohibitions, free to trade with America, and little bothered by unsound royal policies, built their industry to market specifications.

While other factors contributed to industry's success in Valencia and Catalonia, still others obstructed growth in Castile and Leon. Such natural advantages, for example, as populous cities, nearness to sources of raw materials, fine seaports, and clear, swift streams gave the Mediterranean littoral an advantage over central Spain, where rugged terrain, inadequate rainfall, a small supply of wood and other natural resources, poor communications, and relatively small cities militated against economic growth. Perhaps in their efforts to develop Castile and Leon kings were being quixotic and striving after the impossible. Perhaps they would have failed no matter what. Unquestionably they would have been more successful had they centered more of their attention on the coastal regions and had they emphasized the economic considerations of their policies.

The years from 1750 to 1800 in Spain were thus filled with the deeds of an extraordinarily active government and the uneven responses of an industry that dominated the economy and received the full force of government's attention. In contrast, the first fifty years of the century experienced only slight industrial growth. It was a time of organization, of planning, and of experimentation, when the groundwork was being laid for future expansion. After 1800, again in contrast with the years 1750 to 1800, Spain fell victim to Napoleon; the wars, the political upheaval, and the physical destruction that followed undid much of the advance of the previous half-century. The period 1750–1800 is therefore a unique, historical unit. Spain's experience with her textile industry during these years offers a provocative example of an early attempt at economic development.

II

Growth in the Spanish Textile Industry

Industry in Western Europe, following nearly a century of irresolute development, awakened after 1750 to the prodding of technical advances, widening markets, and the enlightened policies of kings. Cotton manufacturing in England virtually exploded forward, introducing the factory system and production on a large scale; manufacture of woolens, silks, and linens also expanded, but at a much slower rate. Only in Alsace-Lorraine did cotton production grow markedly in France, and then not until early in the nineteenth century. The Spanish textile industry, after suffering through at least one hundred years of depression, began in 1750 to scramble back to the respectable place it once held. This chapter investigates the growth in silks, cottons, woolens, and linens, in that order, that occurred between 1750 and 1800 in Spain.

Growth in Silk Production

Chinese legend reveals that Hoang-ti, a great prince, instructed Si-ling-chi, his legitimate wife, to try and obtain thread from silkworms so she might thereby enhance the pleasure of his subjects.[1] Obediently, Si-ling-chi collected a number of these larvae, patiently cared for them, studied them, and presently discovered the means of securing silk threads from their cocoons and therewith introduced fabrics of silk. For this contribution to mankind, Si-ling-chi took her place among Chinese deities as the Goddess of Silkworms.[2]

These events, which supposedly transpired about 2640 B.C., imply an early beginning for the manufacture of silks. After knowledge of the industry had drifted to Japan in the third century A.D.,

---

[1] Perry Walton, *The Story of Textiles* (New York, 1925), pp. 45-46.
[2] *Ibid.*

[7]

it spread to India and then on to Constantinople in the sixth century, from where Arab and Saracen warriors carried it with their invading armies across North Africa and into Spain. Beginning in the eighth century, the Muslims developed thriving centers of silk manufacture in southern Spain. One such center was Seville, where, at the height of its prosperity in the early thirteenth century, the industry may have employed as many as 16,000 looms and 130,000 workers.[3]

After being set back in the second half of the thirteenth century by wars of the reconquest, the industry recovered, especially at Toledo and Seville, only to be engulfed again by the economic disaster that swept the peninsula during the seventeenth century.[4]

Thus it was that 1700 found silk production struggling for its existence once again. Toledo, Seville, Granada, Murcia, and other traditional centers, with their shriveled populations and deserted workshops, were witnesses to the industry's decay. Thereafter, as the Bourbon kings actively stimulated Spanish industry from 1750 to 1800, the different areas of silk manufacture in Spain experienced three patterns of growth: some continued to decline, others stood still or expanded insignificantly, while a few blossomed into prosperity. On balance, the output of silks in Spain increased over these fifty years.

Production continued to drop throughout this period in the provinces of Aragon, Extremadura, Granada, and Toledo. At Zaragoza, where most fabrication of silks in Aragon took place, the number of looms fell from 219 in 1777 to 127 in 1798.[5]

---

[3] Antonio Ponz, *Viaje de España . . . Hay en Ella* (Madrid, 1772-1794), Tomo IX, Carta VIII, p. 833; Joseph Townsend, *A Journey Through Spain in the Years 1786 and 1787* (London, 1792), II, 332; Jean Francois de Bourgoing, *Modern State of Spain*, translated from the 1807 edition, 4 vols. (London, 1808), III, 130; Manuel Escudé Bartoli, *La Producción Española en el Siglo XIX* (Barcelona, 1895), p. 245; Moreau de Ionnes, *Estadística de España* (Barcelona, 1835), pp. 185-187; Gerónimo de Uztáriz, *Theórica, y Práctica de Comercio y de Marina* (Madrid, 1757), p. 240. Ponz, writing in the eighteenth century, belittled these statistics by pointing out that a working force of 130,000 attached to this industry at Seville implies a total population for that city of at least 500,000, a transparent exaggeration (*loc. cit.*).

[4] Townsend, *loc. cit.*; Bourgoing, *loc. cit.*; Escudé Bartoli, *op. cit.*, pp. 245-246; Ionnes, *op. cit.*, p. 185.

[5] Ignacio Jordán de Asso del Río, *Historia de la Economía Política de Aragón* (Zaragoza, 1798), pp. 123, 138, 139; *Censo de la Población de España de el Año de 1797, Executado de Orden del Rey* (Madrid, 1797); *Censo de Frutos y Manufacturas de España é Islas Adyacentes, Ordenado sobre los Datos Dirigidos por los Intendentes, Por el Oficial Don Juan Polo y Catalina* (Madrid, 1803). The Censo de Frutos can be found in the following: Marcelino Graell, *La Industria Sedera*

Whereas Zarza la Mayor (Extremadura) possessed 128 looms in 1751, the entire province of Extremadura contained only eleven looms in 1796.[6] But the province of Toledo experienced the greatest decadence. After the Company of Toledo had coaxed the number of wide looms at Toledo from 239 in 1747 to 610 in 1752, its fortunes began to decline disastrously, and with it crumbled the silk industry of Toledo—only 272 wide looms remained in 1767;[7] by 1774 whole sections of the city had been deserted by artisans; and only 176 wide looms remained in 1787.[8]

The decay of Toledo's silk industry probably was hastened by competition from the royal manufactory for silks at Talavera de la Reina. Begun in 1748 by Ferdinand VI, this factory maintained between 329 and 354 looms during the years 1750 to 1800, and with its exclusive privileges and royal subsidies it proved a formidable rival for all silk producers in central Spain.[9]

Several places preserved their levels of output or at least witnessed little decline during the period 1750–1800. At Valladolid, where producers specialized in passementerie, the number of operating looms varied from 79 in 1746, to 126 in 1753, to 79 in 1778, to 102 in 1789.[10] The village of Requena, in the province of Cuenca, possessed 448 looms which produced substantial quantities of silk cloth in 1735. After expanding mildly until about 1760, the industry declined as the number of looms fell to about 300 and possibly lower;[11] but prosperity returned quickly, and by 1790 between 500 and 600 looms consumed 50,000 pounds of silk as compared to 78,850 pounds in 1735.[12]

(Barcelona, 1926), pp. 20–28; and José Canga Arguëlles, *Diccionario de Hacienda*, 2 vols. (Madrid, 1833–1834), I, 465–467.

The *Censo de Frutos*, taken in 1799, specifically reported that the manufacture of silks in Aragon was decaying and the artisans were poverty-stricken.

[6] Archivo General de Simancas [hereafter cited as AGS], *Secretaría de Hacienda*, leg. 852; Eugenio Larruga y Boneta, *Memorias Políticas y Económicas sobre los Frutos, Comercio, Fábricas y Minas de España*, 45 vols. (Madrid, 1787–1800), XXXIX, 167, 270.

[7] Biblioteca Nacional, *Sección de Manuscritos* [hereafter cited as BN], MS 13066; Larruga y Boneta, *op. cit.*, VII, 114, 364, 389, 416.

[8] *Ibid.*, VII, 418, 419. Apparently the production of passementerie and ribbons also declined, though less severely (*ibid.*, VIII, 59, 61, 69).

[9] By controlling all mulberry trees within ten leagues of Talavera, the royal factory reduced the supply of raw silk available to artisans at Toledo and thereby forced them to seek much of their silk in the provinces of Granada and Valencia (*ibid.*, 166–167, 226, 230, 233).

[10] *Ibid.*, XXIV, 193, 194, 259.

[11] *Ibid.*, XVIII, 265, 266, 274, 275.

[12] *Ibid.*, 289, 296, 301.

The output of silks at Madrid, Seville, and Murcia increased slightly during this fifty-year period. While the number of active looms for wide silks fluctuated around 100 at Madrid, the number of looms for narrow silks ascended from 266 in 1757 to 414 in 1787 and thus probably caused the total output to expand.[13] At Seville, growth concurred with the formation and activities of the Company of Seville;[14] and the increase in output at Murcia followed the creation of a factory for spinning and twisting silk in 1772.[15]

Compared to these rather languid activities, substantial growth occurred in the silk industry in Catalonia and Valencia from 1750 to 1800. A pattern of geographical specialization evolved in Catalonia as production of handkerchiefs centered at Manresa, stockings at Barcelona, and broad and narrow fabrics at both Manresa and Barcelona. Weaving of silks on a smaller scale existed in a number of villages, including Reus, Mataro, Tortosa, Cardona, Vich, Igualada, and Olot.

Evidence suggests that this activity at Manresa grew by about 15 to 20 percent from 1750 to 1800. Manufacturers had 1,105 looms for all silks in 1760,[16] whereas by 1780 they had at least 1,200 with which they wove 70,000 dozen handkerchiefs, as well as taffeta, ribbons, and other silks;[17] and they obtained permits to import 89,791 pounds of silk in 1759. In 1784 they actually im-

    [13] *Ibid.*, II, 93, 96, 97, 155, 187, 189, 261.

    [14] *Ibid.*, 334. The Economic Society of Seville reported in 1775 that the industry maintained 462 looms for wide silks, 62 looms for galloons with gold and silver threads, and 1,779 looms for all types of narrow silks. Another source reported the existence of 34 factories for all types of silks in 1804 (Jaime Carrera y Pujal, *Historia de la Economía Española*, 5 vols. [Barcelona, 1943–1947], IV, 182; *Almanaque Mercantil ó Guia de Comerciante para el Año de 1804* [Madrid, 1804], p. 301).

    [15] Carrera y Pujal, *op. cit.*, IV, 180; AMH, *Catastro de Ensenada*, 7469, Murcia, G; AGS, *op. cit.*, leg. 792.

    [16] Biblioteca Central de Barcelona, *Sección de Manuscritos* [hereafter cited as BCB], *Real Junta Particular de Comercio de Barcelona* [hereafter cited as *Junta de Comercio*], leg. 65; Jaime Carrera y Pujal, *Historia Política y Económica de Cataluña, Siglos XVI al XVIII*, 4 vols. (Barcelona, 1946–1947), IV, 112; Carrera y Pujal, *Historia de la Economía Española*, V, 321.

    [17] Jaime Caresmar, *Discurso sobre la Agricultura, Comercio y Industria, con Inclusión de la Consistencia y Estado en que se Halla cada Partido ó Vegueria de los que Componen el Principado de Cataluña* (handwritten manuscript dated 1780, located at the Biblioteca Central de Barcelona, *Sección de Manuscritos*), pp. 371–373; Carrera y Pujal, *Historia Política y Económica de Cataluña*, IV, 121; Pau Romeva Ferrer, *Historia de la Industria Catalana* (Barcelona, 1952), p. 193; Archivo Histórico Municipal de Barcelona [cited hereafter as AHMB], *Junta General de Comercio*, XXXIX, 106.

ported about 106,700 pounds of silk from other provinces and
foreign nations.[18]

At Barcelona the industry concentrated on stockings, braids,
veils, and velvet.[19] Output of stockings expanded markedly. Orig-
inating in 1730 with twelve looms, the guild of stocking producers prospered as its membership increased nearly 300 percent
from 1750 to 1800.[20] Guildsmen operated 111 looms in 1748 and
600 in 1772. Only 200 remained in 1778; but recovery came soon
and in 1788 the producers used 1,300 looms for weaving silk
stockings.[21] Expansion probably continued until 1796 when war
with England shut off the colonial markets.[22]

Manufacture of braids, velvet, and veils at Barcelona also rose
during the period, though the extent of the growth was less striking than that of silk stockings. The number of artisans weaving
braid increased by over 70 percent, while those making velvet
climbed more than 50 percent.[23] On the other hand, the number
of weavers of veils grew only about 5 percent.[24] The booming
calico industry provides an explanation for this relatively slow
expansion. In the first place, producers of calico hired many weavers of veiling to make cotton fabrics; and in the second place, the
outputs of the calico industry competed successfully with some of
the products of the veil weavers.[25]

[18] BCB, *Junta de Comercio*, leg. 65; AHMB, *op. cit.*, XLIX, 3.

[19] A visitor to Barcelona in 1785 guessed that 12,000 people worked in the manufacture of silks. Although this report may have exaggerated actual employment, it
illustrates how active and therefore impressive the industry must have been (Ponz,
op. cit., Tomo XIV, Carta I, p. 1235).

[20] AHMB, *op. cit.*, XVII, 142; *ibid.*, *Catastro, Gremio de Barreteros Fabricantes
de Medias y demás Maniobras de Aguja;* Carrera y Pujal, *Historia de la Economía
Española*, V, 317.

[21] AHMB, *Junta General de Comercio*, XVIII, 86.

[22] While the output of stockings fell during the war with England, which lasted
from 1796 to 1802, it again picked up as 285 manufacturers in Barcelona produced
stockings as well as small net, caps, gloves, and trousers in 1804 (*Almanaque de
1804, op. cit.*, p. 323).

[23] AHMB, *Catastro, Gremio de Galoneros*, 1750–1800; *ibid., Gremio de Terciopeleros*, 1750–1800.

[24] *Ibid., Catastro, Gremio de Texedores de Velos de Seda*, 1750–1800.

[25] Reus and Mataro were two other important centers of silk production. The
village of Reus contained 185 looms for handkerchiefs in 1760 and 300 in 1804,
besides 250 looms for narrow fabrics. Considerable activity centered in the village
of Mataro where in 1759 the administrator of taxes issued permits to ship 6,159
pounds of silk; in 1784 the producers in this city imported 9,147 pounds and 9
ounces of silk and concentrated on the production of stockings. Manufacture on
a small scale existed at Tortosa, Cardona, Vich, Igualada, and Olot (BCB, *op. cit.*,
legs. 57, 65; AHMB, *Junta General de Comercio*, XLIX, 3; Caresmar, *op. cit.*,
p. 585; *Almanaque de 1804, op. cit.*, pp. 331, 337).

The most important center of the silk industry in Spain evolved at Valencia after the War of the Spanish Succession.[26] A climate ideally suited for growing mulberry trees and propagating silkworms, united with a moderate tax system and a commercial policy designed by kings to aid this industry, propelled the manufacture of silks forward. Beginning after the war with less than 800 looms, the industry grew quickly until it had 1,765 looms for wide silks in 1750.[27] Although the number of looms had nearly doubled by 1767, only 1,519 actively wove fabrics as a temporary decline slowed the industry.[28]

But in the early 1770's prosperity waxed throughout the city and motivated several visitors to assert that five thousand looms for wide silks existed;[29] actually, the number was closer to three thousand. In 1785, the College of the Greater Art of Silks counted 3,485 looms for wide silks of which 299 were idle.[30] The number of active looms probably ascended until March, 1788, when 3,242 operating and 300 idle looms were reported.[31] Depression struck soon thereafter and by 1790 only 2,755 looms actively wove silks. The decline continued. Active looms fell to 2,616 in 1795,[32] and then war with England, lasting from 1796 to 1802, occasioned a further drop to 1,747 in 1804.[33] After a short respite from war, the industry declined again when Napoleon ravaged Spain, and in 1812 only 510 looms remained at Valencia.[34] When the industry had reached its peak in about 1788, it was fashioning 2,278,404 varas of wide silks yearly; output fell to 1,816,200 varas in 1795 and to 1,335,700 in 1804.[35] These data lead to the conclusion that production of wide silks at Valencia expanded by about 80 percent

---

[26] The Greater Art of Silk at Valencia entered the eighteenth century with 3,667 active looms (Eduard Martinez Ferrando, *La Industria Valenciana de la Seda* [Valencia, 1933], p. 14).

[27] Carrera y Pujal, *op. cit.*, V, 457, 460; Townsend, *op. cit.*, III, 254; Martinez Ferrando, *loc. cit.*

[28] Archivo del Colegio del Arte Mayor de la Seda de Valencia [hereafter cited as ACSV], *Manuscritos Sobrantes*, no. 11.

[29] Carrera y Pujal, *op. cit.*, V, 506; Townsend, *op. cit.*, III, 255; Bourgoing, *op. cit.*, III, 243.

[30] ACSV, *Mano de Anotaciones . . . Reyno de Valencia;* Carrera y Pujal, *op. cit.*, V, 516.

[31] ACSV, *op. cit.*

[32] *Ibid.;* ACSV, *Varios*, leg. 1, no. 6; Cavanilles counted 2,658 looms in 1795 (Antonio Joseph Cavanilles, *Observaciones sobre la Historia Natural, Geografía, Agricultura, Población, y Frutos del Reyno de Valencia*, 2 vols. [Madrid, 1795–1797], I, 135).

[33] *Almanaque de 1804, op. cit.*, p. 358.

[34] ACSV, *loc. cit.*

[35] *Ibid.; Almanaque de 1804, loc. cit.; Censo de Frutos, op. cit.*, p. 83.

from 1750 to 1788, and then declined by about 40 percent from 1788 to 1804.

Recordings of new apprentices, journeymen, and masters by the College of the Greater Art of Silks at Valencia, confirm this surge and ebb in output. Except for periodic fluctuations caused by war, variations in silk harvests, and changes in the commercial policy of the kings, the rate at which apprentices, journeymen, and masters joined the College increased from 1750 to about 1790 and thereafter declined.[36]

GROWTH OF THE COTTON INDUSTRY

Cotton fabrics had taken their place with woolens, silks, and linen in the wardrobes of the ancients long before recorded history. Yet textiles of wool, silk, hemp, and flax dominated apparel in Western Europe as the centuries passed. By the eighteenth century, however, with appetites whetted by imports from Calicut, India, consumers delighted in colorful calicoes, and merchants and producers attended to this demand. Despite the vigorous efforts of manufacturers of traditional textiles to throttle it, production of calicoes took root and by the end of the eighteenth century was flourishing in several European countries.

Although the industry might have begun earlier, reliable evidence implies that Spaniards were making calicoes in 1737.[37] In that year Jacinto Estaba of Barcelona, pestered by thieves who stole cotton cloth from his bleaching fields, requested permission to supply two watchmen with shotguns.[38] Some writers believe that Estaban Canals and Buenaventura Canet, with the technical assistance of a Swiss artisan, constructed the first factory for calicoes at Barcelona and started that city on its climb to ascendancy in calico fabrication.[39] In 1738, the two men owned, among other

---

[36] ACSV, *Libros de Cuenta y Razón (Mayorales)*.

Changes in the number of apprentices hired each year varied substantially, for masters looked upon apprenticeship as an inexpensive and simple method of obtaining labor and hence they increased or decreased their apprentices as economic conditions warranted. Although the College apparently succeeded in keeping the number of masters and journeymen from rapid and extensive fluctuations, it permitted a gradual rise of membership in these ranks. Short-run increases or decreases of output, therefore, came about as masters varied the number of their looms and apprentices.

[37] Carrera y Pujal, *op. cit.*, V., 328; Carrera y Pujal, *Historia Política y Económica de Cataluña*, IV, 135.

[38] Carrera y Pujal, *Historia de la Economía Española*, V, 328.

[39] Ángel Ruiz y Pablo, *Historia de la Real Junta Particular de Comercio de Barcelona, 1758–1847* (Barcelona, 1919), p. 59; Ponz, *op. cit.*, Tomo XIV, Carta II, p. 1234. Manuel Colmeiro y Penido claimed that this industry began after a

items, 12 looms, 700 molds or patterns for printing, 6 tables for printing, 1 rolling press, and 4 cauldrons. Philip V granted them exemptions from taxes and personal services in 1741; and, as the industry rapidly expanded during the next decade, he and Ferdinand VI awarded other producers similar privileges.⁴⁰

Just how great was the growth up to 1750 is not known. Nevertheless, substantial progress may be inferred from conditions affecting the supply and price of raw cotton. The Maltese, who supplied most of the industry's spun and bulk cotton, raised their prices in 1752 in response to the increased demand for these materials by Catalonians and thereby induced producers to search for new sources of cotton.⁴¹ Bernardo Gloria, for example, obtained permission and tax concessions from Ferdinand VI to import bulk cotton from the colonies.⁴²

By 1760, at least nine producers with 353 looms occupied 10,000 persons in constructing calicoes at Barcelona.⁴³ Three years later, the industry consisted of fifteen manufacturers, many of whom operated on relatively large scales. Juan Pongem, who owned one of the larger factories, possessed 75 looms, 11 printing tables, 32 winding looms, 1 rolling press, and 2 burnishers; he employed 127 persons at his factory and 32 at his bleaching field.⁴⁴

Expansion continued during the 1760's, even though Charles III, on May 15, 1760, lifted the ban from calico imports and imposed a 20 percent import duty on raw cotton.⁴⁵ The number of producers at Barcelona licensed under the royal ordinances of 1767 increased from 20 in 1767 to 25 in 1768. They owned, in June, 1768, 1,111 looms, of which 718 were running.⁴⁶ Complaining of

---

merchant from Barcelona purchased the equipment of a bankrupt producer of calicoes at Marseilles sometime after 1746 (*Historia de la Economía Política en España*, 2 vols. [Madrid, 1863], II, 225).

⁴⁰ For examples, see: Carrera y Pujal, *Historia Política y Económica de Cataluña*, IV, 136, 139, 140, 161; BCB, *op. cit.*, leg. 53, nos. 1, 2, 7, 30; Archivo de la Corona de Aragón, *Real Audiencia* [hereafter cited as ACA], *Diversorium*, no. 1187, fols. 19–23, 85; no. 1188, fols. 75–76; AMH, *Colección de Órdenes Generales de Rentas*, XXIX, 289.

⁴¹ Carrera y Pujal, *op. cit.*, IV, 141. There is no evidence of a decrease in the supply of cotton on Malta.

⁴² *Ibid.*

⁴³ Carrera y Pujal, *Historia de la Economía Española*, V, 332; Ruiz y Pablo, *op. cit.*, p. 58; Romeva Ferrer, *op. cit.*, I, 157. Wyndham Beawes reported in 1760 that 372 looms existed (*A Civil, Commercial, Political and Literary History of Spain and Portugal* [London, 1793], p. 413).

⁴⁴ BCB, *op. cit.*, leg. 53, no. 1; Ruiz y Pablo, *op. cit.*, p. 106.

⁴⁵ See chapter viii, pp. 142–143.

⁴⁶ BCB, *op. cit.*, leg. 53, nos. 4, 40; Ruiz y Pablo, *op. cit.*, p. 97; Carrera y Pujal, *Historia Política y Económica de Cataluña*, IV, 148; Carrera y Pujal, *Historia de la Economía Española*, V, 333.

ruinous competition from imported cottons, industry spokesmen reported that since 1760 eight new entrants and 137 looms had perished; but they failed to mention that sixteen new entrants had survived and that, although the industry had 393 unemployed looms in 1768, it had more than doubled the number of manufacturers and active looms from 1760 to 1768.[47]

In any event, Charles banned imports of cotton textiles on June 24, 1770, and November 4, 1771.[48] Thereafter the industry expanded at a quickening rate. Twenty-five producers had 741 active looms that consumed 741,000 pounds of spun cotton each year by May 24, 1771.[49] Output varied between 80,000 and 90,000 pieces of calico and employment exceeded 50,000 persons by 1775.[50] Spinning cotton in their homes occupied a substantial number of these workers. Thirty-seven producers operated under the king's ordinances on December 14, 1778, while thirty others ignored them—all at Barcelona.[51]

Industry leaders reported on December 15, 1784, that sixty producers working under the ordinances possessed 2,102 looms and 984 printing tables, employed 4,082 men, 1,380 women, and 2,131 children at their factories and bleaching fields, produced 248,000 pieces of calico and 159,750 pieces of printed linen, and used 2,141,250 pounds of spun cotton.[52] Twenty others, who still operated beyond the rules, possessed 350 looms and 60 printing tables, employed 525 men, 360 women, and 160 children at their factories and bleaching fields. They produced 25,000 pieces of calico and printed linen, and used 166,000 pounds of spun cotton. Of these eighty producers, five were situated at Manresa, one at Mataro, and the remainder at Barcelona.[53]

So swiftly had their outputs risen—more than threefold between 1775 and 1784—that producers were forced to extend their spinning operations far into the hinterland in search of labor. There they antagonized manufacturers of woolens by bidding away their spinners. Attempting to checkmate this unexpected invasion of

[47] BCB, *op. cit.*, leg. 53, nos. 4, 40.

[48] AMH, *op. cit.*, XVII, 228; XIX, 97–104, 105–108; XX, 247–252; Archivo Histórico Nacional [hereafter cited as AHN], *Consejo, Libros de Govierno,* 1770, fols. 334–337, 339–341; 1771, fols. 498–501; AHN, *Biblioteca, Colección de Reales Cédulas,* 1770, VI, fols. 270, 273, 1771, fol. 318; Carrera y Pujal, *op. cit.,* V, 333; Ruiz y Pablo, *op. cit.,* p. 99.

[49] BCB, *op. cit.,* leg. 53, no. 9.

[50] Carrera y Pujal, *Historia Política y Económica de Cataluña,* IV, 156.

[51] BCB, *op. cit.,* leg. 53, no. 23.

[52] *Ibid.,* leg. 53, no. 29; Carrera y Pujal, *Historia de la Economía Española,* V, 337.

[53] BCB, *loc. cit.*

their labor market, producers of woolens in 1773 requested the Special Council of Commerce of Barcelona to oblige the women and girls to spin wool instead of cotton, regardless of the higher alternative wages and cleaner work.[54] The Special Council procrastinated. But pressure from the woolen interests mounted as the burgeoning calico industry absorbed more and more spinners. Finally, on January 16, 1784, the Council forbade women and girls to spin cotton in a number of villages in Catalonia, but then modified this order on February 20 by allowing them to spin cotton only if producers of woolens failed to equal the wages paid by calico manufacturers. Quashing this threat to the further expansion of the industry on July 2, 1784, the General Council of Commerce and Money overruled the Special Council and permitted women in all Catalonia to spin for whomever they pleased.[55]

When Charles IV authorized the import of muslins on September 7, 1789,[56] after they had been excluded for nineteen years, the industry declined until 1,082 looms and 4,125 workers were idle on July 9, 1790.[57] Charles reimposed the ban on September 22, 1793, and the industry prospered for the next three years.[58] Then a war with England, beginning in 1796 and lasting until 1802, cut the industry off from its colonial markets and from its supply of raw materials.[59] One source estimates that one-third of the factories shut down and the other two-thirds reduced output, discharged employees, and canceled orders for materials.[60]

When peace returned in 1802, the thoughts of Catalonian industrialists turned to their American markets, for the English had moved into the commercial vacuum during the blockade of Spain and the colonials themselves had begun to manufacture calicoes

---

[54] AHMB, *op. cit.*, LXXIX, 138, 188, 190; Carrera y Pujal, *Historia Política y Económica de Cataluña*, IV, 155.

[55] *Ibid.*, 157; AHMB, *loc. cit.*

[56] AMH, *op. cit.*, XXXII, 348–351; AHN, *op. cit.*, 1789–1790, XX, fol. 907; AHN, *Consejo, Libros de Govierno*, 1789, fols. 691–693; Carrera y Pujal, *Historia de la Economía Española*, V, 340.

[57] BCB, *op. cit.*, leg. 51, no. 20.

[58] AMH, *op. cit.*, XXXVII, 353–356; AHN, *op. cit.*, 1793, fols. 825–827; AHN, *Biblioteca, Colección de Reales Cédulas*, 1793–1794, XXII, fol. 1066; Archivo Histórico Municipal de Barcelona, *Depósito Santa Cruz* [cited hereafter as AHMB Santa Cruz], *Judicial Corregidor;* AHMB, *op. cit.*, XXVI, 93; Guillermo Graell, *Historia del Fomento del Trabajo Nacional* (Barcelona, 1911), p. 18.

[59] AHMB, *loc. cit.; Censo de Frutos, op. cit.*, p. 16; Canga Argüelles, *op. cit.*, I, 29.

[60] Bourgoing, *op. cit.*, III, 306. Bourgoing, a traveler from France, blamed the poor quality of Catalonia's calicoes for this decline. Despite the aid of skilled artisans from Lyons and Nîmes, reported this Frenchman, Catalonians were unable to create superior fabrics (*ibid.*, III, 307).

in Mexico and elsewhere.[61] On June 15, 1804, therefore, industry spokesmen asked the king to stop the contraband and destroy the calico factories in the colonies and thus to preserve the colonial market exclusively for themselves. Otherwise the industry in Spain would be wrecked, so they argued, for it depended on the colonies to consume two-thirds of its output.[62] At the same time they claimed that over one hundred producers with four thousand looms employed one hundred thousand persons and produced about 3.82 million varas of calicoes worth nearly 100 million vellon reals each year (a vellon real equaled 20 U.S. cents in 1792). Undoubtedly the producers exaggerated their case and sought merely to fortify their position and insure their future in America rather than to rescue their industry from imminent destruction.

To attain so impressive a size had taken the industry sixty-seven years of amazingly rapid development. Beginning in 1737 with one manufacturer, the industry raced ahead until one hundred producers existed in 1804; the number of looms expanded from 353 in 1760 to 4,000 in 1804—more than a tenfold increase. Between 1775 and 1784 output trebled; employment mushroomed from a handful in 1737, to 10,000 in 1760, to 50,000 in 1775, to 100,000 in 1804.

This revolutionary growth overshadowed developments in the production of cotton stockings and caps in Catalonia. Archival and printed sources fail to state exactly when this activity first got under way. It must have happened before June 13, 1773, for Charles III on that date awarded Pedro Calvet and Company certain privileges to assist him in this field.[63] Calvet built his factory at the hamlet of Guils, near the village of Puigcerda in northern Catalonia, and by 1775 operated 45 looms and employed 16 French and 29 Spanish artisans.[64] Charles subsequently granted similar privileges to other entrepreneurs.[65]

During the next several decades the output of cotton stockings and caps in Catalonia mounted rapidly. The town of Olot had 100 looms in 1785 and 500 in 1794.[66] In all Catalonia the industry maintained more than one thousand looms prior to 1796, but

---

[61] BCB, *op. cit.,* leg. 53, no. 37; Carrera y Pujal, *op. cit.,* V, 342.

[62] BCB, *loc. cit.;* Carrera y Pujal, *loc. cit.; Almanaque de 1804, op. cit.,* p. 320; Federico Rahola y Tremols, *Cámara Oficial de Comercio y Navegación de Barcelona* (Barcelona, 1931), p. 151; Romeva Ferrer, *op. cit.,* p. 184.

[63] BCB, *op. cit.,* leg. 33, no. 2; AHMB, *op. cit.,* XXI, 86, 129.

[64] *Ibid.,* XXI, 86.

[65] *Ibid.,* XXI, 165; AHN, *Consejo, Libros de Govierno,* 1785, Tomo II, fols. 383–384; AMH, *op. cit.,* XXVII, 246–249.

[66] Ponz, *op. cit.,* Tomo XIV, Carta III, p. 1255; AHMB, *op. cit.,* XXVI, 95.

reduced this number by at least 50 percent during the war with England that lasted from 1796 to 1802.[67] Shortly after the war, the industry's 330 producers owned 1,463 looms and fashioned 73,200 pairs of stockings and caps each year.[68]

Throughout the eighteenth century Catalonia remained the center of cotton manufacturing. Only small, usually unsuccessful factories appeared elsewhere. A few illustrations should make clear how insignificant were these establishments. Josef de Llano y San Gines in 1783 established a small cotton manufactory on the Island of Leon where he made some coarse textiles, calicoes, and hats.[69] Two producers at the city of Leon wove 1,200 varas of dimity or fustian and 1,000 pairs of cotton stockings in 1799.[70] While traveling through Spain at the turn of the century, Bourgoing noted a mill for coarse cottons at the village of Villalta in La Mancha.[71] At the same time, the Duke del Infantado had a factory at Santander completely outfitted for carding, spinning, weaving, bleaching, and dyeing.[72] Cotton textiles were produced only on a small scale at Valencia.[73]

The largest center for making calicoes outside of Barcelona was created at Avila in 1788 by the king. Beginning operations in 1790 with 18 looms and other necessary equipment,[74] the factory grew until it had 210 looms in 1796.[75] Two years later the king's investment had reached 11 million vellon reals.[76] But on August 29, 1799, after several years of misfortune, Charles IV acknowl-

---

[67] *Ibid.*, 19, 44, 149.

[68] *Ibid.*, 20.

[69] AMH, *op. cit.*, XXVI, 434–436.

[70] *Censo de Frutos, op. cit.*, p. 43.

[71] Bourgoing, *op. cit.*, III, 72.

[72] *Almanaque de 1804, op. cit.*, p. 261. Other insignificant cotton mills existed at Villaviciosa (Asturias), La Coruña, Cuenca, and in Aragon (Francisco Gallardo Fernandez, *Origen, Progresos y Estado de Rentas de la Corona de España*, 7 vols. [Madrid, 1805–1808], II, 411; AMH, *op. cit.*, XI, 434–439; Larruga y Boneta, *op. cit.*, XIX, 75).

[73] AMH, *op. cit.*, XXXVI, 334–335; *Censo de Frutos, op. cit.*, p. 83. Production of cotton textiles at Madrid failed to prosper despite several attempts to develop it. In 1773 a Catalonian manufacturer began to print some cloth, but failed within several years. The Greater Guild of Grocers, Notions, and Drugs owned a factory for brown hollands in 1774 and by 1782 had extended production to buckram. Even though assisted by concessions in 1772, 1782, and 1789, the Guild supplied only the local market with these products (Larruga y Boneta, *op. cit.*, II, 349–350, 398–400; AMH, *op. cit.*, XX, 400, XXV, 325–327; XXXII, 197–198; Gallardo Fernandez, *op. cit.*, II, 399).

[74] AGS, *op. cit.*, leg. 756.

[75] *Ibid.*

[76] *Ibid.*, leg. 757.

edged failure and ceded the manufactory to a private citizen who in turn abandoned the mill before 1807.

GROWTH OF THE WOOLEN INDUSTRY

The art of spinning and weaving woolens probably first began when prehistoric man quit his life as a hunter and turned to the pastoral existence of caring for flocks of sheep. In Western Europe the craft had reached a high level of development by the tenth century when Flemish artisans wove English wool into exquisite fabrics that brought dear prices at commercial fairs. The fine wool of Spain's Merino sheep provided that country with the means by which it developed a considerable industry in the fourteenth, fifteenth, and sixteenth centuries. But catastrophe struck down this activity, as it did all industry in Spain, during the economic decline of the seventeenth century.

Production of woolens responded sluggishly to the efforts of kings to rebuild Spanish industry during the period 1750–1800. Although a wealth of statistics does not exist, sufficient data are available from which general conclusions as to the industry's growth or decline can be deduced. They show that overall output in Spain rose slightly during these fifty years. But this growth was uneven: in some provinces output continued to fall, in others it remained constant or varied only slightly, and in a few it increased.

Woolen production dropped in the provinces of Extremadura, La Mancha, Cuenca, Soria, Palencia, and Toro. Extremadura, its plains swept every winter by over 4 million sheep migrating from the north, experienced a steadily falling output. By 1778 only 767 looms existed;[77] 726 looms wove 1,333,760 varas of ordinary quality woolens in 1785, and 687 looms turned out 771,245 varas in 1797.[78] Output in the province of Cuenca decreased more strikingly. Camlets, fine fabrics woven with silk and wool threads, had been made at the city of Cuenca since Humberto Mariscal had come from Flanders in 1686.[79] After he wove camlets on ten looms in 1691, other entrepreneurs started to imitate his success and by 1727 sixty-six looms for camlets existed.[80] Thereafter the number of looms fell until only nineteen remained in 1764. Antonio Ponz reported in 1774 that this industry, once famous for its products,

[77] Larruga y Boneta, *op. cit.*, XL, 107.
[78] *Ibid.*, 117–118.
[79] *Ibid.*, XIX, 1–4.
[80] *Ibid.*, 27.

was in great decadence.[81] The output of camlets in the province in 1799 was a trifling 22,816 varas.[82] Endeavoring to stimulate the manufacture of standard woolens, Charles III permitted the investment of one million vellon reals of public funds in a community factory at Cuenca. But failure was his only reward.[83]

Decreasing outputs also marred the industry in Palencia and Toro. Two hundred and ninety-two looms wove flannel and serge at Palencia in 1747; this number fell to 236 in 1750, to 224 in 1783, and thereafter remained constant.[84] Production of flannel and serge behaved similarly.[85] An analogous decline occurred in the province of Toro as output of sackcloth, serge, and grosgrain increased slightly from 111,500 varas in 1761, to 114,700 in 1785, but then fell precipitously to 68,000 varas in 1790, and then to 43,640 in 1793.[86]

There appears to have been little variation in the output of woolens in quite a few provinces. At Segovia, where a world famous center for the production of woolens once supplied Europe and Africa with fine cloth, the industry maintained a flow of between 3,500 and 6,000 pieces of stuffs each year from 1750 to 1790.[87]

---

[81] Ponz, *op. cit.*, Tomo III, Carta V, p. 278.
[82] *Censo de Frutos, op. cit.*, p. 22.
[83] Gallardo Fernandez, *op. cit.*, II, 395; AGS, *op. cit.*, leg. 787.
[84] Larruga y Boneta, *op. cit.*, XXXIII, 69–222.
[85] *Ibid.*
[86] *Ibid.*, XXXIX, 69–70.
[87] *Ibid.*, XI, 345–348; XII, 1–225.

1700—3,078 pieces	1723—4,105 pieces	1746—4,084 pieces	1769—3,545 pieces
1701—3,751	1724—3,895	1747—4,511	1770—3,621
1702—4,177	1725—3,920	1748—4,812	1771—4,232
1703—4,294	1726—4,310	1749—4,984	1772—4,175
1704—4,215	1727—3,463	1750—4,853	1773—4,338
1705—4,124	1728—4,345	1751—5,154	1774—4,131
1706—3,975	1729—3,831	1752—5,389	1775—3,974
1707—3,975	1730—4,489	1753—5,013	1776—3,969
1708—3,381	1731—4,439	1754—4,965	1777—4,221
1709—3,197	1732—4,899	1755—4,004	1778—4,053
1710—3,200	1733—4,688	1756—4,700	1779—4,587
1711—3,329	1734—3,926	1757—4,710	1780—4,850
1712—3,612	1735—	1758—5,111	1781—4,438
1713—3,417	1736—4,118	1759—6,161	1782—4,094
1714—3,220	1737—4,084	1760—6,067	1783—4,669
1715—2,763	1738—4,109	1761—5,577	1784—4,356
1716—2,900	1739—4,450	1762—4,591	1785—4,531
1717—2,749	1740—4,089	1763—4,770	1786—4,359
1718—3,346	1741—4,122	1764—5,076	1787—4,220
1719—3,529	1742—4,004	1765—4,602	1788—4,155
1720—3,073	1743—3,057	1766—	1789—4,214
1721—3,612	1744—4,154	1767—3,681	1790—4,399
1722—3,843	1745—4,091	1768—3,852	

Variation in ouptut during this time exhibited no trend; most of the short-run increases or decreases were caused by wars, tariffs, and other factors influencing the prices of textiles and wool. Woolen production at Valladolid also remained approximately constant. Eighty masters with two hundred looms wove fine, medium-fine, and domestic serge, sackcloth, grosgrain, and half flannels in 1761.[88] After increasing from 200 in 1778 to 231 in 1784, the number of looms dropped to 215 in 1789 and to 206 in 1791.[89] Output of all woolens in the province fell correspondingly from 521,530 varas in 1784 to 499,500 in 1789.[90] Apparently the villages in the province of Valladolid experienced a slight overall decline from 1750 to 1800.[91]

Although the number of looms at Toledo increased from 26 in 1748 to 61 in 1786, the provincial villages apparently lost more looms than they gained over the same period.[92] No significant changes occurred in the outputs of woolens in the provinces of Avila, Burgos, Aragon, Salamanca,[93] Granada, Madrid, Murcia, Seville, and Zamora—some appear to have increased slightly while others appear to have dropped slightly.

In contrast to this quiescence throughout most of Spain, ascending production marked Valencia, Guadalaxara, and Catalonia. Construction of woolens at the village of Alcoy, in Valencia, for example, grew swiftly; and by the last decade of the century that village had 14 fulling mills and 18 presses serving a yearly output of about .5 million varas of woolen stuffs, flannel, coating, and blankets.[94] If these data are authentic, they make Alcoy one of the larger centers of woolen production in Spain. More impressive, however, was the great royal factory at Guadalaxara, in the province of Guadalaxara. Begun in 1719, it had 51 looms for woolen stuff and serge in 1731, 105 in 1745, 142 in 1754, and a grand total of 670 in 1784—all in one factory.[95] In the latter year two thousand employees labored in all aspects of woolen fabrication

---

[88] *Ibid.*, XXV, 200; Beawes, *op. cit.*, p. 408.

[89] Larruga y Boneta, *op. cit.*, 252, 275, 299.

[90] *Ibid.*, 275, 299.

[91] *Ibid.*, XXVI, 1–35.

[92] *Ibid.*, IX, 11, 17, 18, 22–135, 176–197.

[93] The village of Bejar, in the province of Salamanca, had begun to produce fine woolen stuffs at the end of the seventeenth century when Flemish artisans settled there. One of the largest and most industrious centers in central Spain, Bejar maintained about 150 looms from 1750 to 1800 and wove fine and medium fine stuff (*ibid.*, XXXV, 116–144).

[94] Cavanilles, *op. cit.*, II, 192–193; Larruga y Boneta, *op. cit.*, V, 470–471.

[95] For a discussion of royal factories, see chapter iii.

at the factory, while 15,000 others at 168 locations scattered throughout six provinces spun wool for Guadalaxara's looms. At Brihuega and San Fernando kings built branch factories. From these royal establishments came a river of woolens that varied from ordinary to superfine quality and that, from warehouses astutely placed in major Spanish cities, flooded markets in Spain and her colonies.

The king's manufactories, completely free from all private, municipal, and royal taxes and customs duties, with a huge monthly subsidy, a network of fourteen warehouses, first call on Spain's finest wool, and staffed with some of Europe's finest artisans, proved a formidable competitor to independent producers in the province of Guadalaxara and, for that matter, in all central Spain. Without doubt, the failure of the woolen industry in many parts of the peninsula to respond more than it did must be blamed partly on the oppressive influence of this factory and its branches.

Far from Guadalaxara and the king's mills, Catalonia's woolen industry expanded by at least 30 percent from 1750 to 1800. Output of flannel grew from 3,511 pieces in 1760 to 5,200 pieces in 1804; and output of serge increased from 9,593 pieces in 1760 to 12,500 pieces in 1804.[96] The amount of wool consumed yearly in the province probably increased by over .8 million pounds from 1755 to 1802.[97]

Besides this moderate growth, a geographical redistribution of the producing centers took place. Barcelona, where seven hundred masters fabricated woolens in the sixteenth century, lost nearly all traces of this activity as the calico and silk industries expanded, forcing wages and prices of materials upward. Membership of the guild of woolen producers fell from fifteen in 1750 to ten in 1800.[98] Of these ten, four were masters with workshops and six were masters without workshops; the guild had no journeymen nor apprencties. A fall of more than 50 percent in active membership of the guild of wool dressers (*pelaires*) at Barcelona bears witness to this decline.[99]

While production of woolens decreased at Barcelona, it climbed in a number of nearby towns and villages where swift, clear streams and relatively cheap labor and fuel existed. Tarrasa, Sabadell, Esparaguera, Olesa, Igualada, Monistrol de Monserrat, Cas-

[96] Carrera y Pujal, *Historia Política y Económica de Cataluña*, IV, 106; BCB, *op. cit.*, leg. 65.

[97] AHMB, *op. cit.*, LIV, 152; leg. II (73), 17.15 (6).

[98] AHMB, *Catastro, Gremio de Texedores de Lana*, 1750–1800.

[99] AHMB, *Catastro, Gremio de Pelayres*, 1750–1800.

telltersol, and Moya became more important centers for woolens, especially after 1765. In that year Barcelona was free to trade directly with ports in the West Indies, and in 1770 the *bolla*, a harsh sales tax on woolens and silks, was abolished. The number of looms in Tarrasa, for example, increased from 32 in 1755 to 53 in 1763; Sabadell made 24,000 varas of woolens in 1760, 31,000 varas in 1763, and 45,00 in 1789;[100] the number of looms at Monistrol de Monserrat doubled between 1763 and 1780; and from 1760 to 1780 producers at Castelltersol increased their looms from 194 to 290.

While expanding their outputs, the Catalonians also varied the quality of their woolens. In Castelltersol they wove a light woolen fabric, similar to serge, unequaled in fineness in the province.[101] Though never equaling the exquisiteness of the fine and superfine cloth from Guadalaxara and San Fernando, woolens from Catalonia found markets in America, the Levant, and even in countries of northern Europe.[102] A chief reason for the success of these manufacturers was their ability to produce cheaply; they used less expensive wool, employed shortcuts in production, and marketed their textiles efficiently.

GROWTH OF THE LINEN INDUSTRY

Weaving of flax and hemp had been practiced in Spain since time immemorial. The ancient Iberians, Celtics, Celtiberians, Romans, and Moors, all wove linens on their simple looms. Women traditionally prepared the flax and hemp, spun the thread, and wove the fabrics, working in their homes during their spare time. Thus it was that in the eighteenth century this industry was mainly in the hands of women—not women of large towns and cities but women of villages and hamlets. There were exceptions, of course; true factories of production on a large scale existed at La Coruña, Leon, Valencia, and Barcelona.

From 1750 to 1800 manufacture of linen products expanded in Spain. In 1799, 48,000 individuals in 24 provinces wove more than 20 million varas of linens, of which only 1,494,849 varas were of fine quality, the rest being ordinary household variety.[103] Catalonia led all provinces with over 4 million varas; Valencia was

---

[100] José Ventalló Vintró, *Historia de la Industria Lanera Catalana* (Tarrasa, 1904), pp. 482, 498, 499; AHMB, *Junta General de Comercio*, L, 62; leg. II (73), 17.15 (2); BCB, *op. cit.*, leg. 65.

[101] Carrera y Pujal, *Historia de la Economía Española*, V, 311.

[102] *Ibid.*, 314.

[103] Canga Arguëlles, *op. cit.*, I, 435; II, 59.

next with over 3.5 million varas; then followed Galicia with more than 1.5 million varas; Aragon and Asturias both made over 1 million varas.[104] Although this output may seem excessive, it should be remembered that linens had multiple uses—bedspreads, tablecloths, napkins, drapes, washcloths, and underclothing of all kinds, to mention several. Linens were also cheaper than fabrics of wool, cotton, or silk, and required little skill to make. Consequently, these textiles, except for 2,549,250 varas exported to America, found a ready market in Spain.[105]

During this period of general growth, some provinces experienced a decline in the output of linens, many witnessed only little expansion or contraction, while a few saw the output increase significantly. The provinces of Avila, Cuenca, Extremadura, Guadalaxara, and Segovia, among others, probably produced less linen in 1800 than in 1750. Extremadura, for example, had 1,668 looms in 1780 which made 957,066 varas of linens, while the output fell to 490,940 varas in 1797 and to 466,921 varas in 1799.[106] Three hundred and sixty-six masters and 81 journeymen wove linens in the province of Guadalaxara in 1756; but apparently only 265 workers remained in 1799.[107] Similarly, Segovia had 36 masters, 409 journeymen, and 373 apprentices in 1756 and only 453 individuals employed in 1799.[108]

While little change either upward or downward occurred in most provinces, progress did take place in the provinces of Burgos, Catalonia, Galicia, Salamanca, Soria, and Valencia. Linen production in Burgos and Salamanca grew by 30 to 40 percent, and the number of individuals manufacturing linens in Soria increased by over 50 percent.[109] Output of these fabrics in Catalonia mounted until in 1799 it reached 4,163,000 varas of ordinary linen cloth and 538,000 varas of other linen products.[110] To reach this large volume, employment increased; at Barcelona, for example, the Guild of Linen Weavers expanded by 75 percent from 1750 to 1800.[111] At the town of Reus, 3,000 women made 125,000

---

[104] *Ibid.*, II, 59.

[105] *Ibid.*

[106] Larruga y Boneta, *op. cit.*, XL, 138, 151; *Censo de Frutos, op. cit.*, p. 25.

[107] AMH, *Catastro de Ensenada*, 7449, Guadalaxara, G; *Censo de Frutos, op. cit.*, p. 34.

[108] AMH, *op. cit.*, 7482, Segovia, G; *Censo de Frutos, op. cit.*, p. 67.

[109] Larruga y Boneta, *op. cit.*, XXXI, 304; XXXV, 191; *Censo de Frutos, op. cit.*, pp. 13, 64, 73; AMH, *op. cit.*, 7489, Soria, G.

[110] *Censo de Frutos, op. cit.*, p. 16.

[111] AHMB, *Catastro, Gremio de Texedores de Lino*, 1750–1800.

pounds of linen thread each year by 1804, whereas hardly any had been made there fifty or sixty years earlier.[112]

Although the women of Reus, specializing in linen thread, attained a large volume of output, they usually performed their tasks at home. Rarely in Spain was the manufacture of linen cloth or thread organized in factories. Exceptions were the royal factories at Leon and San Ildefonso and a factory at La Coruña, the latter supplying linen for the royal family. We do not know much about the king's factory at Leon: in 1756 it employed 13 masters, 93 journeymen, 16 apprentices, and 64 other individuals, not including spinners. When Antonio Ponz visited Leon in 1782, he did not mention the factory, but stated that, while in the recent past 170 looms had woven linens, the industry was decaying.[113] In 1804, 34 to 39 looms at the poorhouse made linen of which 16,000 to 20,000 varas were sent to Madrid each year[114]—perhaps this was all that remained of the factory. The mill at San Ildefonso, its history remaining even more shrouded by a nearly total absence of extant manuscripts, apparently was begun in the 1780's and disappeared before 1800.[115]

The manufactory at La Coruña, in contrast, existed for many years. Charles II, in 1686, permitted Adrian Roo and Baltasar Kiel, two Flemish merchants who manufactured rigging and canvas for the Spanish navy, to import ten families from Holland and start a factory for table linen.[116] Roo and Kiel received a contract for fifty years that gave them a monopoly of producing these items in Galicia, tax concessions, and preference in renting or buying land and buildings. In return, they agreed to supply the royal family with tabble linen. Despite contract difficulties and other problems, the relationship between factory and king still existed in 1767. In that year, 18 looms and 89 employees made linens. From 1760 to 1767 the factory remitted to Madrid 913 sets of first-class table linen, 5,460 single napkins of first class, and 4,000 single napkins of second class.[117] By 1785 it had passed from the heirs of Roo and Kiel to Josef Coderque who employed sixteen persons on tablecloth looms, thirty-six on napkin looms, fifteen others in related processes, and six hundred spinners.

[112] *Almanaque de 1804, op. cit.,* p. 336.

[113] AMH, *op. cit.,* 7457, Leon, G; Ponz, *op. cit.,* Tomo XI, Carta VI, p. 1013.

[114] *Almanaque de 1804, op. cit.,* p. 429.

[115] AGS, *op. cit.,* leg. 756; Townsend, *op. cit.,* II, 114.

[116] Larruga y Boneta, *op. cit.,* XLV, 58, 59.

[117] *Ibid.,* 113; Carrera y Pujal, *op. cit.,* IV, 178.

SUMMARY

Textile production in Spain expanded during the years 1750 to 1800. Silk output on balance rose, even though it fell in some areas and remained constant in others. In the provinces of Aragon, Extremadura, Granada, and Toledo manufacturers were weaving less silk in 1800 than in 1750, while at Valladolid and Requena they were making about the same. Madrid, Seville and Murcia, on the other hand, experienced a slight increase in output of silks over these years. The most substantial growth of all took place in Catalonia and Valencia. Barcelona and Manresa became centers for silks in Catalonia; the villages of Mataro, Tortosa, Cardona, Vich, Igualada, and Olot, among others, also produced some. The most important center of silk production in all Spain developed at Valencia where the number of wide looms rapidly increased from 1,765 to 1750 to 3,242 in 1788.

Beginning in about 1737, the calico industry at Barcelona exploded forward—nine producers used 353 looms and employed 10,000 persons in 1760; twenty-five producers used 741 looms and employed nearly 50,000 persons in 1771; and perhaps as many as 100 producers used 4,000 looms and employed 100,000 persons in 1804. The output of cotton stockings and caps also grew in Catalonia, though not as spectacularly as calicoes. During the last quarter of the century, the manufacture of these two products expanded from practically nothing to an output of 73,200 pairs of stockings and caps annually. Centers for cotton production rarely existed outside of Catalonia and then only on a small scale. The Island of Leon, the cities of Leon, Santander, Valencia, and Avila, and the village of Villalta contained makers of cotton fabrics.

Production of woolens ascended somewhat, though unevenly, during the period 1750–1800. Output dropped in the provinces of Extremadura, La Mancha, Cuenca, Soria, Palencia, and Toro; it varied only slightly in Segovia, Valladolid, Toledo, Avila, Burgos, Aragon, Salamanca, Granada, Madrid, Murcia, Seville, and Zamora. But in Valencia, Guadalaxara, and Catalonia, output of woolens rose significantly. The village of Alcoy in Valencia had a large, rapidly growing industry. The king's huge factory at Guadalaxara dominated production of fine woolens in central Spain. Growing about 30 percent from 1750 to 1800, Catalonia's woolen industry migrated from Barcelona to, among other villages, Tarrasa, Sabadell, Esparaguera, Olesa, and Igualada.

Linen production followed a pattern similar to silk, cotton, and woolen manufacture. While some provinces experienced a decline in the output of linens and while others had little change, Burgos, Catalonia, Galicia, Salamanca, Soria, and Valencia enjoyed expanding production.

III

Royal Textile Factories

INTRODUCTION

An uneven wave of progress thus moved across the land from 1750 to 1800. Many regions experienced little if any growth, a few responded with spectacular ascents. These unbalanced results were the handiwork of numerous promoters of change as well as agents of poverty that intermingled on the peninsula throughout this half-century. Of all the factors touching industry, the most remarkable were those initiated by kings. Using methods that ranged from direct intervention in the production process to subtle encouragement of private enterprise, monarchs created royal factories, chartered joint-stock companies, imported foreign artisans and technology, attacked the monopoly power of craft guilds, reformed the internal tax structure, reorganized tariffs and commercial arrangements, and removed a host of other barriers to industrial growth.

As diversified as they were in method and emphasis, these programs placed notable stress on stimulating the production of fine cloth. From the onset, however, an imposing obstacle threatened their success; Spain lacked vital skills and technology—a legacy of her century of decline. To overcome this handicap, Philip and his successors created royal factories, fitted them with modern equipment, and staffed them with foreign artisans.[1] These manufactories received two mandates. First and most important, they were to act as technical institutions, diffusing the requisite knowledge and skills throughout the peninsula and laying the founda-

---

[1] The term "royal factory" (*fábrica real*) commonly appeared during the period 1750–1800, for kings granted this label to many workshops and factories in recognition of their special achievements. Although kings awarded a few of these "royal factories" direct monetary aid along with the title, they conceded the majority of them only tax reductions on sales of their products and purchases of material and machinery. Hence the title was but one element in a package of concessions and served only as an honorary distinction. This chapter ignores factories of this type.

tion for awakening the production of fine cloth. Second, they were to provide Spain with superior textiles and thus reduce her dependence upon foreign suppliers. Rather than spreading the manufacture of delicate textiles through central Spain, however, the mills obstructed private enterprise and cost Spain dearly in resources and hope.

This chapter first inquires into the creation and development of royal mills, with emphasis on foreign artisans, scales and organization of production, and methods of financing; it then examines the shortcomings generally associated with the factories; and concludes with an explanation for their ultimate failures as makers of fine cloth and as stimulators of industry.

THE CREATION AND DEVELOPMENT OF ROYAL MILLS

Spanish kings established and operated their textile manufactories along three general lines. In the majority of their mills, they chose to play the role of entrepreneur and closely supervise all financial and managerial activities. Woolen manufactories at Guadalaxara, Brihuega, and San Fernando, linen mills at Leon and San Ildefonso,[2] and a silk factory at Talavera de la Reina came into being under these circumstances. When kings wished to

---

[2] For a description of the mills at Leon and San Ildefonso, see above, p. 25.

The Marquis de la Ensenada, acting on the suggestion of the Intendant of Valencia and for the government of Spain, brought four highly trained artisans from France to Valencia in 1753. He hoped to create a factory from which the knowledge of producing fine fabrics with threads of silver, gold, and silk would be diffused throughout Valencia. Ensenada, however, withdrew the government's support of the factory after the arrival of the artisans and, instead, permitted the Five Greater Guilds of Madrid to finance and develop it as a private venture (AGS, *Secretaría de Hacienda,* legs. 789, 790; Miguel Capella and Antonio Matilla Tascón, *Los Cinco Gremios Mayores de Madrid* [Madrid, 1957], pp. 134–145; Jaime Carrera y Pujal, *Historia de la Economía Española,* 5 vols. [Barcelona, 1943–1947], V, 491).

On November 25, 1781, Charles III established the most novel, though perhaps the least successful, royal factory at Seville. The novelty arises because at least fifty skilled Englishmen offered their services to this project rather than to remain in prisoner-of-war camps at Seville and Ecija. They had been interned after capture on the high seas by the Spanish navy during the current war. Although each artisan received a gift of 1,000 vellon reals, plus wages, bread, and subsidies for clothing, nearly all returned to England when the war ended and the king ignored their requests for higher wage rates (AGS, *op. cit.,* leg. 802; AHMB, *Junta General de Comercio,* LII, 3).

Manuel Colmeiro y Penido, José Luis Barcelo de la Mora, and André Mounier mention the establishment of a royal factory for woolens at Chinchon (Manuel Colmeiro y Penido, *Historia de la Economía Política de España,* 2 vols. [Madrid, 1863], II, 218; José Luis Barcelo, *Historia Económica de España* [Madrid, 1952], p. 243; André Mounier, *Les Faits et la Doctrine Economiques en Espagne sous Philip V, Gerónimo de Uztáriz* [Bordeaux, 1919], p. 103).

evade part of the responsibility, they limited their participation to supplying capital and left management in the hands of partners, usually foreign artisans with special skills. Woolen mills at Seville and Almarzo and a cotton factory at Avila were formed by this arrangement. In several instances kings avoided financial as well as managerial burdens by permitting local funds to be employed as capital and by relegating the administration of the institutions to city authorities. Such provisions formed the basis for woolen factories at Cuenca and Avila.

It was not by chance that royal manufactories sprang up at places such as Guadalaxara, Bihuega, San Fernando, Talavera de la Reina, Avila, and elsewhere, all clustering about Madrid. Because Merino sheep, source of the world's finest wool grazed during the summer months in the mountains to the north of Madrid and on the plains of Extremadura during the winter, royal ministers assumed that central Spain had a comparative advantage in the production of fine woolens as well as it apparently had in growing fine wool. Furthermore, the traditional hostility that alienated Castile from Valencia and Catalonia without doubt influenced crucially the locations of these institutions. For the ministers, most of whom were Castilians by birth, envied the flourishing activity in silks, linens, cottons, and woolens at Valencia and Barcelona and then concentrated their efforts on overcoming the inactivity in their cherished interior provinces.

These industrially backward regions, however, possessed few of the skills and technology required for making superior cloth. Confronted with this serious deficiency, kings organized the majority of their factories around nuclei of foreign artisans so as to provide the technical know-how for producing fine textiles and the ability for training skilled workers.[3] It was soon apparent, however, that an original core of foreigners was not enough to maintain a satisfactory level of technology. For a lack of that intangible "something" so essential to originality and therefore to continuing innovation, plus the rapidly advancing technology in competing countries, kept royal factories persistently in the backwash of technical and stylistic changes. The king's mills kept pace only by receiving a continuous flow of skilled aliens.

To obtain these foreign artisans, the government armed its agents with tempting financial offers and dispatched them to cen-

---

[3] Colmeiro y Penido, *op. cit.*, II, 218; Eugenio Larruga y Boneta, *Memorias Políticas y Económicas sobre los Frutos, Comercio, Fábricas y Minas de España*, 45 vols. (Madrid, 1787–1800), XIV, 186; AHN, leg. 51501, no. 1.

ters of textile production in Western Europe. Although these recruiters occasionally sent lone workmen to Spain, they focused their efforts on supplying integral groups of artisans containing all or most of the skills needed at a manufactory.[4]

One of the first mass recruitments of this nature occurred in 1718 when the Baron of Ripperda brought a group of Dutch workmen to Spain.[5] They formed the basis for the Royal Factory at Guadalaxara. The history of this factory, above all others, illustrates the special emphasis placed on foreign artisans. As the century progressed and the mill expanded, its labor force became an heterogeneous mixture of workers from many nations of Europe. England, Ireland, France, and Holland supplied the majority, though Poland, Prussia, Switzerland, and Italy provided substantial numbers. Some of these immigrants, especially adventurers with lesser skills, traveled to Guadalaxara on their own initiative, drawn there by rumors of high wages, but the highly skilled artisans usually came to Guadalaxara only after receiving the security of a government contract.

Such was also the case for workers who came to the mills at San Fernando and Talavera de la Reina. Guadalaxara's branch at San Fernando, whose superfine stuffs may have rivaled the exquisite fabrics of Abbeville,[6] consisted of three interrelated units at three separate locations. Artisans imported *en masse* from Ireland staffed the units at the hamlets of Vicalvara and Torrejon de la Rivera, and workers brought from Holland especially for this purpose staffed the third and central unit at the royal site of San Fernando.[7] The French city of Lyons unwillingly provided a sizable

---

[4] AGS, *op. cit.*, legs. 759, 761, 765, 766, 768, 771, 772, 774, 776, 784, 785; Larruga y Boneta, *op. cit.*, VIII, 95; XX, 133.

[5] Cardinal Alberoni, with the approval of Philip V, in 1718 commissioned John William, Eighth Baron of Ripperda, to form this factory. The Baron imported fifty artisans from his homeland in Holland and installed them at the Castle of Azeca (Jaime Vicens Vives states that they were sent first to Santander and then to El Escorial [*Historia Social y Económica de España y America*, 4 vols. (Barcelona, 1957–1959), IV, 176]); then, in November, 1719, he transferred them to Guadalaxara. Apparently the factory operated continually until 1820 in which year it ceased operating forever (AGS, *op. cit.*, leg. 759; Larruga y Boneta, *op. cit.*, XIV, 113, 117, 118; *La Vuelta por España, Un Sociedad de Literatos* [Barcelona, 1872], p. 106; Jean Francois de Bourgoing, *Modern State of Spain*, translated from the 1807 edition, 4 vols. [London, 1808], I. 101; Mounier, *op. cit.*, p. 102).

[6] AGS, *op. cit.*, legs. 764, 765; Bourgoing, *op. cit.*, I, 103; III, 19.

[7] AGS, *op. cit.*, legs. 764, 765. In 1768 Charles III moved the facilities to Brihuega, abandoning the buildings to the Guardia Españolas and Walloons. Then, after ten years, he transferred the facilities for making superfine woolens from Brihuega to Guadalaxara where these delicate fabrics still retained the name of San Fernando Paños (*ibid.*, legs, 768, 772).

group of highly skilled artisans for one of Spain's largest royal manufactories, that for silks at Talavera de la Reina. While this mill owed its excellence to these Frenchmen, it owed its existence to John Rulière, a Frenchman with rare ability in mechanics and textile production, who designed, built, and directed the mill at the behest of Ferdinand VI in 1748.[8] Though he may have exaggerated, one author suggested six hundred French artisans came to Talavera at Rulière's request.[9] In any event, the record shows that Rulière did entice enough workers out of France to fill the mill's important positions and to cause considerable consternation north of the Pyrenees.[10]

While Spanish rulers vigorously and successfully sought foreign skills and technology, they almost entirely ignored foreign methods of industrial organization in their more important mills. In the English system, for example, merchants usually supplied wool to the spinners, yarn to the weavers, cloth to the fullers, and so on until the fabric was completed; but the Spanish method relied on vertically integrated factories capable of producing on a large scale. Within its specialized structures, a royal mill could carry the raw materials through the entire production process, barring some exceptions in spinning and weaving, without "putting out" any task.

This departure from English procedure was a natural result of Spain's deficiency in the talent and knowledge so vital for producing superior textiles. Striving to remedy this inadequacy by importing artisans, kings found it was not enough to bring just weavers. An absence of the complementary skills, such as fulling, dyeing, and shearing, debased the quality of the products. Once they had committed their mills to the manufacture of fine cloth, kings therefore had to import a full spectrum of skills and provide facilities for their coördinated operation. Thus from necessity came the development of fully integrated units capable of producing on a large scale. This chapter first considers the aspect of size and then discusses the matter of integration.

By far the largest producing unit evolved at Guadalaxara. Philip V created this mill as a true factory in 1719, despite a strong sentiment for dispersing the looms throughout the city, as was the custom in other countries.[11] After twelve years the factory em-

---

[8] *Ibid.*, leg. 786; Larruga y Boneta, *op. cit.*, VIII, 19; Carrera y Pujal, *op. cit.*, IV, 166.

[9] Larruga y Boneta, *op. cit.*, VIII, 161.

[10] *Ibid.*

[11] *Ibid.*, XIV, 148.

ployed 1,097 persons and operated 44 looms for woolen stuffs and 7 for serge. Starting a period of growth in 1745, Philip increased the stuff looms to 75 and the serge looms to 40.[12] Expansion continued under Ferdinand VI; the number of looms for woolen stuffs and serge had reached 100 and 42 respectively by 1754.

Twenty years elapsed without much growth. Then an increase in demand for wool serge, which apparently occurred around 1777, prompted Charles III to expand the serge division at Guadalaxara. Architects designed and builders raised a structure with a capacity for over five hundred looms.[13] Named San Carlos in honor of Charles III and constructed at a cost of more than a million vellon reals, this building housed an amazing total of 506 looms by September, 1782. Separate rooms enclosed, among other things, worsted dispatch, wool dyeing, ordinary wool storage, rolling press, serge shining, shearing, burling, pressing, and stacking. Ten rooms existed solely for weaving.[14] Surely the San Carlos Serge Division was one of Europe's largest and most compact textile factories.[15]

During the period 1784–1791 the plant at Guadalaxara reached its maximum size. Six hundred and seventy looms wove superfine and fine stuffs and serges in 1784.[16] The various production steps from washing of the wool to final packaging and shipping of the finished product employed more than two thousand persons. And scattered throughout six provinces, an additional fifteen thousand workers spun wool for the mill. The entire labor force had grown to 24,000 by 1791.[17]

While the mill at Guadalaxara required about fifty years of uneven growth to reach such massive proportions,[18] the Royal Factory for Fine Silks at Talavera de la Reina achieved a grand scale from the outset. This manufactory blossomed swiftly under the skillful guidance of John Rulière and after only twelve years contained all facilities for making fine silks, including 128 looms for rich cloth *(telas ricas)*—material woven from threads of silver,

[12] AGS, *op. cit.*, leg. 763; BN, MS 13005.

[13] AGS, *op. cit.*, legs. 772, 773.

[14] *Ibid.*, leg. 773.

[15] Bourgoing, *op. cit.*, I, 101–102; AGS, *op. cit.*, leg. 772.

[16] Larruga y Boneta, *op. cit.*, XVI, 86, 87.

[17] AGS, *op. cit.*, leg. 780; Larruga y Boneta, *op. cit.*, XVI, 108; Bourgoing, *op. cit.*, I, 103.

[18] Like many industrial organizations of the twentieth century, Guadalaxara developed branch factories. Ferdinand VI began the first at the Royal Site of San Fernando in 1746, and on April 1, 1750, he created another at the village of Brihuega (AGS, *op. cit.*, legs. 765, 776).

gold, and silk. Two hundred and seventy other looms wove such
fabrics as plain silk cloth, smooth velvet, heavy crepe, *grodetures,*
taffeta, stockings, ribbons, sashes, and braids. An additional six
looms for cut velvet existed at Cervera, a village two leagues distant.[19] After reaching this total of 404 in 1760, the number of
looms fell to 321 in 1785. Two years later the factory worked 354
looms, employed 863 individuals, and occupied eleven factory
buildings at Talavera, which contained nearly 270,000 square feet
of floor space.[20]

Since Philip V created the Royal Factory for Woolen Textiles
at Guadalaxara and Ferdinand VI the Royal Factory for Fine Silks
at Talavera de la Reina, it seems in a certain sense appropriate
that Charles III created the third factory with capacity for large-
scale production—the Royal Factory for Cotton Textiles at Avila.
John Berry and Thomas Milne, who had formed a partnership
with Charles to construct and operate this mill in 1788,[21] had
started production by 1790 with eleven looms at the factory and
seven in the houses of artisans. Perhaps because of limited space
at the mill and the backgrounds of Berry and Milne in English
industry, the separation of looms between the factory and private
homes continued. The manufactory held 13 looms and houses of
artisans contained 197 by December, 1796, at about which time
the mill reached its peak size.[22]

As the mills at Guadalaxara, Talavera, and Avila attained relatively large scales, so they developed high degrees of vertical integration. They would have gained nothing from their ability to
weave hundreds of pieces of cloth yearly unless they also were
capable of fulling, shearing, burling, dyeing, and otherwise trans-
forming woven fabrics into finished textiles of superior quality.
To farm out these tasks was not possible, for private industry in
central Spain could not accomplish any of them with the appropriate degree of expertness. If royal mills were to manufacture
fine textiles, they obviously had to possess all stages of production.
This explains why Guadalaxara's San Carlos Serge Division could
manufacture serges entirely within its own walls. Vertical integration at Guadalaxara, however, went further than merely carrying
the production process through the preparation of raw wool to the
completed textiles. This mill constructed most of its own equip-

[19] Larruga y Boneta, *op. cit.,* VIII, 179.

[20] Antonio Ponz, *Viaje de España . . . Hay en Ella* (Madrid, 1772–1794), Tomo
VII, Carta II, p. 600; AGS, *op. cit.,* leg. 786.

[21] *Ibid.,* leg. 756.

[22] *Ibid.,* legs. 755, 756.

ment; it even maintained within its walls a complete unit for making scissors, including the production of high-grade steel.[23]

Extensive vertical integration likewise characterized the mill at Talavera de la Reina. When Rulière first came to Talavera, he found that not only did the region lack the knowledge and skills for producing silks of fine quality, it lacked the workmen capable of producing the intricate and delicate machinery, as well as those who could forge the instruments needed to make the machinery.[24] Obtaining the help of numerous French artisans, the ingenious Rulière first created the tools, then the machinery, buildings, and all other paraphernalia required in making fine silks. Most spectacular of all Rulière's accomplishments was the mill for twisting silk at Cervera. A sophisticated complex of machinery, it could wind, double, and twist 7,072 silk strands at one time.[25] Rulière had even included at Talavera a division for producing thread from gold and silver with facilities for refining, drawing, and twisting the metals.[26] Not only did the factory produce machinery, process raw materials, and manufacture fine textiles, it also created designs for its own products. This artistry originated in the mill's drawing school where French artists trained young Spaniards to design fabrics. Eugenio Larruga y Boneta described the entire factory as being composed of forty different divisions, all so delicately interrelated that they resembled components of a complex watch mechanism, which, when lacking one piece, lost their concert.[27]

Perhaps the factory for cotton textiles at Avila possessed an even greater degree of vertical integration. Antonio de Velasco, who operated the king's warehouse for textiles at Madrid, inspected the mill in June, 1791, and enthusiastically praised it, especially the water-driven machines for carding and spinning created by Thomas Milne.[28] About these, Velasco was ecstatic. He found them superior, even "difficult to describe," when compared with machines for twisting and spinning silk at Talavera. While Velasco was visiting Avila, several wool buyers from foreign lands told him of the cotton factories at Manchester, Orleons, and Montarsis and unanimously agreed to the superiority of the mill

---

[23] *Ibid.*, legs. 765, 768, 769, 771, 773; Larruga y Boneta, *op. cit.*, XVI, 86–87.

[24] *Ibid.*, VIII, 160.

[25] Ponz, *op. cit.*, Tomo VII, Carta II, p. 600. By 1787 this mill had been transferred to Talavera and waterpower substituted for the oxen (AGS, *op. cit.*, leg. 786; Ponz, *op. cit.*, Tomo VII, Carta II, p. 601).

[26] Larruga y Boneta, *op. cit.*, VIII, 180, 181.

[27] *Ibid.*, 164.

[28] AGS, *op. cit.*, leg. 755.

at Avila. In other countries, they related, steam engines (*bombas de fuego*) powered the carding and spinning machines while independent artisans carried out all other operations. At Avila, however, the complete production process, from raw material to finished product, could be accomplished within the factory; and, to the knowledge of the visitors, such an integrated factory was unique in all Europe.[29]

Although these factories at Gudalaxara, Talavera, and Avila combined considerable vertical integration with capacities for relatively large volumes of output, none of the other royal mills exhibited similar traits. The Royal Factory for Woolens at Avila, for example, normally operated about eighteen to twenty looms, while the manufactories at Almarzo, Cuenca, Seville, and San Ildefonso at no time operated more than these numbers.[30] Nor did any of these smaller mills possess near the vertical integration of the larger establishments.

This network of large and small royal factories, representing thousands of artisans, hundreds of looms, many buildings, and large quantities of other equipment and materials, required huge sums of money for construction and, in many cases, for meeting operating expenses. Though most of the mills received their funds from provincial and tobacco tax receipts and from treasury payments, several factories obtained theirs from local excise taxes and public lands. When he created the Royal Factory for Woolens at Avila, for example, Charles III endowed it with rental income from pasture land, which, previous to the formation of the factory, had been divided between the city and the township of Avila (*tierra* or *sexmo de Avila*).[31]

The factory at Guadalaxara depended entirely upon income from local tax revenue and treasury grants, as it sent all sales receipts directly to the royal treasury. For meeting operating expenses, Guadalaxara received monthly remittances from provincial and tobacco tax receipts; and for purchasing wool and dye ingredients, it relied on annual financial grants from the royal treasury. The monthly remittance had reached 160,000 vellon reals by 1750 and continued to soar as the factory and its branches expanded.[32]

---

[29] *Ibid.*

[30] AHN, *op. cit.*, legs. 41066, fol. 46; 50135; AGS, *op. cit.*, legs. 767, 790, 802; Larruga y Boneta, *op. cit.*, XVII, 291; XX, 85.

[31] AGS, *op. cit.*, leg. 756.

[32] AMH, *Colección de Órdenes Generales de Rentas*, X, 27; Larruga y Boneta, *op. cit.*, XVI, 5.

It rose from 200,000 a month in 1767, to 300,000 in 1769, to 400,-
000 in 1776, to 600,000 in 1779, and to 700,000 in 1788.[33] Apparently no more changes occurred during the century.[34]

Treasury grants for the purchase of wool for Guadalaxara came
to 1,150,000 vellon reals in 1768; by 1773 the amount exceeded
1,887,000 vellon reals.[35] After the San Carlos serge division had
been constructed, yearly expenditures of from about 1,256,000
vellon reals to over 1,650,000 vellon reals were needed to supply
just these serge looms with wool. This was in addition to the average yearly expenditure of 1,210,000 vellon reals on fine wool
required to supply the other looms at Guadalaxara and its branch
at Brihuega.

Similar financial arrangements supported the factories for cottons at Avila and for silks at Talavera. From 1788 until 1798
Charles IV expended at least 11 million vellon reals on his cotton
mill at Avila; and by March, 1798, he had authorized a monthly
payment of 100,000 vellon reals for meeting expenses.[36] At least
part of this money came from provincial taxes in Avila. Also depending upon monthly income from tax receipts, the silk factory
at Talavera de la Reina received about 12 million vellon reals
for construction and operation during the period 1748–1762.[37]

To supplement these direct financial payments, kings indirectly
subsidized their mills with nearly absolute freedom from all exactions.[38] Royal textiles, as a consequence, escaped the government's
harsh transaction taxes (*alcabala* and *cientos*), internal transport
duties, export duties, and colonial taxes when sold by agents of
the kings. This policy likewise exempted raw materials and machinery from all levies when destined for royal factories. But private individuals who occasionally purchased the king's products

---

[33] AGS, *op. cit.*, legs. 771, 773.

[34] *Ibid.*, leg. 779; Joseph Townsend, *A Journey Through Spain in the Years 1786
and 1787*, 3 vols. (London, 1792), I, 240. These amounts do not rise nearly as swiftly
when corrected for changes in the general level of prices. Using Earl J. Hamilton's
index of nonagricultural prices in New Castile for the period 1651–1800, I found
the deflated monthly subsidy to change in this fashion: 155,039 in 1750, to 166,528
in 1767, to 230,592 in 1769, to 320,770 in 1776, to 453,172 in 1779, and to 458,415
in 1788 (Earl J. Hamilton, *War and Prices in Spain, 1651–1800* [Cambridge, 1947],
pp. 172–173).

[35] AGS, *op. cit.*, legs. 768, 770.

[36] *Ibid.*, legs. 757, 758.

[37] Larruga y Boneta, *op. cit.*, VIII, 106.

[38] AMH, *op. cit.*, X, 418–419; XI, 19–26, 442; XII, 19–20; XIII, 58, 65, 66; XX,
615; XXII, 566; XXIX, 605–606; XXXI, 207; XXXIV, 267–268; XXXIX, 58; AHN,
op. cit., leg. 50135; Francisco Gallardo Fernandez, *Origen Progresos y Estado de
Rentas de la Corona de España*, 7 vols. (Madrid, 1805–1808), II, 397–398.

and resold them, paid a 2 percent tax in lieu of the royal transaction taxes.[39]

THE MISFORTUNES OF ROYAL FACTORIES

One might reasonably expect that factories endowed with the newest skills and technology, ample funds, and complete tax exemptions would prosper. Yet, such expectations did not materialize; instead, all of the king's mills suffered perpetual deficits. This chapter now examines these financial misfortunes and discusses the various methods taken to overcome them. Since the factory at Guadalaxara grew to so great a size, existed for at least a hundred years, and generally dominated the kings' attitude toward other royal factories, it appears as a source of illustration more often than any other mill.

Deficits haunted this mill for nearly all of its one hundred years.[40] During Guadalaxara's formative period, Philip looked on the losses as the costs of establishing a going concern. He invested 12 million vellon reals in plant and equipment and received sales receipts of only 21,102 vellon reals during the first five years of operations.[41] It was with mounting concern, however, that he witnessed expenses exceed revenue by over 490,000 vellon reals in 1735 and by over 476,000 vellon reals in 1736. Deficits continued to expand along with the mill, despite all efforts by Philip, Ferdinand VI, Charles III, and Charles IV. More than 3 million vellon reals were lost from April 1, 1774, to December 31, 1776.[42] Moreover, sales receipts for each of the years 1782, 1783, 1784, 1786, 1787, and 1788 averaged 8,832,207 vellon reals, while remittances for operating the factory and grants for purchasing wool and other materials surely exceeded 10 million reals annually.[43]

The year 1798 was a profitable one, as remittances and grants came to at least 11,507,748 vellon reals and sales reached 15,499,-

---

[39] AMH, *op. cit.*, XXXI, 547; AGS, *op. cit.*, leg. 778; Gallardo Fernandez, *op. cit.*, II, 283, 399.

[40] Colmeiro y Penido, *op. cit.*, II, 219.

[41] Larruga y Boneta, *op. cit.*, XIV, 166.

[42] AGS, *op. cit.*, leg. 772.

[43] *Ibid.*, leg. 779. No data were found for the year 1785. When corrected for changes in the level of prices, it appears that losses may have peaked around 1775–1776. The index numbers of nonagricultural prices in New Castile, 1651–1800, constructed by Hamilton, were used here. Losses in constant vellon reals (base period 1726–1750) rose from 478,983 in 1735 to 935,768 in 1775. They fell to 844,391 in 1782 and varied thereafter by from 50,000 to 60,000 vellon reals annually (Hamilton, *loc. cit.*).

634 vellon reals and 33 maravedis.[44] Perhaps the war with England, which lasted from 1796 to 1802, and the consequent boycott of all English textiles, as well as the civil turmoil in France, explain this balance. Since archival records for the royal factories after 1800 are not extant, it is only conjecture to suppose that losses returned with peace and the reappearance in Spain of English woolens.

Guadalaxara's branch factory at San Fernando started losing when Ferdinand VI opened it in 1746 and continued losing until Charles III closed it in 1768. Reopened with a staff of English artisans in August, 1788, after twenty years of inactivity, it struggled for three fruitless years before Charles IV abandoned the factory and, along with it, over 338,000 vellon reals.[45] He then turned the facilities over to a company formed by John and Christopher Bertrand, a Frenchman and his son, who intended to produce textiles of cotton and silk. Like the English artisans before them, the Bertrands were unsuccessful and by 1798 had lost over 400,000 vellon reals, not a small portion of which the Spanish government had lent or given in subsidy.[46]

Most other royal manufactories also found profits elusive. The silk factory at Talavera de la Reina showed signs of promise under the management of John Rulière; however, by 1760 Rulière's enemies at Madrid had finally disgraced and imprisoned him. For two years thereafter his successors fumbled. Unwilling to accept the burden of the subsequent deficits, Charles III leased Talavera to the House of Uztáriz in 1762 and to the Five Greater Guilds of Madrid in 1785.[47] Established by Henry Doyle on May 11, 1757, the Royal Factory for Serges at Almarzo had cost the government at least half a million vellon reals by the time of its demise in 1759.[48] Avila's Royal Factory for Woolens consumed more than 1.6 million vellon reals of public funds from 1776 to 1788;[49] yet by 1790 that city's woolen industry had never been in greater decadence. And there is little doubt that tremendous

---

[44] José Canga Arguëlles, *Diccionario de Hacienda*, 2 vols. (Madrid, 1833–1834), I, 468; AGS, *op. cit.*, leg. 783. Canga Arguëlles held that sales receipts in 1798 amounted to only 5.7 million vellon reals and, as a result, losses reached 5,805,748 vellon reals. There is sufficient archival support, however, to insist that sales exceeded 15 million vellon reals in 1798.

[45] *Ibid.*, legs. 784, 785.

[46] *Ibid.*

[47] *Ibid.*, leg. 786; Larruga y Boneta, *op. cit.*, VIII, 317.

[48] AGS, *op. cit.*, legs. 767, 783; Larruga y Boneta, *op. cit.*, XVII, 286–291.

[49] *Ibid.*, XX, 107. Another source indicates that only 1,329,326 vellon reals had been invested (AGS, *op. cit.*, leg. 756).

losses dogged the mill for cottons at Avila from its beginning in 1788 until its dissolution in 1799.[50]

These discouraging experiences must have seemed to the kings much like pouring funds into a bottomless pit. Yet they continued to pour, but not without searching for the causes of, and cures for, the deficits. They had only to look at sales to find the immediate source of their losses. At the offered prices, the quantities purchased by consumers fell short of the quantities supplied by royal factories. Nowhere was this more evident than at Guadalaxara. From the time it began operations on February 4, 1719, until 1726, this factory produced more than 160,000 varas of woolens, yet sold only 10,000 varas.[51] One year later the director of the warehouse at Madrid reported an inventory of 120,000 varas and suggested that only by drastically reducing prices would the market absorb them.[52] It was not until the last years of the century that the surplus problem diminished; first a destructive revolution in France and then wars that engulfed Europe with Napoleon's ascendancy reduced the imports of woolens into, and therefore the supply of woolens in, Spain. With foreign substitutes thus blocked, Guadalaxara sold nearly all of its output.[53]

During the seventy or more years before, however, kings struggled to overcome surpluses at Guadalaxara. They approached the dilemma in three ways. Employing an obvious method, they lowered the prices of their textiles and thereby increased the quantity demanded. The use of extensive merchandising to increase sales at the established prices was perhaps their most important approach. And as a last resort, they avoided altogether the problem of additional surpluses by leasing, giving away, or abandoning the factories.

Though price reductions were an obvious method of reducing surpluses, they were used sparingly and with little success.[54] When Ferdinand VI lowered prices on fine Guadalaxara stuffs by

---

[50] AMH, *op. cit.*, XL, 167–172; Canga Arguëlles, *op. cit.*, I, 467; AGS, *op. cit.*, legs. 757, 758. Perhaps the Royal Factory of San Nicolas, established by Charles III on July 30, 1787, in an abandoned Jesuit seminary at Guadalaxara, was an exception. Through the efforts of Samuel Bird, its director, the factory announced profits of 26,179 vellon reals and 16 maravedis in 1791 and 66,854 vellon reals in 1793. Unfortunately, this promising factory was shortlived, for when Bird died unexpectedly in 1797 the king moved his seven looms to the main factory (*ibid.*, legs. 775, 776, 780, 781, 783, 784).

[51] *Ibid.*, leg. 759; Larruga y Boneta, *op. cit.*, XIV, 213.

[52] AGS, *op. cit.*, leg. 759.

[53] *Ibid.*, legs. 782, 783.

[54] *Ibid.*, leg. 765.

four vellon reals a vara in 1750, for example, the quantity sold increased substantially and surpluses started to diminish.[55] Soon, however, textiles again piled up and deficits rose in response to competitive price reductions by foreign producers and rising costs of production. Reacting violently, the king raised prices in 1753 above the 1750 level, only to watch sales fall by more than 50 percent during the twelve following days as consumers swiftly substituted foreign for royal textiles. Ferdinand quickly reduced prices.[56]

One might ask why, in the light of their inability to reduce surpluses by lowering prices, kings did not simply produce fewer textiles. As we shall see, they went further than cutting back production when they eventually abandoned some factories and leased or gave others to private individuals. But with Guadalaxara, kings preferred to maintain output at a high level. Apparently they believed that this mill was serving its purpose as a center for the diffusion of skills and technology and that any reduction in output would impair this function.

As an alternative to manipulating prices and output in Guadalaxara, kings turned to merchandising. They endeavored to increase the demand for the mill's products by enlarging the markets and by gaining the favor of consumers. Since they regarded the peninsular market as the most important, kings and their ministers placed high priority on its development. In one of his first efforts to boost sales, Philip V established a warehouse at Madrid on March 7, 1722.[57] Gross inefficiency—operating costs exceeded receipts by 60 percent—forced the government to reorganize it in 1727 and again in 1730. Although the warehouse extended credit to purchasers of large quantities after 1730, it failed to lessen substantially the surplus.[58]

Even during these early years Philip realized that sales would rise only if he penetrated markets other than Madrid and Guadalaxara. In 1727 he therefore asked the merchant guilds in fifty-one villages and cities to sell royal textiles. A few accepted and many refused. Nevertheless, sales in the following two months exceeded

---

[55] *Ibid.*

[56] Though kings found themselves unable to use successfully price reductions during the short run, they permitted prices of Guadalaxara's fabrics to rise slowly over the century. Serges sold for 7, 9½, and 11 vellon reals a vara, depending upon the color, in 1740; this range stood at 11, 12, and 13 vellon reals a vara in 1786. During this period the price range for fine stuffs rose from 48–68 vellon reals to 62–84 vellon reals a vara (Larruga y Boneta, *op. cit.*, XV, 163; XVI, 97).

[57] *Ibid.*, XIV, 126.

[58] *Ibid.*, 231–234, 251–257.

those of the previous seven years.[59] But the problem of surpluses continued, and textiles still piled up at the factory and the warehouse. Then, in 1738, government attorneys presented Philip with a drastic proposal for resolving the dilemma; the king should compel woolen merchants and other dealers in these goods to purchase only from warehouses supplied exclusively by royal factories. Citing laws of the kingdom in support of this opinion, they argued that city officials could obligate citizens to buy surplus goods at set prices, even though the citizens had no need for them, and even though the goods were spoiled and worthless. Moreover, peasants often had to rent the gristmills and pasturelands of princes, at the insistence of the princes, in preference to those owned by others. Philip therefore should seize this legal advantage, they concluded, and force merchants to buy royal textiles rather than those from foreign countries.[60]

Apparently Philip rejected such arbitrary action, for there is no evidence that he compelled merchant guilds to accept royal cloth against their will. Yet the threat posed by this counsel evidently prodded the Guild of Woolen Merchants of Madrid into a marketing agreement with the factory at Guadalaxara.[61] As a consequence of this pact, the factory abandoned its retail and wholesale functions at Madrid in 1744, leaving the Guild as sole seller of royal textiles. In provincial cities and villages, however, the factory opened sales outlets. By 1754 it had established them at Seville, Cadiz, Granada, Cordova, Zaragoza, Valencia, Vitoria, Logroño, and Zafra.[62]

Even with outlets scattered over the peninsula and merchandising assistance from guilds, Guadalaxara could not sell all of its output in Spain at the offered prices. So kings turned to the colonial market. Philip V and his ministers sent more than 300,000

---

[59] AGS, *op. cit.*, leg. 759; Larruga y Boneta, *op. cit.*, XIV, 199.

[60] *Ibid.*, XV, 70–74.

[61] AGS, *op. cit.*, legs. 762, 763; Larruga y Boneta, *op. cit.*, XVI, 1–2.

[62] AGS, *op. cit.*, legs. 765, 766. Surpluses continued; and to escape them, Ferdinand VI leased the mill to the Guild of Woolen Merchants of Madrid from 1757 to 1767. The Guild abolished the provincial warehouses, reduced the output of textiles by one-third, raised prices, and offered easier terms of sale. When Charles III took back the factory in 1768, at the Guild's request, he immediately began reëstablishing provincial outlets and by 1776 operated them at Madrid, Cadiz, Seville, Zaragoza, Valencia, Santiago, Oviedo, Granada, Valladolid, Cartagena, La Coruña, and El Ferrol. Hoping to encourage independent merchants to sell his cloth, Charles closed these competing outlets in 1785 and gave merchants substantial discounts on royal textiles. Within four years, however, he had abandoned the discount method and had reopened his provincial establishments (*ibid.*, legs. 768, 771, 774, 780; Larruga y Boneta, *op. cit.*, XVI, 58).

varas to Spanish America from 1723 to 1744.[63] English merchants dominated this market, and in the fierce competitive struggle that resulted, Philip often sold his textiles for less than the transportation expenses.[64] Sales receipts in the Indies for the period July 1, 1746, to March 31, 1757, reached 2,692,370 vellon reals and 27 maravedis—only a fraction of the cost of the textiles.[65] Often defective, usually tightly woven, heavy in texture, and dark in color, Guadalaxara's textiles competed poorly with the cheaper, lighter, and more colorful products manufactured in England and elsewhere.

Markets in Western and Eastern Europe also received royal textiles. Here, too, success at least partially eluded the Spaniards. To cite an example, Antonio Abancino took fifty pieces of woolen stuffs from Guadalaxara to the Italian cities of Genoa, Rome, Naples, Milan, and Placensia in 1754 and lost more than 37,600 vellon reals.[66] Charles IV suffered additional losses in transactions with Russia. On a shipment sent in August, 1791, consisting of two hundred pieces of fine woolens valued at about 505,000 vellon reals, he lost approximately 16,338 vellon reals.[67] He tried again on November 24, 1794, sending 150 pieces and this time losing nearly 59,000 vellon reals. Undaunted by his ill fortune, Charles exported at least 750 pieces to Russia in 1795 and 1796. He would have met all costs at a price of 6½ rubles an arshin (a measure of twenty-eight inches), but the highest offers did not exceed five rubles.[68]

Royal textiles still remained unsold despite these intensive efforts to merchandise them. So at times kings turned to arbitrary and coercive measures. In not a few instances they paid overdue salaries of their employees in fabrics.[69] And they regularly destined royal cloth, often defective in quality, for the livery of the royal cavalrymen, uniforms of the king's guards and halberdiers, and clothes of the royal servants.[70] Charles III even revised the

---

[63] AGS, *op. cit.*, leg. 759.

[64] Larruga y Boneta, *op. cit.*, XIV, 215.

[65] AGS, *op. cit.*, leg. 766.

[66] *Ibid.*, legs. 765, 766. The Spanish government carried the risk in this venture (*ibid.*, leg. 765).

[67] *Ibid.*, leg. 782.

[68] *Ibid.*, leg. 781. One should not too quickly condemn these overseas transactions as being without merit. When Spanish kings shipped part of their surpluses to foreign and American markets and succeeded in selling them for more than the transport costs, they recovered at least part of their production outlays and thus minimized their losses.

[69] Larruga y Boneta, *op. cit.*, XV, 65.

[70] AGS, *op. cit.*, leg. 782; Larruga y Boneta, *op. cit.*, XIV, 164, 215, 269.

ordinances for the Army and the Navy and thereby obligated all officers to have their uniforms tailored from royal textiles.

Only their intense desire to implant the manufacture of fine textiles throughout central Spain induced kings to accept the discouraging performance of their mills and restrained them from quickly giving up their efforts. Even so, deficits eventually forced them either to abandon the factories, lease them to private individuals and organizations, or give them away. The Royal Factory for Serges at Almarzo, the Royal Factory for Woolens at Seville, the Royal Factory of San Nicolas, and the Royal Factory for Woolens at Avila all were abandoned.[71] Moreover, Charles IV ceded outright the factory for producing textiles from silk and wool at San Fernando and the Royal Factory for Cotton Textiles at Avila to private individuals in 1791 and 1799 respectively.[72] When they wished to maintain ownership and still avoid financial responsibility, kings leased their manufactories. By this fashion the Guild of Woolen Merchants of Madrid operated Guadalaxara from 1757 to 1767. Charles III leased his mill at Talavera to the House of Uztáriz in 1762 and to the Five Greater Guilds of Madrid in 1785. The latter also obtained a lease on the king's factory at Cuenca in 1786.[73]

REASONS FOR THE FAILURE OF ROYAL FACTORIES

Undoubtedly the explanation for the dismal record of royal factories lay in a concatenation of numerous factors all of which adversely affected the relative efficiency of Spanish industry. Despite this complex chain of causes, a few major determinants of inefficiency stand out. One such cause was, strangely enough, the large size and vertical integration of several mills. The large-scale factories prevalent in Europe in the nineteenth century evolved only after innovations permitting the mechanization of certain operations, such as spinning and weaving, made profitable the installation of machinery in specially designed buildings.

---

[71] The factory at Almarzo closed when Charles III refused to advance more funds for its completion; the factory at Seville ceased to exist when a majority of English prisoners returned to England after the war; and the Royal Factory at San Nicolas, as stated above, died with Samuel Bird in 1797 (AGS, *op. cit.*, legs. 767, 783, 802; Larruga y Boneta, *op. cit.*, XVI, 47; Carrera y Pujal, *op. cit.*, IV, 101).

[72] Charles IV ceded the factory at Avila to Agustin Betancourt, a celebrated French machinist (AMH, *op. cit.*, XLIII, 167–172; Enrique Herrera Oria, *La Real Fábrica de Tejidos de Algodón Estampados, de Ávila, y la Reorganización Nacional de esta Industria en el Siglo XVIII* [Valladolid, 1922], p. 40; AGS, *op. cit.*, leg. 785).

[73] *Ibid.*, legs. 786, 787, 788; Ponz, *op. cit.*, Tomo VII, Carta II, p. 601; Larruga y Boneta, *op. cit.*, VIII, 314–315, 317; XVI, 37, 42, 43, 47.

Previous to these developments, however, Spanish kings invested huge sums in large, specialized buildings for holding all elements of the production process, for storing materials, for merchandising textiles, and for housing administrative facilities. Interest on these investments, besides payments for maintenance and depreciation of buildings and equipment, occasioned relatively high fixed costs; wages paid to a myriad of bookkeepers, foremen, guards, porters, scribes, and so forth, also gave rise to relatively high variable costs. And the vastness of the organizations made management difficult. Compare these circumstances with what was common in England, for example, where entrepreneurs supplied materials to specialized artisans who worked in their own houses or workshops. After a worker finished his task, the entrepreneur carried the unfinished textile to another artisan, who, also working in his own house or workshop, in turn applied his specialized skill, moving the textile nearer to completion. Fixed costs were virtually absent; at zero output the entrepreneur held only raw materials, finished and unfinished textiles, and cash. While the English artisan lived and worked in his house, the artisan in a Spanish royal factory lived in his own house and worked in the factory; hence kings duplicated facilities.

Rather than economies of scale, the Spaniards thus probably experienced diseconomies of scale when they built large, integrated factories in advance of the more spectacular cost-reducing inventions. Data to support this position, in the form of cost comparisons between small and large plants in Spain, are not extant; however, a less sophisticated form of evidence does exist. This evidence is bureaucracy. A flagrant symptom of such diseconomies, this malady spread as each mill grew beyond the capacity of one man's leadership, as employees other than those directly employed in production multiplied, and as the internal structure of the mills became split into quasi-independent departments and subdivisions. These conditions often muddled the channels of communication and replaced the drive for efficiency with a desire for personal aggrandizement.[74]

It is not surpising, therefore, that disorder and confusion often plagued the organizations. A typical incident occurred early in Guadalaxara's history. When Philip V established this factory in 1719 he permitted the Dutch artisans to use their language, accounting procedure, and weights and measures in keeping records. Twenty years later, the factory was still using them, even

---

[74] *Ibid.*, XX, 159.

though Spanish officials, who had long since replaced the Dutch in management, had difficulty understanding them.[75] Similar lags in decision-making frequently led to inexcusable waste. Monsieur Cayrol, a French dyer, for example, spent two years at Guadalaxara, plus about 100,000 vellon reals, displaying his proficiency before the Spaniards in charge discovered that he possessed only mediocre talents.[76]

Several mills nearly perished when their administrative procedures collapsed and chaos set in. Indeed, the Royal Factory for Cotton Textiles at Avila did perish amid disorganization and discord. After receiving numerous complaints from workers and officials, Charles IV sent an investigating committee to Avila on August 6, 1797.[77] Conditions at the factory appalled the committee. The books were poorly kept, the storage facilities were unguarded, the apprenticeship system had been abandoned, the products were imperfect and nearly unsalable, most of the looms were idle, and fraud was clearly evident. All efforts by Charles to improve conditions failed. He finally gave up the factory in 1799.[78]

Avila's difficulties did not arise solely from its attributes of large-scale production and vertical integration. Incompetent leadership surely must share the blame. Nor was inept management unique at Avila.[79] Kings invested millions on technical excellence, but practically ignored administrative skills in most of their mills. In fact, they frequently confused the ablity to create a fine piece of cloth with a high degree of competency in management.[80] And too often the kings or their ministers chose as directors men of little experience in either production or leadership, but with much political influence. For example, the intendant of the province of Guadalaxara, beginning in 1857, doubled as the director of the king's mill at Guadalaxara and as the government's representative in that province. As a member of the grossly in-

---

[75] *Ibid.*, XV, 146.

[76] AGS, *op. cit.*, legs. 771, 779.

[77] *Ibid.*, leg. 757; AMH, *op. cit.*, XLI, 282–289; Herrera Oria, *op. cit.*, pp. 28–29.

[78] AMH, *op. cit.*, XLIII, 167–172.

[79] AGS, *op. cit.*, legs. 756, 767, 784, 785; AHN, *op. cit.*, legs. 50134, 51524, 53176; Larruga y Boneta, *op. cit.*, XVII, 286.

[80] For example, neither Henry Doyle, who directed the factory at Almarzo, nor Patrick Boulger, who directed the mill for woolens at Avila, had had experience in managing a textile factory, let alone a workshop. And John Riley obtained the directorship of the factory at Seville even though his reputation as a drunkard had spread north of Seville (AGS, *op. cit.*, legs. 756, 767, 783, 802; AHN, *op. cit.*, legs. 41066, fols. 46, 313; 50135; Larruga y Boneta, *op. cit.*, XVII, 286).

efficient Spanish bureaucracy, the intendant more often than not proved to be inept at managing the factory. An on-the-scene observer questioned the wisdom of this method of selecting managers.

. . . a position of this nature [director of royal factories] is not compatible with the actions of many employees who wish to govern the business of a large factory from their chairs or from their beds by means of oral or perhaps written messages delivered by their attendants. If, for such positions, we do not avail ourselves of men who have acquired the necessary and indispensable art of political calculation by means of their talent, application, and continual love of beneficial enterprise, we shall destroy the best establishments and discredit and injure our country.[81]

These were prophetic words, for the fruits of inferior management litter the histories of Spain's royal factories. Inexperienced or irresponsible administrators were not able to coördinate successfully the hundreds of artisans with different skills, the numerous machines, the large quantities of materials, and the many and involved steps in the production process. As one result, nearly all of the royal factories at one time or another manufactured textiles of lesser quality than those from foreign countries. Woolens produced by the factories at Avila and Cuenca were inferior, as were the textiles of wool and silk made by the English at San Fernando from 1788 to 1792.[82] The factories for silks at Talavera and cottons at Avila were also guilty of producing inferior products. Even stuffs manufactured at Guadalaxara during this mill's early years suffered from thick, uneven threads, defective fulling and dyeing, and the smell of rancid oil.[83]

Though Spanish managers stand accused of frequent bungling, many of their actions were quite predictable under the circumstances. Since they received copious revenue from tax receipts, which made them independent of sales income and shielded them from the discipline of market forces, directors evaded the consequences of their own mistakes. This protection diverted managers from seeking more efficient methods of production and from catering to consumers' tastes and thereby often led them, with the king's full support, to emphasize the purely technical aspects of production.

---

[81] *Ibid.*, XX, 158–159.

[82] AGS, *op. cit.*, legs. 775, 777.

[83] Larruga y Boneta, *op. cit.*, XIV, 167.

Here was a basic error. By allowing this concentration on the technical or engineering considerations, the kings unwittingly diverted attention from economic realities. The directors at Guadalaxara succeeded in producing exquisite fabrics after fifty years of introducing highly skilled artisans and technology from Western Europe and after many reforms at the mill.[84] These reforms, however, entailed controls, a hardening of production techniques, and a crystallization of styles. As this inflexibility became more apparent, the mill became less able to adapt to competition from French and English producers who introduced cheaper, lighter, more colorful textiles from mixtures of silk, wool, cotton, and flax. The difficulty went further than mere inflexibility. From the beginning kings had been obsessed with creating an industry to produce fine, traditional cloth in Spain. In their eager pursuit of this goal, they seemed to have ignored the fact that the demand for these fabrics was a small portion of total demand for fabrics. And the outpouring of textiles from their mills, combined with the cloth supplied by foreign producers, flooded the peninsula and left little room for independent producers. This became even more apparent when the fancy of consumers turned from royal fabrics to the newer, more attractive imported textiles.[85] But the kings and their officials, with their attention fixed on limited technical objectives, gave little heed to changing market conditions and the scale of their factories relative to the demand for cloth.

Although kings applied these same rigid technical objectives to all of their mills, they did not supply their smaller factories with a high degree of engineering sophistication. These mills were built in areas where the manufacture of fine textiles was unknown and thus where most of the complementary skills did not exist, at least not of the necessary quality. And since these factories were small and did not possess all of the skills needed, they availed themselves of local, semiskilled artisans, and, furthermore, em-

---

[84] AGS, *op. cit.*, legs. 759, 761, 762, 765, 766, 769, 771, 774, 775, 776, 778, 779, 780, 781; Larruga y Boneta, *op. cit.*, XIV, 247; XV, 76, 191; XVI, 11, 119; Bourgoing, *op. cit.*, I, 103.

[85] AGS, *op. cit.*, legs. 762, 766, 767, 770, 775, 777, 779, 782; Larruga y Boneta, *op. cit.*, XV, 190. In order to counteract competition from new fabrics, kings occasionally ordered Guadalaxara to imitate the innovated textiles; but more often they established new factories or adapted old ones to produce the new products. The Royal Factory of San Nicolas, for example, produced superfine stuffs that were both narrower and lighter than customary stuffs. And the English at San Fernando in 1788 wove colorful textiles from silk and wool thread. Moreover, on March 16, 1768, Charles III adapted the branch factory at Brihuega to manufacture second-class woolens with narrower dimensions and from second-grade wool. Nevertheless, these efforts offered only token resistance to the rapid proliferation of styles.

ployed skilled artisans in a multiple of tasks, in only one of which each excelled. They consequently produced inferior textiles and suffered from a lack of division of labor.

Besides internal diseconomies, poor or misdirected management, inferior products, and a misguided emphasis on technical considerations, royal mills encountered other, and perhaps even more formidable, obstructions to their success. Natural disadvantages in the form of rugged terrain, inadequate rainfall, an insufficient supply of important resources, wretched communications, and relatively small cities in central Spain all contributed to the ruin of the kings' factories. One case in point illustrates neatly these drawbacks. The expense of packing cotton from the Mediterranean ports over pathlike roads, which meandered through rugged mountains and crossed over windswept plateaus, to the factory at Avila, added at least 10 percent to that mill's cost as compared to its competitors at Barcelona.[86]

The untimely endings of most royal manufactories would have been less disheartening had production of fine cloth taken root in central Spain. But once Spanish artisans left the mills, they did not spread throughout Castile and Leon creating centers for fine textiles. Outside of the royal establishments, the production of superior fabrics was quite rare in central Spain during the eighteenth century.[87] Even the manufacture of ordinary woolens reacted indifferently to these centers of training and technology. Catalonia and Valencia alone experienced much rise in production. Moreover, the output of silks, linens, and cottons changed little except in Catalonia and Valencia. In these two latter provinces, which kings slighted and therefore in which royal mills did not appear, production of textiles expanded rapidly.

The trifling response by private enterprise in Castile and Leon was due to many factors, such as the lack of adequate communications, the harsh climate, the numerous, severe taxes, and the relative scarcity of, among other important things, firewood and swift, clear streams. But the kings' mills themselves, especially the larger ones, proved greater barriers. Originally a means to the stimulation of independent production, royal factories, after receiving millions of reals and after years of being objects of untold

---

[86] AGS, *op. cit.*, leg. 755.

[87] The village of Bejar, in the province of Salamanca, was an exception (see p. 21, n. 93). Another center for fine woolens appeared in Segovia when Laureano Ortiz de Paz obtained the facilities of the defunct Royal Company of Segovia on August 20, 1779. Ortiz de Paz apparently produced fine and superfine stuffs during the remainder of the century (Larruga y Boneta, *op. cit.*, XII, 262–275).

amounts of planning and expectation, slowly became the embodiment of kingly prestige and ends in themselves. They competed vigorously for labor and materials, and poured endless quantities of textiles into a relatively small domestic market, all the while treating independent producers as rivals. Coercion often supplanted competition. Guadalaxara, for example, obtained a royal order on May 6, 1752, that compelled all persons in the right age bracket, not just the poor and the idle, to work in the factory's spinning schools.[88] Royal mills frequently got first choice of materials; Guadalaxara traditionally took the best Merino wool at prices below the current market, and Talavera de la Reina obtained exclusive rights on all silk harvested within ten leagues of the mill.[89] To merchandise its textiles, Guadalaxara placed retail outlets in twelve major cities on the peninsula, obtained a royal decree that prohibited domestic producers from sending fine woolens to America, and even persuaded the king to forbid the production of fine cloth in a village near Valencia.[90] As these few illustrations reveal, the royal mills strayed far from their original purpose and evolved into barriers rather than aids to private enterprise.

[88] AGS, *op. cit.*, leg. 765.
[89] Larruga y Boneta, *op. cit.*, VIII, 166–167, 226, 230, 233.
[90] Colmeiro y Penido, *op. cit.*, II, 220; Bourgoing, *op. cit.*, I, 106.

IV

Royal Joint-Stock Companies

INTRODUCTION

While Spanish kings energetically constructed their textile mills, they concurrently chartered joint-stock companies, permitting them to erect factories and engage in overseas commerce. This form of business organization first appeared in Western Europe during the sixteenth century when traditional means of organizing economic activity were unable to cope with the growing complexities of farflung trade and the expanding scale of production. Borrowing the corporate principle from the merchant guild and the idea of a synthesis of capital from the medieval partnership, the joint-stock company emerged as an hybrid institution with a continuity of existence and the capability of controlling large sums of money.[1] It became more than an efficient method of organizing private business activity; it soon took its place as a tool of economic development, wielded by kings and their ministers for the industrial and commercial well-being of nations.

In England the joint-stock device evolved early and spread rapidly throughout commerce and industry, replacing the older methods of arranging economic endeavor.[2] A close relationship linked the first companies and the English crown; they received grants of privilege from the king, and His Majesty's naval and maritime strength prospered from the masts, cordage, copper, and other items supplied by these companies. As time passed, joint-stock enterprises supported privateering ventures, expanded their trade with distant lands, and financed and implanted overseas

[1] William Robert Scott, *The Constitution and Finance of English, Scottish and Irish Joint-Stock Companies to 1720*, 3 vols. (London, 1910–1912), I, 1–15.

[2] Whereas the Russia Company and the Adventurers to Africa, the only two joint-stock companies known to have been in existence between 1553 and 1560, had capital of less than 10,000 pounds, the many companies operating over a century and a half later on the eve of the South Sea Bubble had capital in the aggregate of about 50 million pounds (*ibid.*, I, 439).

[51]

colonies.[3] In about 1687 a remarkable extension of the joint-stock
device into domestic industry began, and by the early eighteenth
century Englishmen were forming companies to build roads, improve rivers, sell insurance, produce glass, sugar, and textiles, and
generally to establish large-scale industry.

Most other European powers employed joint-stock companies
much as England had done, first as privileged institutions closely
related to the crown's welfare in maritime and naval affairs and
later as developers of domestic industry and commerce. Spain was
an exception. She rejected this type of enterprise during the
sixteenth and seventeenth centuries, adopting a unique relationship with her boundless and opulent provinces in America.
Within fifty years after the epoch voyage of Columbus, a system of
colonial trade, which funneled all commercial activity from
American ports into Seville, San Lucar de Barrameda, and Cadiz,
had appeared and remained essentially intact until the last half
of the eighteenth century.[4] A prerequisite for engaging in American commerce was membership in the Consulate of Seville. Originally a merchant guild with relative ease of entry, the Consulate
soon evolved into a tightly closed organization and resembled a
huge regulated company. It monopolized colonial trade.[5] The
source of its power emanated from the Spanish kings. By protecting and encouraging this small, favored group, Spain's rulers were
able to control the flow of merchandise to and from America and
thereby attain for the royal treasury a large share of revenue from
colonial commerce.

Throughout the sixteenth and seventeenth centuries, Spaniards
who were not affiliated with the Consulate longed to participate
in America's riches, but lacking membership in the Sevillian
coterie they yearned in vain. They nevertheless attempted to
circumvent the Consulate's monopoly. Hence it was that enter-
prising Spaniards from time to time advanced schemes for launching joint-stock companies into colonial trade. Here was a way,
they reasoned, to gain entry into this profitable activity and at
the same time to reduce individual risk, to obtain a large working capital, and to secure valuable rights and prestige from a
governmental grant of privilege. Powerful vested interests at

---

[3] *Ibid.*, I, 440–441.

[4] Roland Dennis Hussey, *The Caracas Company, 1728–1784* (Cambridge, Massachusetts, 1934), p. 5.

[5] *Ibid.*, pp. 6–7; Clarence Henry Haring, *The Spanish Empire in America* (New
York, 1947), p. 321.

Seville thwarted them until 1728.[6] Then, on September 25 of that year, Philip V awarded a group of Basque merchants at San Sebastian a monopoly of trade with Venezuela, and thus began the Caracas Company.[7] The Havana Company, chartered on December 18, 1740, to trade in Cuban tobacco, and the Barcelona Company, founded on May 24, 1755, to trade with the islands of Santo Domingo, Puerto Rico, and La Margarita, joined the Caracas Company as newcomers in colonial commerce.[8] Although these enterprises may appear to have been significant encroachments on the Consulate's monopoly, they were not. For their activities were restricted to areas that merchants of Seville had virtually abandoned to foreigners. Nevertheless, these companies secured valuable privileges in their respective American regions, oriented their affairs toward overseas trade, and experienced some prosperity, though limited and fleeting.

Other joint-stock companies were created by the crown during the eighteenth century. To induce greater entrepreneurial effort and thereby to assist the expansion of industry and commerce in Spain, kings awarded charters for a number of privileged enterprises. These institutions essentially were tools of economic development. Supplied with funds from the sale of stocks and the proceeds of loans and given special prerogatives, they built factories to manufacture textiles and other items and engaged in domestic and foreign commerce. Their initial years were heartening, their final ones bitter and calamitous.

This chapter investigates the use of these domestic joint-stock companies as instruments for improving Spain's economy during the period 1750–1800; it discusses the founding of the institutions and the success they enjoyed in selling shares and in their initial efforts in industry and trade; it concludes with a statement of their universal failure and with an analysis of why this tragedy occurred.

CORPORATE STRUCTURES OF THE JOINT-STOCK COMPANIES

A new era began for this impoverished land with the ascension of Philip V to the Spanish throne in 1700. Immediately upon his

---

[6] For a discussion of these attempts to form joint-stock companies, see Hussey, *op. cit.*

[7] *Ibid.*, p. 60. Hussey tells of a short-lived joint-stock company formed on February 1, 1714, for the purpose of trading with Honduras. He says it "was more or less the early type of mercantile association: a joint-stock company, not a corporation" (*ibid.*). Manuel Colmeiro y Penido also mentions this Company (*Historia de la Economía Política en España*, 2 vols. [Madrid, 1863], II, 460).

[8] Hussey, *op. cit.*, pp. 207–208, 217.

arrival from France, the new king set about to reëstablish Spain's industry and commerce, which had slipped away disastrously during the previous one hundred years. He initiated a number of reforms designed to improve trade and manufacturing; his successors expanded this start into a broad, sweeping program for economic development. As part of their comprehensive plan, Ferdinand VI and Charles III chartered nine domestic joint-stock companies during the period 1746–1773.[9] They assigned each company special objectives. The companies of Extremadura, Granada, Toledo, and Requena were to build factories for silks, to promote the manufacture of these fabrics in their respective provinces by providing artisans with equipment and material, and to sell textiles both at home and abroad.[10] Commerce was the major aim of the Company of Seville, though it was permitted to build factories for making textiles.[11] The Company of Aragon received the broadest mandate. It could engage in overseas trade and build factories to manufacture all types of products.[12] The companies

---

[9] They were: the Royal Company of Commerce and Factories of Aragon (July 27, 1746), the Royal Company of Commerce and Factories of Extremadura (May 11, 1746), the Royal Company of Commerce and Factories of Granada (March 24, 1747), the Royal Company of San Fernando of Seville (August 7, 1747), the Royal Company of Commerce and Factories of Toledo (February 10, 1748), the Royal Company of Commerce and Factories of Requena (April 2, 1753), the Royal Company of Woolen Stuffs of Segovia (January 12, 1763), the Royal Company of the City of Burgos (November 21, 1767), and the Royal Company of Santa Barbara and San Carlos of the Village of Ezcaray (November 7, 1773) (AGS, *Secretaría de Hacienda*, legs. 852, 855, 856, 857; AMH, *Colección de Órdenes Generales de Rentas*, VII, 412, 435; XI, 372–383; BN, MS 13006, fol. 34; Ignacio Jordán de Asso del Río, *Historia de la Economía Política de Aragón* [Zaragoza, 1798], p. 138; Eugenio Larruga y Boneta, *Memorias Políticas y Económicas sobre los Frutos, Comercio, Fábricas y Minas de España*, 45 vols. [Madrid, 1787–1800], VII, 59–60; XII, 227; XVIII, 301–310; XXXI, 185).

[10] AMH, *op. cit.*, X, 381; XI, 372–383; Larruga y Boneta, *op. cit.*, VII, 63–71; XVIII, 301–303; XXXIX, 122–126; BN, MS 13006; AGS, *op. cit.*, legs. 852, 853, 857.

The Company of Requena, however, did not become a reality, for its backers failed to sell a sufficient number of shares of stock (Larruga y Boneta, *op. cit.*, XVIII, 310).

[11] Archival and secondary sources are nearly silent on the Company of Seville. About all the writer found is the following: Ferdinand VI founded the Company on August 7, 1747, and provided it with the customary privileges; on December 31, 1753, he conceded freedom of import duties on materials destined to its factories; in 1755 a master from the king's factory at Guadalaxara had returned recently from the village of Caceres where he had established a mill for producing woolen stuffs for the Company; in 1780 the Company was still operating, for it purchased textiles from the Royal Company of Ezcaray; and Hussey found that the Company continued its American trade until at least 1786 (AMH, *op. cit.*, X, 381; XI, 412; AGS, *op. cit.*, leg. 788; Colmeiro y Penido, *op. cit.*, II, 458–459; Hussey, *op. cit.*, p. 22).

[12] AGS, *op. cit.*, leg. 856; AMH, *op. cit.*, VII, 412–435; Asso del Río, *op. cit.*, p. 138.

of Segovia and Ezcaray, in contrast, were restricted to producing fine woolens.[13] Perhaps the most unusual mission of all belonged to the Company of Burgos. Created as a "bank of active commerce" and forbidden to own or operate factories, it was to provide financial assistance to industry and to serve as a merchandiser for regional products.[14]

Although Ferdinand and Charles did not operate the companies, their crowns cast ever-present, domineering shadows upon the firms. This was inevitable, since these monarchs and members of their families owned shares in all of the institutions.[15] Royal holdings varied from 1 percent to 20 percent of authorized stock issues and from 1.6 percent to 43 percent of shares actually sold. Whether the percentage of ownership was large or small, the royal delegates who sat on the boards of directors were ominous reminders of royal authority. If the enterprises felt the authority of kings on their governing bodies, they were even more aware of the royal presence that resided in company charters. It was to these grants of privilege that joint-stock companies owed their corporate lives and extensive prerogatives; and, knowing full well that such favors depended on the royal mood, the firms did not operate independently of the kings' wishes.

From their charters the companies did in fact obtain extensive rights and privileges not ordinarily available to independent producers in Spain. These cedulas of creation also regulated the sale of shares, borrowing of funds, stockholders' meetings, and activities of the firms in much the same way that they control present-day corporations.

Charters permitted companies to sell only a limited number and value of shares,[16] usually restricted ownership of these shares

[13] Larruga y Boneta, *op. cit.*, XII, 227–261; XXXI, 185–194; AGS, *op. cit.*, leg. 788.

[14] All of the companies except Segovia and Ezcaray could explicitly engage in limited foreign and domestic commerce. The charters of Burgos and Aragon, for example, permitted them to export only products of their regions and import only commodities needed in Spain (*ibid.*, legs. 852, 855, 856; AMH, *op. cit.*, VII, 412–435; Asso del Río, *loc. cit.;* Larruga y Boneta, *op. cit.*, VII, 63–71; XXXIX, 123; BN, MS 13006, fols. 34–38).

[15] For example, the royal household purchased 750,000 vellon reals worth of shares in the Company of Aragon, 60,000 in the Company of Extremadura, 60,000 in the Company of Toledo, 200,000 in the Company of Segovia, 280,000 in the Company of Ezcaray, and 220,000 in the Company of Burgos (AGS, *op. cit.*, legs. 852, 855, 856; AMH, *op. cit.*, VII, 412–435; XVI, 279–281; Larruga y Boneta, *op. cit.*, VII, 62; XXX, 5, 95; XXXI, 187; XXXIX, 116; BN, MS 13006, fol. 34).

[16] For example, the Company of Aragon could issue 2,000 shares each with a par value of 3,750 vellon reals; the Company of Toledo, 2,000 shares each with a par value of 3,000 vellon reals; the Company of Segovia, 333 shares each with a par value of 300 vellon reals; and the Company of Ezcaray, 1,000 shares each with

to Spaniards and Spanish organizations, and often stipulated that only Spaniards of certain classes might purchase them. The Company of Toledo could not sell to members of the ecclesiastical estate nor to charitable establishments.[17] The companies of Aragon and Burgos, however, were permitted to accept funds from churchmen, but not from charitable organizations nor from entailed estates.[18] Some charters authorized persons who had lent money to the firms at interest (*censualistas*) to convert their credits into shares. The Company of Ezcaray preferred these creditors over ordinary stock purchasers.[19]

Unlike their counterparts of today, shareholders of most Spanish companies could not dispose of their stocks freely; in some instances, they had to sell their shares back to the enterprise, the latter being obligated to purchase them. In other instances, owners had to give existing shareholders the first option before selling to other buyers.[20] Evidently only Ezcaray and Extremadura permitted their stock to be exchanged freely. Even so, Ezcaray required notification of the sale and the name of the purchaser, and Extremadura demanded a notarized statement of the transaction.[21]

Shareholders regularly gathered together at either annual, biennial, or triennial meetings as required by the charters. Directors then presented the financial position of the companies and shareholders assessed past achievements and determined future courses

---

a par value of 5,000 vellon reals (AGS, *Secretaría de Hacienda*, leg. 856; AMH, *Colección de Órdenes Generales de Rentas*, VII, 435; *Asso del Rió, loc. cit.*; BN, *loc. cit.*; Larruga y Boneta, *op. cit.*, VII, 62; XII, 288; XXXI, 187–188).

Although charters intended most capital to be furnished by stock sales, they permitted funds to be acquired by borrowing. The Company of Burgos' charter, for example, sanctioned borrowing from charitable institutions and entailed estates, but postponed this until the Company had proved itself financially stable. The Company of Aragon could borrow at 3 percent interest from religious sources, and the Company of Ezcaray could borrow up to 100,000 ducats provided it could not raise .5 million ducats by stock sales. Apparently kings hesitated to allow most companies to use the funds of charitable and entailed estates, for the risk of industrial and commercial ventures, they implied, was too great (AGS, *op. cit.*, leg. 856; AMH, *op. cit.*, VII, 435; XVI, 279–281; Larruga y Boneta, *op. cit.*, XXX, 6).

[17] BN, *loc. cit.*; Larruga y Boneta, *op. cit.*, VII, 63.

[18] AGS, *op. cit.*, legs. 855, 856; AMH, *op. cit.*, VII, 435; XVI, 279–281; Larruga y Boneta, *op. cit.*, XXX, 6.

[19] *Ibid.*, XXXI, 191.

[20] When shareholders in the Company of Burgos, for example, wished to dispose of their stock, they had to notify management at the triennial meetings. The Company then had six months in which to pay for the stock (*ibid.*, XXX, 10; AGS, *op. cit.*, leg. 855).

[21] Larruga y Boneta, *op. cit.*, XXXI, 190; XXXIX, 159.

of action.[22] In all companies, stockowners had the right to vote during these meetings, though not in the ratio of one vote to one share. In the Company of Toledo they enjoyed one vote for each block of five shares they owned, while in the Company of Segovia they had one vote for three or more shares.[23] Ownership of eight shares in the Company of Ezcaray equaled one vote; sixteen shares, two votes; and thirty-two shares, three votes.[24] The par value of shares held by each stockholder determined his voting power in the Company of Burgos: 10,000 vellon reals worth commanded one vote, 20,000 vellon reals, two votes, and 50,000 vellon reals or more, three votes.[25]

Even though shareholders had the right to vote, they often were barred from personally exercising it. Various charters excluded members of the ecclesiastical estate, women, and religious communities (*communidades*) from shareholders' meetings, but permitted them to send nonecclesiastical, male representatives.[26] Apparently many shareholders, other than women and churchmen, delegated their votes to others. This practice inevitably led the ambitious and adventuresome to seek domination over the companies. Several shareholders in the Company of Burgos did just this when they successfully solicited proxies from twenty or more stockholders and thereby controlled the firm. Their opponents complained vehemently and frequently to Madrid, and in 1771 Charles III responded by limiting each shareholder to four proxies.[27]

As charters included regulations that furnished a basis for orderly operation, so they contained special exemptions and privileges that attracted investment funds. Tax relief of a wide variety invariably accompanied the array of concessions. Charters exempted raw materials from internal and external customs du-

---

[22] During the first general meeting, shareholders usually elected a slate of officers consisting of a president, a treasurer, directors, and stockholders' representatives (*diputados, vocales*) (AGS, *op. cit.*, leg. 788; BN, MS 13006, fol. 36; Larruga y Boneta, *op. cit.*, VII, 66; XXXI, 191).

Most companies held an initial meeting after they had sold a stated quantity of stock. Before this occurrence, interim committees, headed by the provincial intendants or ministers of the General Council of Commerce and Money, operated the nascent companies (AGS, *op. cit.*, legs. 788, 856; AMH, *op. cit.*, VII, 412–435; XI, 372–383; BN, *loc. cit.*; Larruga y Boneta, *op. cit.*, VII, 66; XVIII, 308; XXXI, 189).

[23] BN, *loc. cit.*; Larruga y Boneta, *op. cit.*, VII, 67; XVIII, 308.

[24] AGS, *op. cit.*, leg. 855; Larruga y Boneta, *op. cit.*, XXX, 10.

[25] *Ibid.*, XXXI, 189.

[26] AGS, *op. cit.*, legs. 788, 855, 856; AMH, *op. cit.*, VII, 412–435; Larruga y Boneta, *op. cit.*, VII, 67; XXX, 10; XXXI, 190; XXXIX, 131; BN, *loc. cit.*

[27] Larruga y Boneta, *op. cit.*, XXX, 20.

ties, tolls, and sales taxes (*alcabala, cientos,* and *millones*);[28] and they exempted the initial sale of the companies' goods from the *alcabala* and *cientos.*[29]

Concessions also promoted exports. Reduced duties on merchandise shipped to the colonies were common.[30] Special grants permitted the firms to send products to America on the various convoys,[31] even though the companies were not members of the Consulate of Seville. In one of his more generous moments, Ferdinand VI gave the companies of Extremadura, Toledo, and Granada a monopoly of trade with Portugal.[32] And a number of charters allowed firms to manufacture textiles with physical attributes different from legal requirements, provided the firms distinguish these fabrics with a special stamp and thereafter export them.[33]

Before they could begin to enjoy concessions of this nature, however, most of the firms had to build textile mills. To lighten the burden and hasten the process of construction, royal charters gave companies the right of preference (*prelación*) for securing buildings or land required for warehouses, factory buildings, and sites for fulling mills, wool-washing operations, and dye shops. The right of preference required that the structures and land be available for rental or sale and that the two parties agree on terms.[34] Resembling the rule of preference and gracing most charters, the right of *tanteo* gave companies the legal prerogative to confiscate raw materials needed in their factories, on condition the present owner did not intend to use the resources himself in production.[35]

---

[28] AGS, *op. cit.,* legs. 852, 856; AMH, *op. cit.,* VII, 412–435; XI, 372–383; Larruga y Boneta, *op. cit.,* VII, 65; XVIII, 308; XXXIX, 125; BN, *loc. cit.*

[29] AGS, *op. cit.,* legs. 855, 856, 857; AMH, *op. cit.,* VII, 412–435; Larruga y Boneta, *op. cit.,* VII, 65; XII, 245; XXX, 12; BN, *loc. cit.* These concessions at times applied only to sales at either the factories, warehouses, or in certain cities.

[30] AGS, *op. cit.,* legs. 852, 856; AMH, *op. cit.,* VII, 412–435; Larruga y Boneta, *op. cit.,* VII, 65; XXXIX, 123; BN, *loc. cit.*

[31] AGS, *op. cit.,* legs. 855, 856; AMH, *op. cit.,* VII, 412–435; Larruga y Boneta, *op. cit.,* XXX, 13.

[32] Antonio Matilla Tascón, *Catálogo de la Colección de Órdenes Generales de Rentas* (Madrid, 1950), p. 91; Larruga y Boneta, *op. cit.,* XXXIX, 162–163.

[33] BN, MS 13006, fol. 38; Larruga y Boneta, *op. cit.,* VII, 69.

[34] AGS, *op. cit.,* legs. 855, 856; AMH, *op. cit.,* VII, 412–435; XI, 372–383; Larruga y Boneta, *op. cit.,* VII, 69; XVIII, 308; XXX, 10; BN, *loc. cit.*

[35] The Company of Toledo, for example, during a silk shortage might requisition the supply of a merchant and then pay him a "fair" price for it. But if the Company and the merchant failed to settle on a price, a magistrate would enter the negotiations and would render a decision binding upon both parties.
On May 11, 1783, Charles III ordered manufacturers of woolens, when using the

While the rights of preference and *tanteo* aided firms in securing land, structures, and materials, other provisions protected the workers of royal companies. Charters commonly ordained that once an artisan contracted to work for a firm he could not resign before fulfilling his contract. Furthermore, employees of companies escaped obligatory personal services, such as quartering of soldiers, military draft, casting of lots for military service, compulsory enlistment, and municipal service.[36] To give still more assurance that workers would remain in the employ of royal companies, charters forbade any person or organization to hire an artisan away from a firm without first obtaining written approval of that enterprise's directors.[37]

INITIAL SUCCESSES OF THE COMPANIES

Armed with the king's generous concessions, royal joint-stock companies enthusiastically set out to market their shares and commence operations. With surprising ease they amassed substantial amounts of capital; and forthwith they built factories, purchased materials, manufactured textiles, and began exporting products. Profits rewarded their initial years of effort and seemed to herald success.

One of the first to get under way was the Company of Extremadura. During the period 1747–1750, it sold 3.6 million vellon reals worth of stock, set up 102 looms, and employed 425 individuals in the production of silks. This manufacturing activity reportedly returned a profit of about 424,900 vellon reals in

---

right of *tanteo,* to compensate wool merchants the full amount of the purchase price, even if merchants had bought the wool the previous year. Charles also directed the producers to refund the storage costs, plus a sum equal to one-half of one percent a month of the merchant's investment, calculated from the day the merchant bought the wool to the day he gave it up.

Although Charles stated that protection of merchants motivated this ruling, he probably recognized fully the benefits it would give producers. That is, by explicitly requiring the producers to pay the original price of the wool, Charles inhibited wool merchants from earning speculative profits by purchasing wool, holding it for a time, and then selling it at a higher price. The king also protected manufacturers of woolens even more by setting forth the terms of *tanteo.* This stopped merchants from charging considerable fees over and above the original price and thus closed another avenue to speculative profits. It must be remembered that producers of woolens would normally have used the *tanteo* during periods of relatively short supply of wool when the price of wool would have reflected that shortage (AHN, *Consejo, Libros de Govierno,* 1784, I, 591; AMH, *op. cit.,* XXVI, 137–140).

[36] AGS, *op. cit.,* leg. 852; Larruga y Boneta, *op. cit.,* VII, 66; XII, 246; XVIII, 309; XXXIX, 126, BN, MS 13006, fol. 36; AMH, *op. cit.,* XI, 372–383.

[37] Larruga y Boneta, *op. cit.,* VII, 68; XVIII, 308–310; XXX, 11; BN, MS 13006, fol. 38; AMH, *op. cit.,* XI, 372–383; AGS, *op. cit.,* leg. 855. All charters encouraged the importation of skilled foreign artisans.

1753,[38] even though the Company's fortunes had already begun to decline. Success in accumulating capital and progress in manufacturing textiles similarly marked the early years of the Company of Granada. After accumulating 3,244,000 vellon reals from stock sales and loans in its first months of existence, this firm saw its assets appreciate by over 14 percent by December 31, 1748.[39] Some of this increase probably resulted from the Company's flourishing textile factories. By 1749, its 604 looms had woven over 190,000 varas of wide silks, 5,700 silk handkerchiefs, 692 pairs of stockings, 8,151 varas of woolens, and 17,803 varas of linens.[40]

The Company of Toledo officially commenced operations on June 1, 1748, with 4,002,000 vellon reals of stock receipts and over 760,000 vellon reals of borrowed funds. Within eighteen months its assets had increased by over 4.5 million vellon reals, due to appreciation of inventory, retained earnings, sales of additional shares, and borrowings.[41] Sometime in 1752 the Company's assets reached a peak value of over 11 million vellon reals.[42] With this extraordinarily large fund, it is not surprising that the Company of Toledo expanded the productive capacity of the silk industry at Toledo. In 1747, that city possessed a total of 2,322 silk looms, of which 239 were for wide fabrics;[43] four years later the city had 4,240 silk looms, of which 610 were of the wide variety.[44] Over 300 of these wide looms belonged to the Company and each year they used silk thread valued at more than 7 million vellon reals.

Shortly after receiving its charter, the Company of Toledo joined the companies of Extremadura and Granada in a venture to trade with Portugal. This came about on April 26, 1748, when Ferdinand VI permitted these firms to pool a fraction of their resources and also gave them a monopoly of commerce with Portugal. The three created a fund of six million vellon reals, of which Extremadura supplied three million, Toledo two million, and Granada one million.[45] Formed solely to exploit the monop-

---

[38] *Ibid.*, leg. 852. By 1751 the Company had 128 looms operating in Zarza and planned to add 71 at Zarza and 30 at Plasencia (Larruga y Boneta, *op. cit.*, XXXIX, 167).

[39] AGS, *loc. cit.*

[40] *Ibid.*

[41] Larruga y Boneta, *op. cit.*, VII, 73–74.

[42] *Ibid.*, 117. Profits for the year were about 535 vellon reals a share (*ibid.*, 113).

[43] *Ibid.*, 114.

[44] *Ibid.*

[45] AGS, *op. cit.*, leg. 853; Larruga y Boneta, *op. cit.*, 70–71.

oly of trade with Portugal, this association was a loosely knit combination of capital: each company retained its autonomy, promoted its own textile factories, sold the outputs to the pool, and shared in the profits in the ratio of its contribution to the pool.

While the companies of Toledo, Extremadura, and Granada specialized in silks, the Company of Aragon diversified its operation by building factories for fine woolens, linens, calicoes, hats, paper, and brandy.[46] To finance these projects, the Company obtained 2,064,000 vellon reals from stock sales and over 1.6 million vellon reals from loans.[47] By 1754, the Company's assets had reached 5,454,054 vellon reals, and its activities appeared to be thriving.

The companies of Burgos and Ezcaray both enjoyed early success. Although Burgos had accumulated a capital fund of only 1,218,000 vellon reals by January 1, 1768, it had already begun to trade in such products as fine wool, sugar, saffron, and fish.[48] Modest prosperity marked the Company's first three years, as profits exceeded 20,000 vellon reals annually.[49] While this firm limited its activities to commerce, Ezcaray engaged solely in the manufacture of woolens. It sold 244 shares of stock for which it received 1,220,000 vellon reals and took over a mature woolen mill which had been functioning for some years under private ownership and whose assets were valued at 1,951,000 vellon reals.[50]

In contrast to the ample resources of most of these royal enterprises, the Company of Segovia began operations in 1765 with only 455,900 vellon reals. The directors had supposedly asked for only one-half of the purchase prices of shares, giving as their reason a shortage of skilled textile artisans at Segovia. As might be expected after such an inauspicious start, the Company produced fine woolens on a small scale.[51]

FAILURE OF THE COMPANIES

It is quite evident that Segovia was an exception. For in their formative years nearly all the companies were successful in gather-

---

[46] AGS, *op. cit.*, leg. 856.

[47] *Ibid.*

[48] *Ibid.*, leg. 855; Larruga y Boneta, *op. cit.*, XXX, 21.

[49] AGS, *loc. cit.*

[50] *Ibid.*, leg. 788.

[51] By 1765 the Company of Segovia was operating only eight looms (Larruga y Boneta, *op. cit.*, XII, 246).

ing investment funds and in starting profitable commercial and industrial activities. However, prosperity soon turned to misfortune, and one by one they failed. The companies of Extremadura, Granada, and Toledo were bankrupt by 1755. After only six years of activity the Company of Burgos ceased to exist, while Ezcaray lasted about twelve years and Segovia about sixteen. The Company of Seville may have been the only one to survive until the end of the century.

Disintegration of these enterprises followed remarkably similar patterns. The first ominous sign of trouble appeared when interest and dividend obligations were postponed. Creditors and stockholders then became alarmed and demanded payment. But either silence or evasion met their requests. Tension and anxiety thereafter rapidly mounted until bitter arguments erupted, involving management, shareholders, and creditors. Inevitably the king intervened. The end came swiftly for some firms; the king declared them bankrupt and ordered the sale of their assets. Others were permitted to reorganize, only to flounder again and end up in liquidation.[52]

It would be pointless to describe the failure of each company. Four examples will suffice to indicate what usually happened. After only six years of operation, the Company of Burgos had squandered about 333,500 vellon reals and with them the confidence of its supporters. Charles III withdrew its charter and dissolved the Company in May, 1773.[53] Although he had invested 100,000 vellon reals in shares, Charles received from the liquidation only 68,435 vellon reals in cash, merchandise, and credits.[54] The Company of Ezcaray ended similarly when the king rescinded its charter and forced it to liquidate sometime between August, 1785, and March, 1787. Creditors and shareholders lost more than 245,000 vellon reals, including over 30,000 by the royal family.[55] Just one year after the dissolution of the pool among Toledo, Granada, and Extremadura, the Company of Toledo acknowledged its bankruptcy; nevertheless, it was reorganized and

---

[52] Apparently the king partly based his decision to withdraw a charter on the stockholders' desires to continue or to dissolve the company.

[53] AGS, *op. cit.*, leg. 855; Larruga y Boneta, *op. cit.*, XXX, 119, 133.

[54] AGS, *loc. cit.* No mention is made as to whether Charles's family received full or partial compensation for its investment of 120,000 vellon reals.

[55] *Ibid.*, leg. 788. Charles III purchased the factory from the Company and leased it to the Five Greater Guilds of Madrid on September 11, 1785 (AMH, *op. cit.*, XXVII, 316–335; Miguel Capella and Antonio Matilla Tascón, *Los Cinco Gremios Mayores de Madrid* [Madrid, 1957], pp. 158–159).

continued to operate until 1788 when the shareholders and the king abandoned all hope for its success.[56]

Of all these debacles perhaps the one experienced by the Company of Extremadura was the most bitter and complete. After a heartening beginning, this firm started to decline in 1749 when the Portuguese restricted imports of Spanish silks.[57] Shareholders soon missed their dividends. They wrathfully turned on the management, especially Blas Caballero, who dominated the Company. Even the Company's president-director, Señor Prieto, in a letter to the General Council of Commerce and Money, attacked Caballero.

. . . without bothering you with a detailed description of the disorders, tyrannies, and swindles that are committed in the government of the Company, I tell you they are of infinite consequence and value; each day they become greater; if not immediately stopped they will continue until the capital is dissipated completely. The difficulty is caused by don Blas Caballero, who, blinded by excessive ambition and supported by you, has taken over the Company and so dominates the employees that no one dares question his orders, for if someone does and is found out he is castigated.[58]

Caballero successfully parried these attacks until a disastrous earthquake and fire razed Lisbon on November 1, 1755, and destroyed a large quantity of the Company's merchandise.[59] A growing clamor from shareholders and creditors then forced the General Council of Commerce and Money to send Pedro Thomas de Alcova de Medina to investigate. When Alcova failed to end the confusion, he was replaced by Marcelino Canals de los Rios.[60] Canals ascertained that of the original capital of 3.6 million vellon reals nearly 2 million had been lost since 1749, which left only 1,634,641 vellon reals on the books in 1755.[61] But Canals found only 530,000 vellon reals worth of assets in existence.[62] He suspicioned Caballero's honesty as well as his managerial competence.

Though supplied with evidence by Canals, the General Council

---

[56] Colmeiro y Penido, *op. cit.*, II, 459; Larruga y Boneta, *op. cit.*, VII, 198.

[57] The Company ceased paying dividends and interest in 1751; in all likelihood the import restrictions placed on silks by Portugal in 1749 precipitated this (*ibid.*, XXXIX, 180).

[58] AGS, *op. cit.*, leg. 852.

[59] Larruga y Boneta, *op. cit.*, 179.

[60] AGS, *loc. cit.*; Larruga y Boneta, *op. cit.*, 180, 181.

[61] AGS, *loc. cit.*; Larruga y Boneta, *op. cit.*, 182.

[62] AGS, *loc. cit.*; Larruga y Boneta, *loc. cit.*

of Commerce and Money dallied until May 28, 1760, before it charged Caballero and several other officials with misconduct. The Council ordered Caballero to repay over .5 million vellon reals within fifteen days or be banished to Africa for eight years.[63] Nothing could save the Company now, however, and when it expired shortly after 1760 shareholders lost about 80 percent of their investment.[64]

SOME EXPLANATIONS FOR THE FAILURES

Extremadura's disaster dramatically illustrates the bitterness and confusion that accompanied these failures. It illustrates how passions became violently aroused, blurring judgments and convincing men that the disputes themselves had produced the bankruptcies. But certainly more than a coincidence of petty arguments and rivalries caused the companies to fail so conclusively. Indeed, several profitless years always preceded the troubles and therefore suggest that more profound difficulties afflicted the enterprises. When dispassionately examined, the evidence reveals that high-cost production, ordained by geographical obstacles, abetted by a lack of external economies, and magnified by unskilled management doomed all of the companies.

A screen of exclusive privileges concealed this weakness when the companies of Extremadura, Granada, Toledo, Seville, and Aragon began. Even grossly inefficient firms might have profited under like protection and succor. But a series of fateful occurrences, starting with the Portuguese restriction on silk imports in 1749 and climaxed by the revocation of all exclusive privileges on June 24, 1752, exposed these companies to rigorous foreign and domestic competition.[65] Without the monopoly of trading with Portugal, rights of *tanteo* and preference, extensive tax exemptions, and freedom from obligatory services, the companies of Extremadura, Toledo, Granada, and Aragon deteriorated rapidly.[66] Ferdinand VI tried to avert the failures on March 30, 1753,

---

[63] AGS, *loc. cit.;* Larruga y Boneta, *op. cit.,* 196.

[64] Two hundred and eight shareholders had paid 3.6 million vellon reals for their shares, but received back only 675,000 vellon reals. In this case, the king recovered all of his investment (*ibid.,* 228–336).

[65] AGS, *loc. cit.;* Francisco Gallardo Fernandez, *Origen, Progresos y Estado de Rentas de la Corona de España,* 7 vols. (Madrid, 1805–1808), II, 384–386; BN, MS 13006; AMH, *op. cit.,* XI, 99–100; Larruga y Boneta, *op. cit.,* XXXIX, 165–167.

[66] Gallardo Fernandez, *loc. cit.;* BN, *loc. cit.;* AMH, *loc. cit.* We do not know whether Seville deteriorated at this time; but since this Company's major concern was American commerce, she probably was less affected by the revocation of the exclusive privileges than were the other companies.

when he restored the right of *tanteo*, tax exemptions, and freedom from obligatory services. But he extended these concessions to all producers in the companies' jurisdictions and, of greater importance, left the Portuguese trade open to all Spaniards.[67] These concessions, much weaker and more widely diffused than those originally granted, could not save the companies.

Without substantial governmental subsidies these institutions just could not operate economically enough to meet their competition. A major cause of the higher costs faced by Toledo, Granada, Extremadura, and Aragon was probably technological in nature. By the beginning of the eighteenth century, the centers of silk manufacture had shifted from Toledo and southern Spain to Valencia and Catalonia where it was cheaper to produce. At Valencia, for example, by 1750 each stage in the productive process had become the specialized task of skilled artisans who made up an industrial labor force. Along with gains from this specialization, a number of economies external to the workshops and factories had appeared. Refined credit and merchandizing facilities and improved public services within the city are examples. In the hinterland, peasants cultivated silk worms and provided the industry at Valencia with silk thread. When the companies decided to establish production in their jurisdictions, they had to achieve not only efficiency at their factories, but also similar external economies if they were to compete. Their rivals at Valencia, Barcelona, and foreign centers of textile production were already benefiting from both external and internal economies—advantages that the companies could not promote at short notice, or possibly ever, in their jurisdictions.

The companies of Segovia and Ezcaray, formed after Ferdinand VI had taken away the companies' privileges in 1752, had to face considerable rivalry from the outset.[68] Here, in these small, isolated towns the absence of external economies also weakened the

---

[67] Gallardo Fernandez, *op. cit.*, II, 386–389; ACSV, *Pragmáticas y Reales Cédulas*, no. 1; AMH, *op. cit.*, XI, 307–310.

On October 26, 1756, Ferdinand VI exempted the Company of Toledo from all customs duties on goods exported to Portugal, but then negated this order on April 10, 1765. Larruga y Boneta claimed that Toledo, Granada, and Extremadura received this exemption on January 22 or February 10, 1756 (AMH, *op. cit.*, XV, 225; Matilla Tascón, *op. cit.*, I, 137; Larruga y Boneta, *op. cit.*, XXXIX, 180, 226).

Hussey states that the General Council of Commerce and Money secured the return, on June 18, 1756, of the concessions that the companies had lost in 1752. A close reading of this cedula of 1756 reveals that such was not the case; rather, Ferdinand VI extended additional concessions to individual producers.

[68] *Ibid.*, XI, 227; XXX, 2; XXXI, 185.

chances for these enterprises to prosper. Created solely to produce
and sell fine woolens, Ezcaray and Segovia never produced cheaply
enough to compete successfully with foreign textiles, particularly
those manufactured in Great Britain. The English bought wool
in Spain for three pounds an arroba, made fine woolens in England, sent them into Spain, and easily undersold domestic fabrics
of the same quality. Even though the Company of Segovia paid
one-third less for identical wool and reportedly made the same
quality cloth, it never sold enough to cover its payroll.[69] Charles
III understandably lost confidence in the Company, withdrew his
investment in 1768, and annulled its charter in 1779.[70] The Company of Ezcaray, beginning with an interest-bearing debt of little
more than 1.4 million vellon reals, manufactured defective textiles and suffered further from an admittedly dishonest manager.[71]

Since the Company of Burgos did not own or operate factories,
it escaped the quicksand of production inefficiency; nevertheless,
within several years it had lost considerable money through transactions in wool, sugar, saffron, and codfish.[72] Insufficient capital,
inexperience and poor judgment of the directors, and unfore-
seeable price fluctuations all played their roles in creating losses
from which the Company never recovered.

Burgos was not alone in lacking able direction. This affliction
seems to have plagued nearly all of the companies. Instead of
leaving their immediate areas for competent and experienced
personnel, the companies picked local men with little training in
industry or international trade. One contemporary writer observed this problem and suggested what characteristics a director
needed. "He should be zealous, disinterested, well traveled, acquainted with Spanish products, and skillful in the practices of
active commerce." [73] He then criticized directors of Spanish companies for lacking these requisites. "These men had never traveled
and possessed neither the valor nor the courage to promote great
and advantageous concepts. They were elected by shareholders
and consequently, in many cases, never moved from behind a
counter and only looked to riches, as if this were enough for

[69] Joseph Townsend, *A Journey Through Spain in the Years 1786–1787,* 3 vols.
(London, 1792), II, 117.
[70] Larruga y Boneta, *op. cit.,* XII, 252–261.
[71] AGS, *op. cit.,* leg. 788. Antonia Bazo, codirector of the Company of Ezcaray,
admitted taking 100,000 vellon reals from the Company and later, after the General
Council of Commerce and Money had investigated the case, died in jail (*ibid.*).
[72] *Ibid.,* leg. 855; Larruga y Boneta, *op. cit.,* XXX, 18.
[73] *Ibid.,* VII, 202–203.

mercantile government." [74] Inexperience, and at times dishonesty, thus numbed management's effectiveness and led inevitably to greater inefficiency.

Had fate relieved the companies of mismanagement and provided them with external economies, geographical barriers would still have remained as a major obstacle to their success. Marked by rugged, lofty plateaus, crisscrossed by gorges, watered by a few unnavigable rivers that flood in winter and wither in summer, and ringed with steep mountain ranges, the Iberian peninsula had physical characteristics that made transportation of any kind extremely difficult and costly. River traffic in most areas was nonexistent, there were few canals, and roads were so bad that even animals foundered on them in winter.[75] Merchandise normally traveled on pack animals, rarely in carts or wagons. Since the majority of these domestic joint-stock companies existed in isolated, interior regions, nature's burden weighed heavily upon them and gravely handicapped them relative to their seaboard competitors.

---

[74] *Ibid.*, 203.

[75] Earl J. Hamilton, *War and Prices in Spain, 1651–1800* (Cambridge, Massachusetts, 1947), pp. 99–100; Larruga y Boneta, *op. cit.*, XXVII, 96, 208, 221, 222; Antonio Joseph Cavanilles, *Observaciones sobre la Historia Natural, Geografía Agricultura, Población, y Frutos del Reyno de Valencia,* 2 vols. (Madrid, 1795–1797), I, 126; Townsend, *op. cit.*, I, 104.

V

Foreign Technology and Spanish Textiles

INTRODUCTION

The rapid decline of Spain's economy in the seventeenth century left her textile industry incapable of producing fine cloth. Foreign fabrics had displaced the domestic product, forcing many artisans into weaving common textiles, others into new occupations, and still others into beggary. As Spanish workmen deserted the manufacture of fine cloth, they failed to pass on their skills to apprentices and thus bequeathed to the eighteenth century an industry capable of producing only common fabrics. Spain's position relative to her neighbors to the north deteriorated substantially, for other nations of Western Europe continued to produce textiles of high quality and to improve their technology.

When Philip V became king in 1700 and undertook to rebuild the Spanish economy, a critical deficiency in the knowledge of production thus handicapped his efforts. Removing this obstacle became one of his primary goals. He resolutely sent his deputies abroad to recruit craftsmen with skills that were most lacking at home. Although Philip's efforts bore considerable fruit, his successors intensified and broadened the raiding of labor markets in foreign nations and enjoyed still more rewards. Yet their achievements would have been greater had it not been for powerful barriers that slowed the flow of human resources between nations and retarded the diffusion of technology by borrowing. National hostilities, industrial and commercial rivalries, intolerance, and human emotions discouraged artisans from emigrating to Spain and troubled them after their arrival. An even more distressing development, however, was the indifferent reception given many of the technological improvements by domestic industry. In most of Spain, artisans rejected the new, sophisticated methods and retained their traditional ways. Only in Catalonia, and to a lesser extent in Valencia, did diffusion of imported techniques take place.

RECRUITMENT OF FOREIGN ARTISANS

Kings of Spain used a simple method to recruit workmen. In the vanguard of their operations they placed Spanish ambassadors and consuls, sometimes allowing these envoys complete autonomy in managing the affairs of enlistment and sometimes closely directing their activities.[1] In their roles of respected statesmen, these officials were ideally situated to keep a close watch for skilled workers who might serve Spain and to investigate freely the backgrounds of prospective emigrants. Yet their diplomatic positions rarely permitted them to contact workmen directly; and so they delegated this task to special agents who usually were natives of the countries from which Spain was seeking craftsmen.[2]

With striking success these diplomats and their persuasive deputies recruited foreign workmen. As their first priority, they sought artisans who possessed those skills most needed on the peninsula. John Rulière, who came to Spain in a most fortuitous manner, was a man of extraordinary talent. While this Frenchman was waiting at The Hague for passage to, and asylum in, England in 1748, he chanced to meet an agent of the Marquis del Puerto, Spanish ambassador to the Netherlands. The Marquis quickly made arrangements for Rulière to serve Spain, and during the next twelve years Rulière created and directed the Royal Factory for Fine Silks at Talavera de la Reina and staffed it with many artisans who came from France at his request.[3] Of special interest to recruiters were small groups of workers forming nuclei of important skills. Thus it was that Jerónimo Ortiza, a Spaniard in the service of Ferdinand VI, persuaded four highly skilled Frenchmen to leave Lyons in 1753 and settle at Valencia where they created the nucleus of a factory for fine silks.[4] Spanish kings on occasion instructed their agents and diplomats to secure large

[1] AGS, *Secretaría de Hacienda*, legs. 765, 768, 775, 778.

[2] For example, William Fitzimmons and Bartholomew Nesbit, both Englishmen, and Ambrose Berry and Henry Doyle, both Irishmen, recruited for Spain in their respective homelands (*ibid.*, legs. 764, 766, 776, 780, 781, 784; Eugenio Larruga y Boneta, *Memorias Políticas y Económicas sobre los Frutos, Comercio, Fábricas y Minas de España*, 45 vols. [Madrid, 1787–1800], XVII, 286).

[3] AGS, *op. cit.*, leg. 786; Larruga y Boneta, *op. cit.*, VIII, 161.

[4] AGS, *op. cit.*, leg. 789; Miguel Capella and Antonio Matilla Tascón, *Los Cinco Gremios Mayores de Madrid* (Madrid, 1957), pp. 134–136; Jaime Carrera y Pujal, *Historia de la Economía Española*, 5 vols. (Barcelona, 1943–1947), V, 491.

groups of artisans possessing most or all of the skills needed in a factory. One of the most successful episodes of this kind occurred in 1750 when Ambrose Berry recruited enough Irishmen to staff completely one unit of the king's mill for superfine woolens at San Fernando.[5]

As the century progressed and kings intensified their programs of development, recruiters sought an increasing number of skilled aliens to fill positions in the expanding royal textile mills scattered throughout Castile and Leon.[6] The government was not alone in this search; independent manufacturers and organizations in increasing number and with growing vigor joined in the proselytizing of workers from other nations. Catalonians and Valencians, their textile operations booming, led the way. An added incentive for king and subjects was the rapidly rising rate of technological progress in Western Europe, especially during the last third of the century.

The demand for foreign skills and technology thus expanded. Coincidentally, the supply of workers willing to immigrate ascended. Whereas at the beginning of Ferdinand VI's reign diplomats and their agents were searching for skilled workmen, by the end of the reign of Charles III foreign craftsmen were taking the initiative in contacting diplomats and their agents. Some artisans wrote directly to the king or his ministers and offered their services. Others traveled to Spain first and then searched for employment. A simple explanation exists for this turnabout. Spain's persistent and vigorous campaign of enlistment naturally aroused great interest among craftsmen of Western Europe; they heard exaggerated rumors of high wages, low living costs, and pleasant working conditions, all of which conjured visions of a worker's paradise in Spain. And this image seemed more attractive when revolution racked France.[7]

In response to the real and imaginary conditions of employment, many artisans found their way into Spain without promised employment, adding their talents to those of their countrymen

---

[5] AGS, *op. cit.*, legs. 764, 766; Larruga y Boneta, *op. cit.*, XVII, 286. Kings frequently discovered skilled foreigners already residing in Spain. Charles III employed over fifty English prisoners of war interned in southern Spain, and other kings frequently uncovered men with special talents among the Walloons and others in the military service of Spain (AGS, *op. cit.*, legs. 756, 802).

[6] *Ibid.*, legs. 759, 761, 765, 769, 771, 776.

[7] Many skilled workers from outstanding textile factories in France fled the Revolution and swelled the number of Frenchmen in Spain, especially in Catalonia (Jean Francois de Bourgoing, *Modern State of Spain*, 4 vols., translated from the 1807 edition [London, 1808], III, 307).

who had immigrated at Spain's request. The fates of these adventurers varied. Some traveled to royal factories—Guadalaxara, for example, became an entrepôt for them—and applied for work.[8] After demonstrating their skills, the most talented won positions; others traveled to centers of industry with recommendations from the royal mills; and the rest scattered to seek employment on their own. Skilled aliens frequently obtained the king's permission to establish their own workshops or factories expressly for manufacturing new products and using advanced processes.[9] Others served the economic societies and councils of commerce of large cities by teaching their skills to local workmen.[10]

Whether foreign artisans came to Spain with or without promised employment, the majority eventually negotiated written or oral contracts with their employers. The greater number who traveled to Spain on their own initiative received minimum contracts. Since they usually possessed only ordinary skills and were already in Spain, they had relatively little bargaining power. In contrast, those craftsmen whom royal agents wished to lure to Spain were usually more skilled and, besides, were still in their homelands. They could therefore demand more favorable terms prior to setting out for Spain. Merely to allay their qualms about leaving homes and families, these artisans were assured of continuous incomes, return voyages, and religious tolerance. Of course, the greater their skills, the more lucrative were their contracts no matter how they came to Spain.

Terms of the contracts, which reflected both differences in skills and bargaining abilities of the workers, varied greatly. Setting the upper extreme was the extraordinary contract signed by John Rulière in 1751. This agreement awarded Rulière a salary of 45,000 vellon reals annually, 2 percent of the yearly sales receipts

[8] Larruga y Boneta, *op. cit.*, XIV, 239.

[9] For examples, see: AGS, *op. cit.*, legs. 755, 764, 777; AMH, *Colección de Órdenes Generales de Rentas*, XVIII, 25–28; XX, 102–103; XXIII, 269; XXVII, 240–249; XXIX, 289; XXXVII, 7–10; XLIII, 52; XLIV, 375; ACA, *Diversorium*, no. 1183, fol. 2; no. 1187, fol. 19; *ibid.*, *Acordadas*, no. 586, fol. 97; AHN, *Consejo, Libros de Govierno*, 1785, tomo 2, fol. 383; BCB, *Junta de Comercio*, leg. 12, no. 4; leg. 53, no. 30; Larruga y Boneta, *op. cit.*, II, 324; XV, 134; XXIV, 197–199; XXV, 149; XXXI, 1–21; XXXV, 90–91; Bourgoing, *op. cit.*, III, 264; Carrera y Pujal, *op. cit.*, V, 517; Jaime Carrera y Pujal, *Historia Política y Económica de Cataluña, Siglos XVI al XVIII*, 4 vols. (Barcelona, 1946–1947), IV, 129; Francisco Gallardo Fernandez, *Origen, Progresos y Estado de Rentas de la Corona de España*, 7 vols. (Madrid, 1805–1808), II, 409.

[10] BCB, *op. cit.*, leg. 51, nos. 14, 19; Carrera y Pujal, *op. cit.*, IV, 211, 235; Ángel Ruiz y Pablo, *Historia de la Real Junta Particular de Comercio de Barcelona, 1758–1847* (Barcelona, 1919), pp. 77–78.

of the Royal Factory at Talavera, and a pension for his wife and daughter of 12,000 vellon reals annually in the event of his death.[11] He also received the titles of Director of the Factory and Secretary General of the Harvesting, Spinning, and Twisting of Silk, Gold, and Silver of all Spain. As a crowning distinction, Ferdinand VI extended Rulière's contract to include naturalization and status of nobility.[12] The lower extreme of contractual terms was perhaps reached between Charles III and a group of English prisoners of war who staffed a factory at Seville. This agreement called for a gift of 1,000 vellon reals for each artisan, plus meager wages, bread, and a subsidy for clothing.[13]

Between these two extremes lay the majority of contracts. An immigrant worker normally received a daily wage or salary, the amount depending on the skill and the position to be filled. In addition to getting a bonus for settlement, he obtained transportation expenses to Spain for himself and his family and the promise of return fare if he went back to his homeland. The assurance of pensions for his survivors should the artisan die while employed by the king was a frequent provision. And perhaps the most important stipulation of all was the guarantee of religious tolerance.[14] As the contracts provided these concessions, so they exacted a *quid pro quo*. Each workman agreed to remain in Spain for a minimum period; promised to respect the customs of the country as well as the rules and regulations of the factories; and bound himself to teach his skills to a certain number of apprentices each year.[15]

As might have been expected, the nations of Western Europe did not stand idly by while Spanish agents carried off their skilled workmen in wholesale and piecemeal lots. To block the emigration of her artisans, France placed special guards along her Spanish frontiers. England similarly watched her ports and ordered her consulates in Portugal and elsewhere to turn back Irish and

[11] AGS, *op. cit.*, legs. 772, 786; Larruga y Boneta, *op. cit.*, VIII, 103–104.

[12] *Ibid*. Spanish kings awarded the rank of nobility to but a few immigrant artisans during the period 1750–1800. Apparently only a handful of these recipients were in the field of textiles. René María Lamy, Juan José Georget, Pedro Suavan, and Juan Bautista Phelipot, silk artisans from Lyons, France, received this honor in 1751 with an effective date of 1765. Joseph de Payba Manso, Manuel Fernandez de Payba Manso, and Joseph Payo Fernandez, all from Portugal and skilled in making textile scissors, were enobled in 1769. And José Lapayese, a manufacturer of silk threads from France, received a grant of nobility in 1776 (AGS, *op. cit.*, leg. 773; Capella and Matilla Tascón, *op. cit.*, p. 142).

[13] AGS, *op. cit.*, leg. 802.

[14] *Ibid.*, legs. 764, 775, 776, 778, 783.

[15] *Ibid.*, legs. 784, 789.

English workmen.[16] Moreover, both nations attempted to discourage artisans from leaving in the first place. It was to dissuade her workers from abandoning Lyons and traveling to Talavera de la Reina and elsewhere in 1749 that the government of France paid wages to several thousand unemployed silk artisans.[17]

A more persuasive weapon, however, was the imposition of harsh penalties on emigrant workmen. When John Rulière persuaded a group of his countrymen to leave France for Talavera, the French Council of State first erected signs telling of this crime and then, on March 31, 1751, condemned John and Andres Rulière and others *in absentia* for abandoning their country and inducing others to do likewise.[18] Not only did it sentence John and Andres Rulière to perpetual servitude in the galleys of the "Very Christian King," it also ordered them to be branded on the right shoulders with the letters G.A.N. and to be placed in iron collars (*carcan*) for two hours each day for three successive days, during which time a sign was to be placed before them reading "guilty of transporting manufactures to foreign nations and of seducing artisans." [19] Finally, the Council assessed John and Andres Rulière each an oppressive fine.

To remove temptation from the presence of their artisans, nations of Western Europe took action against Spain's recruiters. Prison terms awaited those agents who were unlucky enough to be caught enticing artisans to leave for Spain or buying new machines. William Fitzimmons was unlucky. This Irishman, who had come to Spain in 1786, agreed to journey to England and obtain a machine for shining textiles as well as an artisan to operate it. With this task in mind he visited Dublin, Manchester, Birmingham, London, and elsewhere. When he reached London on the last leg of his trip, authorities uncovered his mission and put him in prison where he remained until the Spanish ambassador finally obtained his release three years later.[20]

Spain's neighbors to the north were not content merely to be on the defensive. As early as 1734 they had organized a counteroffensive and had dispatched agents to Spain to lure their artisans back home. In that year, Milord Stanhope (Estanop), an English diplomat, offered Michael Stapleton (Establecon) seven hundred doubloons and privileges in England if he would leave his post

---

[16] AHN, *op. cit.*, leg. 50135, no. 1.
[17] Larruga y Boneta, *op. cit.*, VIII, 102.
[18] *Ibid.*, 100–101.
[19] *Ibid.*
[20] AGS, *op. cit.*, legs. 776, 780, 781.

at the Royal Factory of Guadalaxara and return to Great Britain.[21] Stapleton refused. Then Stanhope succeeded in luring Diego Bath (Vad), also an artisan at Guadalaxara, back to England with a bribe of only fifty doubloons. Perhaps it was the position of valet to Stanhope's pedigree dogs rather than the offer of money that convinced Bath to leave.[22] A half century later, Quatréme d'Ysjonial, a member of the Royal Academy of Sciences of Paris and Director of the Factory for Woolens at the Château du Parc, accepted an invitation to work in Spain. Within a few months, however, after receiving a lucrative counteroffer from the Duke of Vauguion, he returned to France.[23] Spain, of course, was aware of such efforts and tried to checkmate them. In a typical action of this sort, Miguel Musquiz, Ferdinand VI's minister, warned the Intendant of Valencia on the eve of the arrival of a foreign artisan's wife

. . . to watch carefully that the wife of Phelipot, when she arrives in that city, has not come instructed by the French to induce those artisans to return to their homeland and leave us ridiculed. . . .[24]

SETTLEMENT OF FOREIGN ARTISANS

Despite their defensive and offensive tactics, foreign countries were unable to prevent Spain from acquiring numerous artisans. Working with unusual vigor and cunning, Spanish kings and their subjects overcame all counteractions and directed an increasing stream of craftsmen to Spain. Actually, far greater difficulties were encountered in settling the workmen than in recruiting them. Religious bigotry, guild persecution, and distrust confronted the artisans when they set foot in Spain.

A religious fervor that often bordered on fanaticism led many Spaniards to regard non-Catholics as heretics. Since this state of mind created an hostile atmosphere for Protestant artisans, kings had to protect foreign workers from almost certain religious persecution by granting them individual dispensations.[25] In effect,

---

[21] Larruga y Boneta, *op. cit.*, XVI, 137.

[22] *Ibid.*

[23] AGS, *op. cit.*, leg. 775; Bourgoing, *op. cit.*, I, 104.

[24] AGS, *op. cit.*, leg. 789.

[25] Despite this qualified acceptance of Protestants by the Church and government, the Church, with full approval of the king, vigorously and unrelentingly tried to convert non-Catholic foreigners. In many instances they succeeded. Bentura Argumosa, the director of Ferdinand VI's factory at Guadalaxara, reported on May 19, 1752, that six of the Irishmen who had recently arrived at the branch factory of San Fernando had accepted conversion and would "soon enter the Church's flock." Kings frequently became willing partners in conversion. Thus it

these royal exemptions enjoined the Inquisitor from bothering Protestants who obeyed the laws, did not openly advocate their beliefs, and respected the churches, rites, and sacred ceremonies of Catholicism.[26]

One of the most interesting and revealing examples of religious dispensations took place in Seville in 1781. A group of English Calvinists, who had been captured on the high seas by the Spanish Navy during the current war, agreed to form a woolen factory rather than remain in prisoner-of-war camps. Sixteen of them readily accepted the Catholic faith.[27] Charles III then permitted the others, whom he classified as "heretical subjects with special skills" (*sugetos hereges de especial habilidad*), to remain at the mill under the following conditions: they could not argue religion with Catholics; they could be Calvinists, but they could not hold public ceremonies; they could listen to Catholic ceremonies, but not to sacred ceremonies; they had to make the sign of the cross, then genuflect, and so forth, when entering churches; and they could possess Calvinist books, provided they had them marked as "prohibited" and did not show them to Catholics.[28]

Even though Protestants received some form of royal protection, they nonetheless suffered persecution. Religious intolerance was especially strong in the villages. There, a pious dogmatism, nourished by local priests and sustained by ignorance, moved villagers to fear, suspect, and harass Protestants. The reception given John Berry and Thomas Milne by the inhabitants of Avila illustrates the hostility that foreign Protestants faced. Because the local priest had taught that all heretics devoured Catholic children, the people of Avila feared these two Englishmen, threatened to stone them, and walked long distances to avoid passing their houses.[29] The larger and more cosmopolitan the population, however, the less offensive was the bigotry. In Barcelona, with its many, industrial, and mobile people, the beliefs of a non-Catholic tended to fade with the anonymity of the individual. But even there Protestants felt themselves penalized to some extent.

Charles IV addressed himself to the religious problem on June

---

was that Charles III on January 21, 1768, issued a pension to Mrs. William Scheercraft, the widow of an immigrant from Ireland. Charles wished to dissuade Mrs. Scheercraft from returning home, for he feared that her daughter, who had recently been converted, would "fall into evil ways in Ireland" (*ibid.*, legs. 765, 768, 802).

[26] AMH, *op. cit.*, XLI, 230–232.
[27] AGS, *op. cit.*, leg. 802.
[28] *Ibid.*
[29] Bourgoing, *op. cit.*, III, 25.

23, 1797, when he permitted foreigners of any religion, except Judaism, to enter Spain and engage in any trade they wished.[30] At the same time, he prohibited the Inquisitor from molesting Protestants provided they respected public customs. Charles added nothing new with this ruling; he merely echoed the policy of his predecessors by generalizing a ruling that previous to that time had been restated whenever a religious dispensation was granted. Unfortunately, enlightenment and tolerance came not by royal edict.

As religious bigotry tormented foreign artisans who practiced faiths other than Catholicism, so craft guilds frustrated those who practiced trades without being guild members. Only foreigners employed by the royal mills, the economic societies, and the councils of commerce, escaped the authority of guilds. Fierce opposition confronted those who operated their own workshops or factories or who offered their services to independent producers. For immigrants in such situations came within the jurisdiction of guilds, and these privileged institutions inevitably used their power to assail all threats to their monopoly position.

Spanish textile guilds had protected their status for centuries by controlling the physical makeup of fabrics as well as the processes and tools used in their production. They also limited membership in each rank in the guild's hierarchy and controlled the volume of output of each master. It was in this fashion that guilds strictly controlled the quantity and quality of output and thereby simultaneously preserved each master's relative position and promoted monopoly profits. Foreign artisans menaced all of this when they introduced new textiles and modern techniques. Even the simple request of immigrants for admittance into guilds threatened to dilute the power of existing masters. Naturally, Spanish guilds resisted this invasion of foreign masters and journeymen during the eighteenth century.

The controversies that grew out of the clash between recent arrivals and traditional interests centered around guild ordinances. Drawn up by guilds themselves and then accepted by kings, these rules provided the organizations with legal sanction as well as a framework for government.[31] Most ordinances required a period of apprenticeship of from two to four years and a period of jour-

---

[30] AMH, *op. cit.*, XLI, 230–232.

[31] Antonio de Capmany y de Montpalau, *Memorias Históricas sobre la Marina, Comercio y Artes de la Antigua Ciudad de Barcelona*, 4 vols. (Madrid, 1779–1792), I, part 3, pp. 15–47.

neymanship of one or more years. The rules insisted that apprentices and journeymen undergo their training in the city of the
guild and under the supervision of some master.[32] This meant
that a guild in Valencia, for example, could force a silk craftsman
from, say, Lyons, France, to train for as many as eight years before permitting him to practice the art in which he already excelled. Still another obstruction often lay in wait for the foreigner
in the form of exorbitant fees exacted for a proficiency examination and for entrance to the guild.[33]

That such requirements limited the full utilization of foreign
skills the kings were aware, and so they permitted many immigrants to operate independently of these rules. Guilds defended
themselves against these privileged artisans by requesting local
authorities, who were far removed from royal influence and usually sympathetic to the guilds' cause, to enforce the ordinances.
The local justices usually complied by impounding the equipment and materials owned by the offending artisans.[34] This de-
feated many foreigners who did not possess sufficient resources to
carry their fight from local jurisdictions to the General Council
of Commerce and Money.

By thus invoking their ordinances guilds were frequently able
to nullify the protection that royal grants of immunity afforded
individual craftsmen. Kings then moved to nullify the ordinances.
Philip V began the assault on June 2, 1703, when he commanded
all guilds to admit foreign artisans.[35] But this was an empty command, for guilds went right on denying membership to foreigners
by imposing harsh and discriminatory entrance requirements. The
issue simmered for nearly seventy years before Charles III, on
April 30, 1772, ordered all guilds to accept foreign artisans and
permit them to work as masters, provided they possessed original
letters of examinations proving their skills.[36] By this action he
essentially abolished all rules that required masters to take their
apprenticeship and journeymanship in a particular locality.[37]

Rather than diminishing, disputes between guilds and foreign-

[32] ACA, *Acordadas*, no. 587, fol. 239; *ibid., Diversorium*, no. 870, fol. 248.

[33] *Ibid., Acordadas*, no. 563, fol. 149; no. 568, fol. 340; no. 570, fol. 210; no. 574,
fol. 70; *ibid., Diversorium*, no. 874, fol. 219; AHMB, *Junta General de Comercio*,
XV, 108; XXV, 107.

[34] ACA, *Acordadas*, no. 571, fols. 208–213.

[35] *Ibid.*, no. 572, fol. 208.

[36] Carrera y Pujal, *Historia de la Economía Española*, IV, 115.

[37] Guilds generally ignored this ruling, and on March 24, 1777, Charles III commanded all guilds to obey it (AHN, *Biblioteca, Colección de Reales Cédulas*, 1777,
X, 430; ACSV, *Reales Cédulas*, no. 2; Carrera y Pujal, *op. cit.*, IV, 117).

ers multiplied. Then, on July 23 and on December 4, 1797, in perhaps the strongest action taken against guilds during the century, Charles IV restated that guilds should permit all masters to practice their trades provided they had original letters of their masters' examinations and then instructed all guilds to give masters' examinations to artisans who requested them, notwithstanding their lack of apprenticeship, journeymanship, domicile, or for any other reason contained in guild ordinances.[38] He also prohibited guilds from charging fees for those examinations in excess of actual costs.

All of this legislation was inconsequential, despite its powerful wording. In small cities and towns, where economic activity languished and the king's influence gave way to regional authority, strong guilds maintained their alliances with local justices and continued to thwart the hopes of foreign artisans.[39] On the other hand, in the larger cities, such as Barcelona and Valencia, the rapidly expanding textile industry and the spread of the factory system had already created a regular market for labor that readily absorbed not only journeymen and masters from guilds but foreigners as well. This broke the guilds' hold on all artisans and made it easier for outsiders to work at their trades. What this legislation accomplished in these larger industrial cities was merely the sanctioning of modifications in the economic structure that had already occurred; while in other places where there was economic stagnation it had no effect.

As if their troubles with the Church and the guilds were not enough, many foreign artisans clashed with the Spaniards because of personality conflicts. Immigrant workers often disagreed with the methods of their superiors, refused to follow orders, and complained about their treatment to the king.[40] Most regrettable were the personal conflicts that often developed between foreigners in responsible positions and prominent Spaniards.[41] Of all the disputes of this nature perhaps the one involving John Rulière and members of the Spanish Court was the most protracted and vicious.

---

[38] AMH, *op. cit.*, XLI, 230–232; ACSV, *loc. cit.*

[39] Decrees from Madrid dwindled in effectiveness as royal authority became diluted by distance and provincial contempt.

[40] A typical dispute transpired at San Fernando in 1788 when Hugo Keenan, the leader of the English workers there, refused to obey the factory's director. Keenan complained to Madrid of the director's ignorance and harshness. The king rejected these grievances and suspended Keenan's salary. After becoming even more intransigent, this Englishman was finally placed under guard, forced to work, and charged with the expenses of his guards (AGS, *op. cit.*, leg. 784).

[41] *Ibid.*, legs. 775, 776, 777, 779, 780, 781, 782, 783, 784.

Almost immediately after Rulière began to organize the Royal Factory for Fine Silks at Talavera de la Reina in 1748, he aroused the animosity of influential Spaniards at Madrid.[42] For nearly twelve years he survived their extreme personal attacks, thanks to his remarkable friendship with Ferdinand VI and especially with Barbara de Braganza, the queen. But when Ferdinand died and Charles III became king, Rulière's enemies triumphed and had him jailed. All evidence suggests that Rulière was a capable manufacturer and innocent of any wrongdoing.[43]

It would be a mistake to assume that all immigrants had an unhappy experience in Spain.[44] Kings generally treated foreigners well. They scrupulously honored the contracts made with artisans and complied with the stipulations about paying for the voyage home, often providing return transportation for those whose contracts had ignored the provision.[45] In fact, kings made little effort to stop any artisan who desired to return home.[46] And many departed.[47] Surprisingly, enough, however, many decided to stay in Spain for the remainder of their lives.[48]

---

[42] *Ibid.*, leg. 786; Larruga y Boneta, *op. cit.*, VIII, 95–176.

[43] Perhaps most foreigners who came to Spain were honest and capable, as was Rulière. But a minority were rogues or adventurers. John Riley was typical of the latter. This Englishman offered his services to Charles III while a prisoner of war at Seville. After atoning for his reputation as a heavy drinker of wine by embracing Catholicism, he negotiated a personal contract with Charles in November, 1781, which called for a salary of 9,000 vellon reals annually. For his part, Riley pledged to direct a factory for woolens at Seville or to serve in any other way that Charles commanded. Riley's name thereafter appears in the archives only sparingly until 1801, when the royal treasury discovered that he had been receiving his salary for twenty years yet had worked only sporadically up to 1791 and since then had been idle (AGS, *op. cit.*, leg. 802).

[44] During times of war, however, kings frequently confiscated the wealth of natives of enemy nations and then interned or expelled them from Spain. Of course, many exceptions were made and probably most immigrant artisans remained in Spain (AHN, *op. cit.*, 1793–1794, XXII, 1087; 1795–1796, XXIII, 1129, 1155; 1797–1798, XXIV, 1203).

[45] One example will suffice to illustrate this frequent generosity. Juan Bautista Bavoy and four companions came to Guadalaxara from Paris in 1751 without the guarantee of a return voyage. After permitting them to experiment with the production of a new type of cloth for four years, the director of the factory declared their efforts useless and, with the permission of Ferdinand VI, gave Bavoy and his companions 3,000 vellon reals for return passage (AGS, *op. cit.*, legs. 765, 779).

[46] Financial and legal problems actually posed the greatest obstacles to their return. Workers who had not received the promise of return voyages, or who possessed no outstanding talents and hence received relatively small incomes, found it difficult, often impossible, to save the expenses of transportation. Even artisans who had contracts that promised return voyages or who had earned sufficient salaries from which to save the costs of travel hesitated to return to their homes lest their governments condemn them as traitors.

[47] *Ibid.*, legs. 765, 780, 781, 784.

[48] *Ibid.*, legs. 765, 766, 768, 770, 773, 783, 786.

TECHNOLOGY AND FOREIGN ARTISANS

Spanish kings hoped that immigrant craftsmen would bring detailed information about methods, materials, and machinery to Spain along with their precious skills. Their hopes were fulfilled. Mere possession of this technology, however, would serve no purpose for Spain unless her workers were able to implement it. And to the task of giving domestic artisans this capability, kings assigned foreigners. Contracts between skilled immigrants and Spaniards emphasized the obligation of the former to maintain several apprentices at all times.[49] This was especially true at royal factories. To these mills kings sent young Spaniards to be trained by some of Europe's finest craftsmen, and from them kings sent out accomplished artisans to work in the manufactories of Spain. Independent producers, economic societies, and councils of commerce also helped the process of diffusion when they employed foreign artisans to pass on their skills and knowledge to designated workmen.[50] Other foreigners operated schools in which they taught selected crafts.[51]

As foreign craftsmen contributed to Spain's knowledge of production by training workmen, so they also helped diffuse technology by introducing a number of mechanical innovations. Many who immigrated strictly as workmen freely offered knowledge of mechanical advances they had acquired in their native lands. They did this for their own prosperity as well as for Spain's, for in all

---

[49] One source explicitly states that the real purpose of bringing them [foreign artisans] was "to guarantee, by teaching, the nationalization and permanence of a body of technical knowledge superior to that in existence" (Capella and Matilla Tascón, *op. cit.,* p. 141).

[50] BCB, *op. cit.,* leg. 51, nos. 14, 19; AMH, *op. cit.,* XXXII, 290; Ruiz y Pablo, *op. cit.,* pp. 77, 78, 79; Carrera y Pujal, *Historia Política y Económica de Cataluña,* IV, 112, 211, 235; Gallardo Fernandez, *op. cit.,* II, 400.

[51] Though foreign artisans came to Spain in large numbers to teach their skills, many promising young Spaniards traveled to foreign lands to receive their training. Kings, economic societies, and councils of commerce financed these expeditions; others they sent abroad merely to observe and collect information. Independent producers left the peninsula to work in foreign mills on their own initiative. During the last two decades of the century, training in foreign countries became a common practice and part of the government's economic policy. In 1783 Charles III inaugurated a program to send competent students abroad and pay for their education, provided they would agree to return and propagate their skills. On occasion he placed apprentices under the care of Spanish diplomats in France who in turn placed them in the best factories and made certain that they returned after the apprenticeship period (AGS, *op. cit.,* legs. 771, 773; Carrera y Pujal, *op. cit.,* IV, 216–220, 248; Carrera y Pujal, *Historia de la Economía Española,* V, 508–509; Joaquín Manuel Fos, *Instrucción Metódica sobre los Mueres* [Madrid, 1790]).

likelihood they had been recruited to introduce textiles of fine quality and hence needed the requisite machinery to succeed and maintain their employment. But not all workmen could reproduce the contrivances they had once used. Spanish kings therefore recruited foreign machinists to construct advanced equipment; in a more direct action, Spaniards often dispatched agents to foreign lands to secure by subterfuge or otherwise the improved machinery.[52]

Though Spain was the aggressor in seeking technology, as time passed numerous mechanical advances came to her shores without persuasion, borne there by professional vendors from foreign lands.[53] These salesmen appeared more regularly as Spain's reputation as a rich market for technology spread and as foreign improvements in textile machinery multiplied. Arbitrage was their business. John Wadle and Joseph Caldwell typified them. In 1789 these English spinners approached Floridablanca, Charles IV's minister, with an offer to sell a novel machine for spinning and twisting cotton.[54] Floridablanca sent them to Barcelona, where the cotton textile industry flourished. Once there, Wadle and Caldwell installed their machine in the commercial exchange and demonstrated its capabilities to the leaders of commerce and industry, all of whom agreed on its superiority. Nothing came of the consequent negotiations, however, and the Englishmen left in search of more eager buyers.[55]

Innovations in product were often as important as innovations in process. For profits reacted favorably to the adoption of demand-increasing changes in style as well as cost-reducing techniques of production. It was precisely to win markets that countries of Western Europe, especially England, worked hard at differentiating their textiles during the period 1750–1800. Some new fabrics required the use of advanced machines; the majority depended on combinations of greater skills and different compositions of materials. Reacting to the impact of these variations, Spanish kings and their subjects attempted to imitate the new fab-

---

[52] AGS, *op. cit.*, legs. 775, 776, 779, 780.

[53] For illustrations, see: AMH, *op. cit.*, XVIII, 25–28; XXXVII, 7–10; AGS, *op. cit.*, legs. 772, 775, 776, 779; BCB, *op. cit.*, leg. 23, nos. 7, 18, 19, 21, 24; Carrera y Pujal, *Historia Política y Económica de Cataluña*, IV, 240–241, 244–245; Larruga y Boneta, *op. cit.*, IV, 185; Ruiz y Pablo, *op. cit.*, p. 78; AHMB, *op. cit.*, LII, 3; Gallardo Fernandez, *op. cit.*, II, 409.

[54] BCB, *op. cit.*, leg. 23, no. 10; Carrera y Pujal, *op. cit.*, IV, 240–241.

[55] John Wadle teamed with the Duke del Infantado at the Village of Bustrago in 1793 and established a factory for spinning and weaving cotton textiles (AMH, *op. cit.*, XXXVII, 7–10).

rics.[56] Their endeavors along this line generally met with failure.

Spain's efforts to import and diffuse the manufacture of light woolen stuffs called *telillas* may prove illustrative. This type of fabric was smaller in dimension and lighter in texture than most other fine woolens and often exhibited multicolored stripes woven from a delicate mixture of silk and wool threads. Beauty and fineness graced these fabrics and made them favorites. Francisco Morel, a weaving instructor from Lyons, France, was perhaps the first to introduce *telillas* in Spain when he taught artisans at Barcelona how to construct them in 1768.[57] It was the Crown of Spain, however, that made the greatest efforts to promote these new fabrics. Charles III in 1775 showed his interest by establishing the Royal Factory for Woolens at Avila where Patrick Boulger produced *telillas*. The royal mill at Seville, staffed by English prisoners, also manufactured some,[58] and Englishmen working for the king at San Fernando engaged in the same activity between 1788 and 1791.[59] At the Royal Factory of San Nicolas in Guadalaxara, Samuel Bird made the finest woolens of this class during the last decade of the century.[60] Despite these and other efforts, the manufacture of light woolens never prospered in Spain, and England remained the undisputed master in this line.

As English manufacturers were thus strengthening their position in fine cloth, so they simultaneously were attempting to gain ground in common fabrics by reducing the dimensions of, and the number of threads and quality of ingredients in, their standard export fabrics. These innovations escaped the attention of consumers, reduced the costs of production, and thereby yielded a competitive advantage to the innovators.[61] The natural reaction of Spanish manufacturers was to imitate these changes; however, production ordinances, which prohibited variations in the physical makeup of traditional textiles, stood in their way. It was not

---

[56] *Ibid.*, XX, 102–103; XXVII, 240–249; XXIX, 289; AHN, *Consejo, Libros de Govierno*, 1785, II, 383; ACA, *Diversorium*, no. 1183, fol. 2, no. 1187, fol 19; *ibid.*, *Acordadas*, no. 586, fol. 97; BCB, *op. cit.*, leg. 53, no. 30; Carrera y Pujal, *op. cit.*, IV, 129. As one method of keeping up with the proliferation of textiles, kings ordered customs officials to forward to Madrid samples of new types of cloth that entered the country. Official requests of this nature were made on May 12, 1783, June 7, 1784, June 10, 1785, July 21, 1791, and September 23, 1794 (AMH, *op. cit.*, XXVI, 141–145; XXVII, 115, XXVIII, 190–193; XXXV, 282–283; XXXVIII, 278–279).

[57] Ruiz y Pablo, *op. cit.*, p. 77; Carrera y Pujal, *op. cit.*, IV, 211.

[58] AGS, *op. cit.*, leg. 802.

[59] *Ibid.*, legs. 775, 776, 777, 778, 781, 782, 783, 784, 785.

[60] *Ibid.*, legs. 775, 776, 777, 779, 780, 781, 782, 783, 784.

[61] *Ibid.*, leg. 768.

until the last decades of the century that mounting pressure from domestic producers forced the king to remove many of these legal barriers to the freedom of production.[62] Spanish manufacturers, particularly those in Catalonia and Valencia, thereafter adapted their fabrics to meet the challenge of their competitors and changing market conditions.

While Spaniards were eager to vary the quality and style of their textiles, they were often apathetic to adopting mechanical advances. Charles III, the Economic Society of Valencia, and the Special Council of Commerce of Barcelona encountered resistance when they tried to diffuse the Vaucanson and Piedmontese developments in spinning and twisting silk throughout Valencia and Catalonia. Apparently Charles III provided for the introduction of the Vaucanson method in 1769 when he conceded to two Frenchmen, William and Santiago Reboull, the exclusive right to use this process in Vinalesa, near Valencia.[63] Several years later, the General Council of Commerce and Money and the Economic Society of Valencia strove to convince the harvesters of silk in the province, who also spun most of the thread used in Valencia, to adopt Vaucanson's method. To jar these spinners from their traditional techniques, the Council and the Society offered free instruction, free spinning machines, and a bounty on silk spun by the new method.[64]

Authorities also sought to introduce both the Vaucanson and the Piedmontese methods to Catalonia. Charles III obtained 1,500 spinning machines of the Vaucanson model in 1783 and offered 108 of them to harvesters in Catalonia at a discount.[65] The following year the Council of Commerce of Barcelona commissioned Maria Margarita Bertot, a native of Piedmont, to direct the construction of machines for reeling, spinning, and twisting silk as developed in her country and to teach Spaniards how to use

---

[62] ACSV, *loc. cit.;* AHN, *Biblioteca, Colección de Reales Cédulas,* 1789–1790, XX, 910; AHN, *Consejo, Libros de Govierno,* 1789, fols. 976–978; AHMB, *op. cit.,* I, 36; XXXIII, 162; LXI, 164–165.

[63] AMH, *op. cit.,* XVIII, 25–28; Carrera y Pujal, *Historia de la Economía Española,* V, 492. Several years later the Reboulls failed, and Charles transferred the concession to José Lapayese, a Frenchman and financier of the original project. Lapayese enlarged the factory and enjoyed some prosperity (AGS, *op. cit.,* leg. 773; Carrera y Pujal, *op. cit.,* V, 517).

[64] Juan Sempere y Guarinos, *Ensayo de una Biblioteca Española de los Mejores Escritores del Reynado de Carlos III,* 6 vols. (Madrid, 1785–1789), V, 223; BCB, *op. cit.,* leg. 51, nos. 14, 19; leg. 23, no. 11.

[65] Carrera y Pujal, *Historia Política y Económica de Cataluña,* IV, 222. There is confusion as to whether Charles III purchased these or obtained them as booty from a captured English convoy (*ibid.;* BCB, *op. cit.,* leg. 23, no. 9).

them.[66] That the Catalonians employed a woman in such a position reveals their eagerness to improve technology. Nevertheless, the Council released her in 1791, for meanwhile it had decided to concentrate on the promotion of the Vaucanson method rather than on the Piedmontese.[67]

Despite these extensive efforts on the part of officials to diffuse the sophisticated methods of Vaucanson and the Piedmont, the Valencian and Catalonian spinners stubbornly refused to abandon their simple and crude processes. A contemporary observer reported that such diffusion was tardy in Spain because

. . . the progress of almost everything in Spain is yet extremely slow; because the most advantageous improvements, being almost always but feebly patronized, are frequently opposed with all the obstinacy of prejudice, and all the acrimony of envy; because the government itself finds its powers circumscribed by the passions of those by whom its confidence is usurped and betrayed.[68]

Yet most observers as well as most officials failed to recognize that while the new methods of spinning silk were technically superior they were economically inferior to the older techniques; the Piedmontese and Vaucanson processes yielded finer, more even, but more expensive threads.[69] Producers at Valencia and Catalonia sent most of their stockings, handkerchiefs, and broadcloths of silk to colonial markets where colorful, inexpensive, and common-grade merchandise sold readily. They did not market their commonplace products in the large cities of Western Europe where fine and costly silks found buyers. Hence they had little need for finer, more even threads, especially at a higher cost than coarser ones. Had innovations in spinning and twisting silk furnished both more refined and cheaper threads than traditional techniques the Catalonians and Valencians surely would have subscribed to them.

They immediately adopted new techniques for spinning cotton when it became apparent that these advances supplied finer as well as less expensive thread. During the last two decades of the century, the king, the Special Council of Commerce of Barcelona, and producers of calico combined their efforts to transfer technology in this field from England to Catalonia. Their success was remarkable. By 1780 manufacturers in Barcelona were making

---

[66] *Ibid.*, leg. 51, nos. 14, 19; Carrera y Pujal, *op. cit.*, IV, 235–236.

[67] *Ibid.*

[68] Bourgoing, *op. cit.*, III, 160–161.

[69] *Ibid.*, III, 264.

thread with spinning jennies invented in 1767 by James Hargreaves.[70] They had renamed the machines "Bergadanes" or "Maxerines" and had increased the spindles from 24 to 120. Invented by Richard Arkwright or Thomas Highs in 1769 and first used by English industry in 1785, the water frame had appeared in Catalonia by 1791.[71] And by 1805 textile mills in Catalonia were operating the "mule," invented by Samuel Crompton in 1779.[72]

From their conception in England to their diffusion in Catalonia, these processes required only several decades. Catalonians acted with vigor, imagination, and resourcefulness when economies were at stake. And these economies were often substantial. Sometime before 1792 Salvador Pallarola and Manuel Flotats, owners of a cotton mill in the village of Cardona in Catalonia, recruited Bernard Young (Townch) from Manchester, England. Young constructed one machine for ginning, another for carding, and still another for spinning cotton.[73] With the carder two men were said to process a hundred pounds of cotton a day and thereby reduce the cost of this operation from sixty-four maravedis to only four a pound. Using the new spinning machine, one woman could spin nine pounds of cotton each day at a cost of eighteen maravedis instead of sixty-four a pound. The ginning machine could clean a hundred pounds of cotton each day so efficiently that costs fell from thirty-six reals and eight maravedis to only eight reals. After demonstrating how their machines thus reduced costs, Pallarola and Flotats received the king's permission in 1793 to manufacture and sell them throughout Catalonia.[74]

Makers of cotton fabrics at Barcelona habitually were the first Spaniards to embrace new developments. This became apparent to the General Council of Commerce and Money when it communicated its knowledge of industrial advancements to local councils of commerce. After receiving such communications, the

[70] Manuel Escudé Bartoli, *La Producción Española en el Siglo XIX* (Barcelona, 1895), p. 202; Carrera y Pujal, *op. cit.*, IV, 245.

[71] Escudé Bartoli, *loc. cit.*

[72] *Ibid.*, p. 203. Jacinto Ramon, a producer of calicoes at Barcelona, introduced the "mule" and powered it with a steam engine of twenty horsepower. Dr. Francisco Santpons of the Academy of Sciences had developed the steam engine earlier (Carrera y Pujal, *op. cit.*, IV, 256).

[73] BCB, *op. cit.*, leg. 23, no. 21; Carrera y Pujal, *op. cit.*, IV, 244–245.

[74] By 1796 the Special Council of Commerce of Barcelona reported that machines manufactured by Pallarola and Flotats were being used extensively in Catalonia. Nevertheless, some entrepreneurs in the region had already imitated these contrivances and others had imported more advanced models, thus reducing the advantage held by Pallarola and Flotats (*ibid.*, 247).

Council of Barcelona very often replied that producers in Catalonia not only knew of these new techniques but had already adopted them.[75] In those rare instances when Barcelonians heard of better techniques elsewhere in Spain, they boldly went after them. A representative event took place in 1790 when producers of muslin at Barcelona learned that Severo Vela of Tarragona had acquired a new machine for spinning cotton and a unique method for preparing the threads. The manufacturers wrote neither to Severo nor to the General Council of Commerce and Money but directly to Charles IV and requested that Severo be commanded to travel to Barcelona and acquaint them with his techniques.[76] It was much in this fashion that aggressive Catalonians had developed a level of technology far superior to the rest of Spain by the 1780's.[77]

Then came a remarkable irony. Agents from Castile and Leon began to recruit Catalonia's artisans. Perhaps the most celebrated exodus took place when Count O'Reily lured thirty-seven skilled Catalonians to Cadiz in 1785.[78] The Principality responded much as did England and France when Spain raided their labor supply. Acting on behalf of the industrial and mercantile interests, the Special Council of Commere of Barcelona threatened artisans, watched their movements, and in general tried to prevent their emigration. Charles III's government, committed to the industrial improvement of Castile and Leon, on August 31, 1785, prohibited any action that would impede the flow of artisans from Barcelona to other parts of Spain.[79]

CONCLUSION

It is impossible to say with accuracy how many foreign artisans came to Spain during the period 1700–1800. Only a glimmer of the magnitude reaches us from a census of foreigners taken in the summer of 1791, which uncovered 20,569 aliens living permanently and 5,193 living temporarily in the twenty-eight provinces of Castile and Leon.[80] Ignored by this count were Valencia, Aragon, Catalonia, Navarre, and the Basque provinces, and consequently perhaps five to ten thousand more permanent residents

---

[75] *Ibid.*, 255–256.
[76] AGS, *op. cit.*, leg. 756.
[77] For examples, see: BCB, *op. cit.*, leg. 23, nos. 7, 18, 19, 24; Bourgoing, *op. cit.*, III, 309–310.
[78] BCB, *op. cit.*, leg. 12, no. 1; Carrera y Pujal, *op. cit.*, IV, 231.
[79] BCB, *op. cit.*, leg. 12, no. 1.
[80] AHN, *Documentos Curiosos*, leg. 17808, no. 166.

should be added to the total. Of these twenty-five or thirty thousand foreigners, the majority were probably merchants. Even if only 10 to 20 percent were textile artisans, Spain would have possessed three to six thousand potential diffusers of knowledge. Whatever their numbers, they represented the fruits of an enlightened national policy of nearly a century's standing.[81] And much of Europe's technology came to Spain in their minds and luggage.

Upon this knowledge of production rested much of a proul nation's hopes for economic resurgence. Mere possession of technology, however, does not beget industry. A lack of any one of numerous productive factors can render useless the most recent technical developments. Thus it was that fine cloth failed to increase in central Spain other than at royal factories, even though kings made great efforts to diffuse the techniques of making fine textiles throughout this region. Technology in this rugged, wind-swept, treeless, isolated, parched area languished partly for want of requisite factors.

An entirely different state of affairs existed along the Mediterranean littoral. There, new techniques mingled with natural advantages, achieving a blend of ingredients ideal for industrial growth. Barcelona, with its large population, its convenient harbor, its geographical situation, and its extensive and populous hinterland from which came a variety of materials and services, absorbed England's best technology and became one of Europe's leading centers of calico production. Catalonia and Valencia, nevertheless, were selective in the technology they adopted. They spurned methods or machines that did not complement their endowment of resources; for more often than not new developments gave superior technical results but did not yield economies in the making of common fabrics, in which the natural advantages of these regions lay.

---

[81] Some of these artisans, of course, had fled from France and would have come even if Spain had had no policy.

VI

Craft Guilds of Spain

INTRODUCTION

The appearance of craft guilds in Europe's burgeoning towns marked an important milestone in the economic evolution of the Western world. By producing goods and services for a rising urban population, guilds helped transform the self-sufficient manorial system into the sophisticated economy of the late Middle Ages. Guilds were dynamic agents of change. But as the centuries passed they failed to adapt to growing markets and increasing productivity, lapsing into foes of progress and hindering further economic change.[1]

This chapter first examines how guilds plagued Spain's textile industry during the period 1750–1800: the internal structure of guilds are analyzed to illustrate the subservience of guildsmen. It then focuses on the actions taken by kings to reduce the baneful influence of these institutions. In conclusion, the chapter considers how the policies of kings joined with changing economic conditions to bring about a decline in the prominence of guilds.

SPANISH GUILDS AROUND 1750

Craft guilds dominated Spanish industry as the eighteenth century opened. By holding to an hierarchy of masters, journeymen, and apprentices and by limiting membership in each rank, they regulated the supply of labor in the different trades. They controlled output by restricting the quantity, and specifying the quality, of equipment and labor that each master could command. This monopoly power of guilds sprang from ordinances that were sanctioned by kings and rigorously enforced by the guilds themselves.[2]

---

[1] Gaspar Melchor de Jovellanos, *Biblioteca de Autores Españoles* (Madrid, 1859), L, 36–37; Juan Uña Sarthou, *Las Asociaciones Obreras en España* (Madrid, 1900), p. 284.

[2] Antonio de Capmany y de Montpalau, *Memorias Históricas sobre la Marina, Comercio y Artes de la Antigua Ciudad de Barcelona*, 4 vols. (Madrid, 1779–1792). I, part 3, pp. 46–47; AHN, *Consejo, Libros de Govierno*, 1739, fols. 297–302; ACA,

Control over artisans began with apprenticeship. Bound to his master by a written contract, the boy was to work, sleep, and eat in the master's home during the training interval, which averaged four years in the textile industry.[3] Unless dismissed for incompetence, insubordination, or some other just cause, the apprentice remained with his master for the entire period. He might transfer to another, however, and receive credit for his previous schooling if his original master consented. But a dismissed apprentice forfeited all of his training time and had six months added to the normal term as punishment. To preclude competitive bidding for partially trained workers, a master had to obtain the guild's permission before accepting an apprentice who had been employed by another master.[4]

When he had successfully completed his education, the apprentice received a certificate of apprenticeship and thus assumed the rank of journeyman.[5] His trials were far from over. For thereafter he had to spend from one to four years gaining additional experience in his trade. Although he need not remain with the same master during the entire period, he had to obtain permission if he wished to leave. Strict rules again prohibited competitive bidding for workers. Masters had to see the written release of the previous employer before hiring a journeyman.[6] A journeyman who wished to earn a mastership had to complete his training period and then submit to an examination. Given by officials of the guild, this test included practical application of the examinee's skills and oral questions. Once successfully beyond this hurdle, the artisan need only to pay fees and tips to wear the mantle of master.

Acordadas, no. 387, fols. 11–16; AHMB, *Junta General de Comercio*, XXVIII, 95–96.

Although guilds had changed but little from the 1300's to the 1700's, they underwent one important alteration in the early eighteenth century that affected the application of their ordinances. The sovereign authority replaced the municipalities as the legal guardian of guilds (Uña Sarthou, *op. cit.*, p. 286).

[3] AHN, *ibid.*, fol. 300; *ibid.*, *Biblioteca, Colección de Reales Cédulas*, 1778, XI, 451; AHMB, *op. cit.*, XXV, 127; XXVIII, 95; XLV, 168; ACA, *Acordadas*, no. 563, fol. 143; no. 568, fol. 340; no. 569, fol. 125; no. 570, fol. 213; no. 573, fol. 435; no. 574, fol. 68; no. 587, fol. 235; *ibid.*, *Diversorium*, no. 870, fol. 112; no. 872, fols. 12, 183, 269; no. 874, fols. 42, 63; no. 1184, fol. 65.

[4] *Ibid.*, *Acordadas*, no. 563, fol. 451; no. 574, fol. 69; no. 587, fol. 233; *ibid.*, *Diversorium*, no. 872, fol. 185; no. 874, fol. 43; AHN, *op. cit.*, 1778, XI, 451; AHMB, *op. cit.*, XV, 105.

[5] ACA, *Diversorium*, no. 872, fol. 184; no. 874, fol. 221. Only on occasion did guilds charge fees for this procedure.

[6] *Ibid.*, *Acordadas*, no. 563, fol. 141; no. 573, fol. 451; *ibid.*, *Diversorium*, no. 870, fol. 113; no. 872, fol. 186; no. 874, fol. 43; AHMB, *op. cit.*, XXV, 110; XLV, 172; AHN, *op. cit.*, 1778, XI, 45; ACSV, *Memoriales*, no. 3.

His new status elevated him to a privileged position within the guild: only masters could have apprentices, hire journeymen, and own looms, stores, and workshops. Nevertheless, a web of restrictions circumscribed his activities, limiting him to one apprentice, perhaps several journeymen, from one to five looms, and one workshop.[7] He had to follow exact procedures in manufacturing cloth and observe standards of quality that specified even the number and size of threads in each fabric. Gaspar Melchor de Jovellanos, an articulate economist of the eighteenth century, summarized the restraints that were placed on masters.

Once the master is established, the number of apprentices and journeyman that he can hire, and sometimes the number of looms and equipment that he can use, are fixed. He is obliged to share with his colleagues the material he gathers, or else to supply himself from the guild's warehouse, if one exists, or, finally, the guild supplies him with material even if he does not request it. He must work for himself and not for a merchant or trader even though he has no funds. He must adapt his work to the ordinances and sacrifice his hands and talent to them. He must pay taxes and give donations for the objects of the guild society. He must suffer denunciations, inspections, penalties, confiscations, and an infinity of annoyances. Now see if it is possible to multiply the number of artisans and industrial products under this system of oppression and exclusion.[8]

While Jovellanos rightly concluded that restrictions of this nature limited productivity, he wrongly intimated that controls were thrust upon the guilds. A majority of guildsmen clamored for regulations; they wanted absolute control over their trade. By limiting the number of producers, specifying technology, restricting outputs, and regulating the quality and styles of fabrics, they secured monopoly profits. Nevertheless, a few guildsmen, who recognized that even greater profits awaited those who broke the rules, strayed from the accepted path and, when caught, cried out against oppression.

To defend themselves against rebellious members and interlopers, guilds invoked their ordinances. These charters, which furnished guilds with a continuity of existence and governed virtually every act of the artisan from his apprenticeship to his death, provided explicit machinery for enforcement. Inspectors of the

---

[7] *Ibid., Reales Cédulas,* no. 2; ACA, *Acordadas,* no. 587, fol. 237; *ibid., Diversorium,* no. 1184, fol. 67.

[8] Jovellanos, *op. cit.,* 36–37.

guild were to seek out violators, and justices of the peace were to sentence wrongdoers.

Although the content of ordinances had remained essentially unaltered for centuries, their application became tyrannical during the eighteenth century.[9] Basic changes within the guild help explain this more rigorous enforcement. Sometime prior to 1750, economic position replaced technical skill as the source of prestige and as a prerequisite for election to office in the guild. And the guild itself evolved into a family patrimony by limiting the number of masters and by reserving vacated positions for sons of masters.[10] The office of inspector frequently became hereditary or its election was decided by intrigue and bribe.[11] In either event, inspectors became arrogant; they harassed artisans by searching them, by stamping, denouncing, and confiscating their textiles, and by punishing them for minor violations.[12] Oppression and tyranny replaced fairness and honesty in the administration of ordinances.

In some regions of Spain, the rapidly expanding textile industry brought forth changes after 1750 that challenged the very existence of guilds and aroused them to exploit with all their might and subtlety the restrictive potentials of their ordinances. It was in Catalonia where industrial changes were most revolutionary and guild reactions most vehement.[13] Unfettered by regulations, manufacturers of calicoes at Barcelona bid away workers from producers of silks, linens, and woolens. They even imported weavers when local wage rates rose enough to make this profitable.[14] Ascending wages and production on a large scale, which had dominated the calico industry from the outset, not only widened the differences between masters and journeymen but also created a new relationship—the entrepreneur and the day laborer. This development also affected the organization of the silk and woolen industry in Catalonia, though to a lesser extent. Perhaps

---

[9] Uña Sarthou, *op. cit.*, p. 283.

[10] *Ibid.*, p. 284.

[11] Manuel Colmeiro y Penido, *Historia de la Economía Política en España*, 2 vols. (Madrid, 1863), II, 224.

[12] *Ibid.*, 245.

[13] Wyndham Beawes, *A Civil, Commercial, Political and Literary History of Spain and Portugal* (London, 1793), p. 413; BCB, *Junta de Comercio*, leg. 53, nos. 24, 29, 37; Guillermo Graell, *La Cuestión Catalana* (Barcelona, 1902), p. 18.

[14] ACA, *Consultas*, no. 814, fols. 142, 220, 319; *ibid.*, *Diversorium*, no. 1184, fol. 42; Jaime Carrera y Pujal, *Historia Política y Económica de Cataluña, Siglos XVI al XVIII*, 4 vols. (Barcelona, 1946–1947), IV, 154.

several masters might rise to the status of entrepreneur and provide employment to other guildsmen,[15] or the role of organizer
might fall to merchants who gave orders to any number of masters.[16] Clearly, traditional relationships and methods of organizing economic activity were crumbling away.

In defense of a world which they had known for centuries and
which now faced extinction, guilds waged a desperate battle.
Throwing themselves against the swiftly mutating circumstances,
they sought to hold back the rush of events. Guilds made it more
difficult for men to become masters, journeymen, and apprentices,
limited the ability of masters to expand their outputs, and inter-
preted the rules on techniques and quality with overbearing
strictness.[17] Entrance requirements became increasingly severe:
many guilds admitted only apprentices who possessed pure Spanish blood, proof of baptism, and sufficient education to read,
write, and count.[18] Journeymen often had their ambitions of becoming masters frustrated if they had served their apprenticeships
in other cities or nations and hence not under "approved" masters.[19] Candidates who met these harsh requirements frequently
could not pay the registration fees. If they came from another
county or province, they often encountered higher fees than did
natives of the city and its surrounding jurisdiction. Sons and
sons-in-law of masters frequently paid nothing. Others exhausted
their savings by paying fees and tips, while those without funds
"called in vain at the door of the guild, for it was opened only
with a silver key." [20]

For foreigners and Spaniards from other regions that magic
sum was frequently five or ten times greater than that paid by
inhabitants of the city.[21] Discrimination between natives of the

---

[15] AHMB, *op. cit.*, XVI, 152, 155.

[16] Richard Herr, *The Eighteenth Century Revolution in Spain* (Princeton, 1958),
p. 134.

[17] Colmeiro y Penido, *op. cit.*, II, 244–245.

[18] ACA, *Diversorium*, no. 870, fol. 245; no. 874, fol. 66; AHMB, *op. cit.*, XV, 104;
Uña Sarthou, *loc. cit.*

[19] A unique way of limiting the number of masters was the practice of requiring
full periods of apprenticeship and journeymanship with "approved" masters. Guilds
then twisted the term "approved" masters to encompass masters in all of Spain,
only in a particular province, or solely in a particular city. At times they made it
clear that all skills must have been obtained from a master of a particular guild,
and that they would not certify skilled men from nearby cities (ACA, *Acordadas*,
no. 571, fols. 208–213; no. 587, fol. 239; *ibid.*, *Diversorium*, no. 870, fol. 248).

[20] Colmeiro y Penido, *op. cit.*, II, 245.

[21] For instance: the Guild of Veil Weavers and Velveteers at Tortosa requested
acceptance of new ordinances in 1768 which called for fees of three livres for sons
and sons-in-law and twenty-eight livres for all other journeymen. The Guild of

town was even more glaring. While the charge to ordinary journeymen often approached five hundred vellon reals, the exactions
from masters' sons and sons-in-law sometimes amounted to only
one pound of candle wax.[22] Besides paying fees, the unfortunate
journeyman got billed by the guild for the costs of the examination and dunned by the examiners for generous tips.

These responses, despite their fury and bitterness, took place
within the legal framework of ordinances. Providing all of the
authority necessary to control minutely the quantity and quality
of output of guildsmen, these ordinances permitted inspectors to
enter workshops at any time and investigate the number and
types of looms, equipment, employees, the quality of products,
and the processes used.[23] If inspectors discovered deviations from
the letter of the law, they confiscated the looms and fabrics and

---

Wool Weavers at Vich asked for approval of new ordinances in 1774 with fees of
twelve livres and ten sous for sons and sons-in-law, and twenty-five livres for all
other journeymen. Producers at Madrid, the Royal Factory at Talavera de la Reina,
and the attorney for the General Council of Commerce and Money inspected and
passed upon the ordinances for the Guild of Silk Stocking Producers at Barcelona.
These rules included a fee of fifty livres for admittance to the guild; however, sons
and sons-in-law of masters were to pay only ten livres. The Guild of Linen Weavers
at Tortosa sent the royal authorities new ordinances that included a six livre fee
for sons and sons-in-law, sixteen livres and eighteen sous for natives of the area,
and thirty-five livres for all others. In 1784 the ordinances for the Guild of Veil
Weavers at Gerona were approved. They included fees of seven livres for sons born
after their fathers had become masters, and one hundred livres for all others. Approved on November 28, 1790, the ordinances of the Guild of Linen and Cotton
Weavers at Reus charged masters' sons two pounds of wax on completion of their
examinations and exacted ten livres from natives and non-natives of the city (ACA,
Acordadas, no. 563, fol. 149; no. 570, fol. 210; no. 574, fol. 70; *ibid., Diversorium*,
no. 874, fol. 219; AHMB, *op. cit.*, XV, 108; XXV, 107).

[23] Some guilds limited this special treatment to eldest sons, sons-in-law married
to the eldest daughters, or sons who were born after their fathers had become
masters. Journeymen frequently and carefully examined the past and present ordinances of their guilds, hoping to discover an easy path to the rank of master. Juan
Babara, a journeyman weaver of cotton at Barcelona, for example, discovered that
the ordinances in effect during the years 1727 to 1745 awarded the status of master to journeymen who married daughters of masters. New ordinances passed in
1745, however, had abolished this policy. Nevertheless, Babara claimed that since
his wife, a master's daughter, had been born prior to 1745 and after 1727 he should
be made a master. After hearing his case in 1774, the Real Audiencia agreed and
ordered the guild to admit Babara (ACA, *Consultas*, no. 814, fol. 142).

Sons of masters frequently became masters at ridiculously young ages and without completing their apprenticeships or journeymanships. Juan Joseph Ruis
achieved this rank at such a tender age he did not know what a loom was; in 1750
Esteban Casanoba entered a guild as a master at seven years of age; and in 1775
Llarion Lopez was only two and one-half years of age when he became a master
(Eugenio Larruga y Boneta, *Memorias Políticas y Económicas sobre los Frutos, Comercio, Fábricas, y Minas de España*, 45 vols. [Madrid, 1787–1800], II, 3).

[23] ACA, *Acordadas*, no. 570, fol. 215; no. 568, fol. 343; *ibid., Diversorium*, no. 874,
fol. 64.

notified a justice of the peace. A verdict of guilty usually merited a fine. Fines in Catalonia varied between three and ten livres for offenses such as producing faulty goods, hiring nonguild labor, misconduct at meetings, refusing office in the guild, or possessing too many apprentices and looms.[24] Minor transgressions—missing funerals, public functions, or guild meetings—warranted fines of one or two pounds of candle wax.[25] Guildsmen convicted for the second or third time received more severe penalties, public burning of faulty textiles was a particularly disagreeable punishment.[26]

Although guild ordinances often stated what constituted faulty textiles, separate production ordinances, framed by the king but welcomed and enforced by the guilds, set standards for certain provinces and at times for all Spain.[27] Convinced that their country's economic troubles stemmed from inferior products, kings introduced many production ordinances during the sixteenth and seventeenth centuries.[28] Philip II established quality standards for silks in 1590.[29] After being modified at least four times between 1600 and 1685, these precepts remained in force throughout the eighteenth century. They measured quality by the grade of the thread and the weight of the fabric; and to insure high quality, they set forth mandatory weights for about eighteen different silks.[30]

---

[24] For examples, see: AHMB, *op. cit.*, XV, 108; XXVIII, 96; XLV, 172; ACA, *Acordadas*, no. 574, fol. 65; no. 687, fol. 237; AHN, *op. cit.*, 1778, XI, 451.

[25] Ordinances called for the proceeds from fines to be divided into three portions. One part went to the judge or the prosecuting body, another third was awarded to the denouncer, usually the guild inspector, and the last third was received by the legal chamber of the General Council of Commerce and Money (ACA, *Diversorium*, no. 870, fol. 186).

[26] Joaquin Manuel Fos, guild inspector and famous Valencian producer of silks, confiscated and publicly burned some silks in 1783, for they had not been made in accordance with the rules published on March 8, 1778. Heaping insult on injury after he had burned the cloth in the Plaza del Mercado, he displayed a large placard that named the producers and accused them of faulty workmanship. Immediately a great uproar sounded, and the implicated masters claimed one thousand persons had been left unemployed because of this heinous act. Finally, Charles III reprimanded Fos, ordered the fines returned to the masters, and commanded that, in the future, confiscated textiles were to be burned in private by the guild's caretaker after the cases had been reviewed by the General Council of Commerce and Money (ACSV, *loc. cit.*).

[27] ACA, *Acordadas*, no. 563, fols. 141–154; no. 573, fols. 431–453.

[28] Colmeiro y Penido, *op. cit.*, II, 239.

[29] AHN, *Consejo, Libros de Govierno*, 1675, fols. 3–25.

[30] For example, each vara of plain or figured black velvet had to weigh six ounces, with one-quarter of an ounce leeway; plain or figured, colored velvet had to weigh five and one-half ounces a vara. The rules provided fines of 100,000 maravedis (nearly 3,000 vellon reals) for each piece of cloth made incorrectly (*ibid.*, 1675, fol. 4).

In contrast, standards for woolens fixed a minimum number of threads in the warp and specified the length, width, thickness, color, texture, and weight of the different types of cloth.[31] To insure that manufacturers followed these mandates, ordinances closely regulated the production process; those introduced for woolens in Catalonia on January 15, 1769, for example, controlled the manufacture of stuffs and fine flannel from the first washing of selected wool to the final approval of the finished cloth.[32]

Because producers of calico operated on relatively large scales and appeared in Spain only late in the second quarter of the eighteenth century, they escaped domination by guild and production ordinances for some time. When control did arrive, however, it came at the request of the manufacturers themselves. On June 9, 1766, Charles III presented the industry with a general ordinance that regulated entry into the industry and controlled the quality of output.[33] After the enactment of these rules, a new entrant could receive economic privileges from the king only after he passed a proficiency examination and proved he owned a minimum of twelve looms, a field for bleaching cloth, printing tables, molds, and all other utensils needed for a complete factory. The new rules also attempted to thwart the export of technology by providing fines and jail sentences for producers or their employees who left Catalonia to profit by their knowledge of the industry.[34]

In one sense these ordinances were exceptional. For they endeavored to prevent technology from leaving rather than entering an industry.[35] But the philosophy that spawned this difference was indistinguishable from the rationale that lurked beneath most guild ordinances. Swayed by a fierce resolve to defend the group monopoly, this mentality normally revolted before new techniques, unique tools, differentiated products, or any innovation that might give a competitive advantage. Thus it was that arti-

---

[31] After ordinances for the woolen guild at Bejar had been amended and approved by the General Council of Commerce and Money in 1765, they permitted woolen producers to make only two classes of cloth. The first type was to have at least 3,000 threads in the warp and was to be seven-fourths of a vara in width, while the second was to have the same width and to contain at least 2,600 threads in the warp (AHN, *Consejo*, leg. 41067, fol. 2).

[32] AHMB, *op. cit.*, LXXIII, 16–21.

[33] BCB, *op. cit.*, leg. 53, no. 3.

[34] *Ibid.*

[35] Colmeiro y Penido, *op. cit.*, II, 247, 248; Larruga y Boneta, *op. cit.*, XXIV, 258–259.

sans who opposed the majority will and turned from traditional ways usually faced quick reprisals.[36]

Blas Lopez Arroyo, a weaver of passementerie at Valladolid, felt the wrath of his colleagues in 1758 when he sought financial assistance from the General Council of Commerce and Money to introduce a machine loom which he had improved.[37] After two years of vacillation,[38] the Council gave Lopez Arroyo a series of tax concessions. With this aid, he put his looms into operation, only to be confronted immediately with protestations and lawsuits introduced by his fellow guildsmen.[39] After eight years of continuous legal action, the General Council of Commerce and Money apparently ended the dispute by denying a petition that would have prohibited all use of the looms.[40] But the guild continued to resist, and twenty-five years after the controversy started hand looms still outnumbered machine looms at Valladolid.

Spain's textile industry suffered not only from sanctions against technical change but also from barriers to innovations of style and quality. While complicated rules and regulations strangled the ingenuity of Spanish manufacturers, a comparative freedom of production let English and French merchants cater to and cultivate consumer tastes in foreign markets. Producers in Spain could offer American consumers only closely woven, heavy cloth of European style; their competitors abroad easily adapted fabrics to suit the climatic and style conditions of the American colonies.[41] Competition was therefore slow, halting, and exasperating. Spanish producers countered their rivals slowly, first by obtaining revisions of their ordinances and thereafter by adapting to the new modes. By then, however, English manufacturers had designed and introduced new fabrics, frustrating their competitors.[42]

Some Spanish manufacturers refused to abide by production ordinances and defiantly adapted their goods to consumers'

---

[36] *Ibid.*, XVII, 270.

[37] *Ibid.*, XXIV, 217.

[38] The Council of Commerce, as it was wont to do, asked artisans in other cities to pass judgment on product samples from this loom. The consensus at Madrid was that looms of this advanced type did not exist—such weaving machines had not been seen at Madrid, therefore they did not exist (*ibid.*, XXIV, 218).

[39] *Ibid.*, 259.

[40] *Ibid.*

[41] Colmeiro y Penido, *op. cit.*, II, 248.

[42] Jovellanos lamented these fetters on Spanish inventiveness: ". . . the technical rules of guild legislation, the envious eye of the master, and the hungry vigilance of inspectors and their henchmen continuously discourage talent and dissuade it from these useful but dangerous attempts [at innovation] (Jovellanos, *op. cit.*, 37).

tastes, preferring to fight their guilds than to concede the market to foreign manufacturers. Such a conflict flared when the Guild of Silk Stocking Producers at Barcelona received an order on April 13, 1752, fixing the weights of stockings as well as the method of producing them.[43] Three or four masters, who had begun to expand and produce for export, disregarded the instructions, while the other guildsmen, many of whom worked as day laborers, clamored for enforcement and condemned the violators for discrediting the industry and harming the commerce and public. From this furor came more extensive regulation on July 7, 1777.[44]

The split within the Guild widened. Spurred on by a majority of guildsmen, the Special Council of Commerce of Barcelona tightened the regulations. After July 28, 1778, producers whose stockings had not been inspected by officers of the Guild were denied customs guides;[45] and beginning August 17, 1778, inspectors were to stamp each pair of stockings and collect a small fee from the owners.[46] To catch those who ignored these regulations, inspectors made surprise searches, discovering and confiscating many dozens of "faulty" hosiery. This infuriated the adventuresome masters and even moved some to violence.[47] After two years, however, enforcement slowed, and confiscations and fines dwindled as war with England closed the colonial market from June, 1779, to September, 1783.

The dispute abruptly surfaced again on March 14, 1787, when the Special Council of Commerce of Barcelona, responding to complaints that some masters were successfully evading all controls, reaffirmed the regulations.[48] In a fiery rebuttal, dominant producers declared that quality of silk stockings depended less on their weight than on the quality of thread in them. If weight were the only factor, they asserted, the poorest and heaviest silk would yield the finest product. They furthermore claimed that stockings made to foreign rather than to Spanish specifications sold more readily; exporters placed orders with them for imita-

---

[43] AHMB, *op. cit.*, XVIII, 152. Most likely the guild had no ordinances, for production of stockings with looms had been in existence only since 1730 (*ibid.*, XV, 104; XVII, 142).

[44] These additional controls set absolute weight limits for silk stockings (*ibid.*, XIX, 136).

[45] *Ibid.*, XV, 95.

[46] The Council apparently added one more important control: the replacement of the inspectors of the guild by those selected by the Council (*ibid.*).

[47] *Ibid.*, XVI, 90–99.

[48] *Ibid.*, XVIII, 39.

tions of foreign stockings, knowing that these items failed to weigh the "correct" amount.[49] The vigorous persistence of these arguments and the sympathy of government for an unfettered economy finally decided the issue: on June 25, 1788, the General Council of Commerce and Money suspended the inspection of silk stockings and thereby left manufacturers free to produce their output as they wished.[50]

MODIFICATION OF GUILD ORDINANCES AFTER 1750

A rising tide of concern for the consequences of restrictive practices of guilds rolled across Spain during the eighteenth century, culminating after 1750 with the decisive action of Charles III and his able ministers.[51] In general, the pattern of these efforts resembled those that lifted the controls from the production of silk stockings. Rather than destroy the guilds, the government initiated general reforms of ordinances or attacked piecemeal those sections of ordinances that obstructed economic progress.

Charles III first ordered a general reform on June 13, 1770, when he gave the General Council of Commerce and Money authority to revise guild rules and remove all obstacles to industrial progress.[52] The General Council had little success. Thus it was that on September 21, 1789, Charles IV commanded the General Council to eliminate once and for all the ability of guilds to frustrate creative genius and to obstruct the growth and prosperity of industry.[53] The influence of Gaspar Melchor de Jovellanos is evident in this action, for in 1788 he had chided the General Council.

. . . let us cut with one blow the chain that oppresses and weakens our industry and restore at once that desired liberty by which its prosperity and growth is cyphered.[54]

---

[49] *Ibid.*, 75.

[50] *Ibid.*, 111.

[51] Pedro Rodriguez, Conde de Campomanes, *Discurso sobre el Fomento de la Industria Popular* (Madrid, 1774), pp. 109–119.

[52] AHN, *Biblioteca, Colección de Reales Cédulas,* 1770, VI, 271; José Ventalló Vintró, *Historia de la Industria Lanera Catalana* (Tarrasa, 1904), p. 546; Jaime Carrera y Pujal, *Historia de la Economía Española,* 5 vols. (Barcelona, 1943–1947), IV, 102.
On January 12, 1779, Charles urged the Council to make some progress and thirteen days later he asked the economic societies to study the guild ordinances in their jurisdictions and to propose reforms (AHN, *op. cit.,* 1779, 1780, XII, 491; Uña Sarthou, *op. cit.,* p. 288).

[53] ACSV, *loc. cit.;* AHMB, *op. cit.,* I, 34; LIX, 156.

[54] Jovellanos, *op. cit.,* 38.

In 1790, however, Charles took the initiative from the General Council and ordered guilds to purge their own ordinances with assistance from the General Council, special councils of commerce in provincial cities, and economic societies.[55] He evidently felt that rewriting the ordinances of all guilds in Spain was too great a task for the General Council of Commerce and Money and hoped to obtain some results by placing the burden on the guilds.

Revisions of ordinances that occurred after 1770, however, demonstrate how futile were these attempts at general reform. Guilds compromised, withdrawing articles they considered nonessential to preservation of their monopoly control. Fines often were reduced or deleted for minor offenses such as refusing guild office or for missing meetings and funerals; sons and sons-in-law of masters no longer were sheltered from examinations or given shortened apprenticeships. And yet, the wellspring of guild strength—discriminatory fees and traditional restrictions on equipment, apprentices, and journeymen—remained solidly in force.[56]

Kings enjoyed more success when they focused upon specific rules within the ordinances that obviously were detrimental to industrial growth and then declared null and void all such restrictions throughout Spain. Control over apprentices and journeymen, a major component of guild power, was one of these limitations. Settlement of disputes arising from this issue generally favored guilds during the first three-quarters of the century, but thereafter a mounting sentiment for economic freedom turned the decisions against guilds.[57] Casting away the customs of apprenticeship and journeymanship on January 14, 1798, Charles IV commanded guilds to examine all nonmasters who sought admission, even if they lacked apprenticeship, journeymanship, domicile, or any other requirement of guild ordinances. Moreover,

---

[55] AHMB, *op. cit.*, I, 35; LIX, 156.

[56] *Ibid.*, XXV, 107–114; XLV, 168–172; ACA, *Acordadas*, no. 569, fols. 123–125; *ibid.*, *Consultas*, no. 814, fol. 180; *ibid.*, *Diversorium*, no. 872, fols. 11–23, 181–186, 266–270; no. 870, fols. 242–252; no. 874, fols. 40–45, 63–68, 219–222; no. 1184, fols. 64–73; AHN, *op. cit.*, 1778, XI, 45.

[57] An exception occurred in 1774 when authorities allowed calico producers to employ journeymen who were not members of the Guild of Linen Weavers, regardless of opposition from that guild. Twenty years later during a recession, authorities prohibited calico producers from employing journeymen who were not members of the Guild of Linen Weavers. On January 25, 1788, the General Council permitted producers of silk stockings at Manresa to employ the number of apprentices they so desired, regardless of any ordinance rule to the contrary (ACA, *Consultas*, no. 814, fols. 142, 220, 319; *ibid.*, *Diversorium*, no. 1184, fol. 42; AHMB, *op. cit.*, XVIII, 106; Carrera y Pujal, *Historia Política y Económica de Cataluña*, IV, 154).

Charles declared that the exercise of any trade was not to be withheld from any artisan who possessed sufficient skill and a master's
letter of examination.[58] As added protection for journeymen, the
king abolished fees and tips, but allowed guilds to collect the expenses of examinations.[59] The Cortes of Cadiz on June 8, 1813,
emancipated all economic activity by allowing any artisan to start
a factory or workshop without the need of requesting anyone's
permission.[60]

While guilds held journeymen and apprentices in near bondage
for most of the century, they were loath to accept women in their
ranks. They limited employment to men in many trades, or gave
them preference in others. As long as male silk twisters were unemployed at Barcelona, for example, their guild denied employment to women.[61] Charles III began the assault on such discrimination when he abolished all guild rules that withheld employment from women in trades compatible with their sex and strength
on January 12, 1779.[62] But royal proclamations spread slowly
through Spain, and frequently provincial authorities even formulated policies in opposition to them. This happened on January
16, 1784, when the Special Council of Commerce of Barcelona
forbade women to spin cotton in many villages of Catalonia. The
women complained bitterly, for they earned more and worked
less by spinning cotton rather than wool. Setting aside this ruling
on July 2, 1784, the General Council of Commerce and Money

---

[58] ACSV, *loc. cit.;* Ventalló Vintró, *op. cit.,* p. 550; Charles E. Kany, *Life and Manners in Madrid, 1750–1800* (Berkeley, 1932), p. 169.

[59] Uña Sarthou writes that a royal order issued on May 26, 1790, allowed any
artisan of known or unknown profession with recognized skill to exercise his trade
without a guild examination. This order, however, which was issued on behalf of
a lather, then extended to all skills, probably did not receive much publicity or
enforcement. In fact, it is not beyond reason that the royal cedula of January 4,
1798, which permitted an individual to engage in any trade if he had a letter of
examination, was enacted without knowledge or remembrance of the order cited
by Uña Sarthou (*op. cit.,* p. 293).

[60] Ventalló Vintró, *op. cit.,* p. 539; Uña Sarthou, *op. cit.,* p. 296. The Cortes of
Cadiz was a reunion of Spanish representatives that met on September 24, 1810, on
the isle of Leon and later moved to Cadiz. The purpose of the convocation was to
form a united and strong front before the French invaders. First of all, the representatives stated the principles of national sovereignty and then turned their attention to legislative matters, one important result of which was the Constitution of
1812. The representatives were predominantly liberal and consequently their legislation had the effect of supporting the economic reforms of the 1780's and 1790's
(C. Perez-Bustamente, *Compendio de Historia de España* [Madrid, 1957], p. 443).

[61] Carrera y Pujal, *Historia de la Economía Española,* V, 320.

[62] Jovellanos, *op. cit.,* p. 33; Carrera y Pujal, *op. cit.,* IV, 120; AHN, *op. cit.,*
1779–1780, XII, 491. This cedula had been preceded by a similar edict published on
January 12, 1679 (Jovellanos, *loc. cit.*).

allowed women to spin materials of their choice.[63] Two months later, Charles III permitted all women in Spain to determine their occupations, provided they chose occupations compatible with their sex, decency, and strength.[64]

As guilds discriminated against women, so they also made it difficult and frequently impossible for foreign artisans to become guildsmen.[65] This hostility met only sporadic, impotent legislative opposition during the reigns of Philip V and Ferdinand VI.[66] Then, near the three-quarter mark of the century, guilds stepped up their opposition to foreigners as the demand for labor increased in Valencia and Barcelona, and as more and more artisans immigrated to Spain on their own initiative, or were induced there by kings.[67] Charles III reacted to this growing intransigence on April 30, 1772, by ordering guilds to admit to membership any foreign artisan who presented proof of his mastership.[68] In a further effort to halt this abuse of foreigners, Charles, on March 24, 1777, commanded guilds to examine and then receive as members all foreign or Spanish journeymen who came to their city. If they failed the first examination, foreign journeymen could request a second one with two new examiners selected by the justice of the peace.[69] This decree again ordered guilds to accept any master who could prove his status with an original letter of examination.

Continuing the policy of his father, Charles IV placed foreign artisans outside the jurisdiction of guilds on July 23, 1797, when

---

[63] AHMB, *Junta General de Comercio*, LXXIX, 138, 188, 190.

[64] *Ibid.*, LXXX, 80; AHN, *Consejo, Libros de Govierno*, 1784, II, fols. 332–334; AMH, *Colección de Órdenes Generales de Rentas*, XXVII, 157–160; Carrera y Pujal, *op. cit.*, IV, 126.
Charles IV strengthened hereditary rights of masters' widows on December 23, 1789, and May 19, 1790 (AHMB, *op. cit.*, I, 21–22; AHN, *Biblioteca, Colección de Reales Cédulas*, 1789, 1790, XX, 938; Uña Sarthou, *op. cit.*, p. 293; Kany, *op. cit.*, p. 169).
According to one contemporary, women should not be restricted to jobs "compatible with their sex, decency, and strength," for these limitations existed only in the minds of men and not in fact. And so, he concluded, why sanctify them by law? (Jovellanos, *op. cit.*, pp. 33–34).

[65] ACA, *Acordadas*, no. 571, fols. 208–213.

[66] Some early attempts were made to ease the burden of foreign artisans in Spain: Philip V commanded on June 2, 1703, that guilds admit foreigners to membership; and in 1706 the Cortes of Barcelona ruled that alien workmen be permitted to work in their trades without need of examination by guilds (*ibid.*, fol. 209; Uña Sarthou, *op. cit.*, p. 292; Campomanes, *op. cit.*, p. 116).

[67] ACA, *op. cit.*, fols. 208–213.

[68] Uña Sarthou, *loc. cit.*; Carrera y Pujal, *op. cit.*, IV, 115.

[69] AHN, *op. cit.*, 1777, X, 430; ACSV, *loc. cit.*; Carrera y Pujal, *op. cit.*, IV, 117; Uña Sarthou, *loc. cit.*

he instructed the General Council of Commerce and Money and the provincial intendants to grant all skilled immigrants, except Jews, permission to establish workshops or factories.[70] Guilds continued to restrain foreigners, however, and additional rulings in 1798 and 1799 once again commanded them to admit immigrants.[71] The culminating decree against restricting foreign and, for that matter, Spanish artisans was issued on June 8, 1813, when the Cortes of Cadiz canceled the need of requesting permission to start a factory and thereby granted absolute economic freedom to all.[72]

Guilds also limited the number of looms a master could possess. Though ambitious guildsmen protested against this restraint, it remained in force throughout the first thirty-five years of the period 1750–1800. Members of the Guild of Silk Stocking Producers at Barcelona, for example, asked for abolition of the limitation of two looms for each master in 1748;[73] they waited thirty-seven years before Charles III permitted them to operate as many as they wished.[74] Extending this decision on June 2, 1787, Charles gave all producers of textiles in Spain the freedom to utilize any number of looms, regardless of ordinances to the contrary. "For these restrictions are harmful to the progress of manufacture and to the promotion of national industry." [75]

During the last quarter of the eighteenth century, Charles III and Charles IV nullified several minor guild rules that impeded the exercise of certain trades. Stigma of illegitimacy had legally excluded many able Spanards from apprenticeship until Charles III voided all such regulations on September 2, 1784.[76] If a man or even his father had been employed in a "vile" trade,[77] he found

---

[70] AMH, *op. cit.*, XLI, 230–232; AHMB, *op. cit.*, I, 155.

[71] The guilds at Barcelona convinced the king that their city should be exempted from these orders (Carrera y Pujal, *op. cit.*, V, 300).

[72] Ventalló Vintró, *op. cit.*, p. 539; Uña Sarthou, *op. cit.*, p. 296.

[73] Carrera y Pujal, *op. cit.*, V, 317.

[74] Published in the *Madrid Gazeta* on March 4, 1785, this cedula received little circulation and possibly never reached Barcelona (AHMB, *op. cit.*, XXII, 145).

Charles had given this privilege to producers of silk stockings at Valencia on July 12, 1780 (Uña Sarthou, *op. cit.*, p. 292).

[75] ACSV, *loc. cit.*; Carrera y Pujal, *op. cit.*, IV, 130; Uña Sarthou, *loc. cit.*; AHMB, *op. cit.*, XLIV, 35.

[76] AHN, *Consejo, Libros de Govierno,* 1784, II, 338–340; Carrera y Pujal, *op. cit.*, IV, 127.

[77] Certain trades, such as leather tanning and wool carding, were considered vile because those who engaged in them were contaminated with an offensive odor, left with stained hands, or otherwise affected in a disagreeable manner. After having worked in a vile trade an artisan found it impossible to be admitted to public office, the ministry, or guilds. He was despised by his neighbors and hated by his relatives (*ibid.*, 179).

himself banned from other professions. To raise the social standing of "vile" occupations, Charles declared them honored on March 18, 1783, and commanded that artisans so employed were not to be excluded from holding municipal office nor from enjoying the prerogatives of nobility.[78]

Thus it was that Charles III and Charles IV annulled the major restrictions in guild ordinances during the last three decades of the century. In 1770 and 1789 they ordered the General Council of Commerce and Money to cleanse these rules of all obstacles to industrial expansion. While this frontal attack enjoyed only meager success, a roundabout, piecemeal offensive earned substantial triumphs. Charles IV abolished all regulations governing apprenticeship and journeymanship in 1798 by forcing guilds to examine anyone who requested membership and to admit any master with an original letter of examination. Women received substantial economic freedom in 1779, 1784, 1789, and 1790. Charles III, Charles IV, and the Cortes of Cadiz banned discrimination of foreigners by successive actions in 1772, 1777, 1797, and 1813. And producers won the freedom to operate any number of looms after 1787.[79]

MODIFICATION OF PRODUCTION ORDINANCES AFTER 1750

At the same time kings were removing the nettle from guild rules, they were undermining production ordinances. Rather than suspend these rules, kings made them ineffective by isolating entrepreneurs from their influence. Imposed by kings on producers in certain provinces or, as frequently occurred, on manufacturers in all Spain, production ordinances were fewer in number and less traditional than guild ordinances and hence were easier to suppress.

---

[78] Colmeiro y Penido, *op. cit.*, II, 222; Uña Sarthou, *op. cit.*, p. 287; Kany, *op. cit.*, p. 168; Carrera y Pujal, *op. cit.*, IV, 126; AHN, *op. cit.*, 1783, fols. 521–522.

Kany writes that in 1803 this ruling was reinterpreted to mean that such vile occupations had been raised above crime, vagrancy, idleness, and dishonor, not that they had been elevated to the rank of highest honor (Kany, *loc. cit.*).

Noblemen had been reluctant to enter industry in Spain lest they lose their status; in 1773, Charles III assured them that their titles would be safe if they engaged in manufacture. A pragmatic sanction issued on December 15, 1682, had permitted Spanish nobles to engage in industry, but had had little effect (Carrera y Pujal, *op. cit.*, V, 116; AHN, *op. cit.*, 1682, fols. 309–311).

[79] Another way by which kings freed textile producers from guild obstacles was to exempt from guild regulations individual artisans who had developed special processes or new products. These dispensations usually preceded the more general actions against ordinances. For some examples, see: AHMB, *op. cit.*, XXI, 165; XXXIX, 2, 4, 8, 13–26; XLVII, 112; BCB, *op. cit.*, leg. 23, no. 3; AHN, *op. cit.*, 1782, fol. 557; Carrera y Pujal, *Historia Política y Económica de Cataluña*, IV, 215–236.

Philip II imposed production ordinances on manufacturers of silks in 1590. Revised a number of times during the seventeenth century, they prohibited innovation and fixed methods of production in this industry.[80] Foreign makers of silks, however, were relatively free to alter their techniques and designs and thus undersold their Spanish rivals.[81] Occupying most of the century, the struggle to free manufacturers of silks from the clutches of these rules first began as a series of exemptions to selected regions, institutions, and persons, then turned into a tug-of-war as Spaniards vied with one another for additional independence, and ended with all winning complete liberty.

Charters of the joint-stock companies of Aragon, Extremadura, Granada, Seville, and Toledo, issued by Ferdinand VI between 1746 and 1748, permitted these companies to manufacture silks without maintaining the legal standards.[82] But these textiles, differentiated by lead stamps, had to be exported.[83] After withdrawing this concession on June 24, 1752, he awarded it again on March 30, 1753, not only to joint-stock companies but also to all other makers of silks at Toledo, Seville, Granada, Zaragoza, and Zarza la Mayor (Extremadura). Textiles made under these circumstances still had to be exported.[84]

To give even more freedom to the industry ,Ferdinand permitted all producers of silks in Spain to vary the weights of their fabrics on September 17, 1750,[85] and allowed the Five Greater Guilds of Madrid, on April 26 and June 25, 1755, to weave silks at their factory at Valencia with narrower widths than legally permitted by the ordinances.[86] Other producers at Valencia complained against this special privilege and obtained similar concessions on September 29, 1756.[87]

Less onerous technical limitations now burdened manufacturers of silks at Valencia than producers of silks elsewhere in Spain.

---

[80] AHN, *op. cit.*, 1675, fols. 3–6.

[81] ACSV, *Pragmáticas y Reales Cédulas*, no. 1.

[82] Larruga y Boneta, *op. cit.*, VII, 64; Colmeiro y Penido, *op. cit.*, II, 458.

[83] Francisco Gallardo Fernandez, *Origen, Progresos y Estado de Rentas de la Corona de España*, 7 vols. (Madrid, 1805–1808), II, 384; BN, MS 13006, fol. 38.

[84] Gallardo Fernandez, *op. cit.*, II, 388; AMH, *op. cit.*, XI, 307–310.

[85] ACSV, *loc. cit.*

[86] *Ibid.*

[87] *Ibid., Reales Cédulas*, no. 2.

Charles III granted producers of silks at Valencia further immunities in 1768 when he permitted them to weave light and heavy serge by methods not included in the ordinances (*ibid., Pragmáticas y Reales Cédulas*, no. 1).

This inequality of treatment triggered widespread charges of unfairness. Relenting before the discontent on March 8, 1778, Charles permitted all manufacturers of silks in Spain to weave fabrics with less weight and width than required by the ordinances.[88] But producers at Valencia balked when asked to respect these rules, for concessions which they previously had received on September 29, 1756, allowed greater independence.[89] When Charles yielded to the Valencians, the Guild of Velveteers and Weavers of Silk at Barcelona and the Guild of Veil Weavers and Velveteers at Tortosa immediately asked for similar treatment. Charles consequently extended the Valencian rules to all of Catalonia on July 5, 1782.[90]

Foreign producers swiftly varied the styles and quality of their fabrics and easily overcame the narrow leeway in weight and dimension now allowed Spanish manufacturers. Finally convinced that the proliferation of styles and the fickleness of consumers made obsolete the hard and fast rules of production, Charles took more determined action on October 25 and November 9, 1786. He permitted producers of silks as well as woolens to innovate and imitate textiles without regard for production ordinances. In order to maintain control over quality, however, he ordered the General Council of Commerce and Money to pass judgment on all deviations from standard fabrics before permitting their manufacture.[91] Charles furthermore commanded producers to stamp all new fabrics to distinguish them from standard textiles, but permitted them to sell these goods in Spain.[92]

Producers of silks, along with producers of all other textiles, received complete independence in manufacturing their fabrics on September 21, 1789. By this action Charles IV permitted them to invent and imitate textiles, and to vary the width, the number of threads in the warp and woof, and the weight of the fabrics. Producers could also modify technical processes and machines. In order to differentiate these new textiles from standard fabrics,

---

[88] *Ibid., Reales Cédulas,* no. 2; AHN, *Biblioteca, Colección de Reales Cédulas,* 1778, XI, 459; AMH, *op. cit.,* XXII, 203–209; AHMB, *op. cit.,* XXVIII, 153; Carrera y Pujal, *Historia de la Economía Española,* V, 323.

[89] ACSV, *loc. cit.;* AMH, *op. cit.,* XXIV, 73–74.

[90] AHMB, *op. cit.,* XLII, 132; XXXVI, 126.

[91] AHN, *Consejo, Libros de Govierno,* 1786; fols. 1340–1342; Carrera y Pujal, *op. cit.,* IV, 130; V, 499.

[92] On June 25, 1788, the government permitted producers of silk stockings in Spain to manufacture stockings of any weight, provided lighter stockings contained finer silk (AHMB, *op. cit.,* XVIII, 111).

Charles required manufacturers to stamp their name and place of residence on the new cloth.[93]

Emancipation of woolen production followed a similar pattern. After granting limited freedom from production controls to manufacturers in restricted locations, kings gradually expanded these concessions and extended them to all producers in Spain.[94] When Charles III freed manufacturers of silks from controls in November 9, 1786, he also allowed makers of woolens to vary their looms, loom combs, and spinning machines with the end of innovating, imitating, or varying fabrics.[95] They, too, had to request permission to institute changes from the General Council of Commerce and Money and then differentiate their fabrics with a special stamp.[96] Producers of woolens, as well as producers of all textiles, received unconditional independence from technical ordinances on September 21, 1789.[97]

Soon after receiving substantial freedom to innovate their fabrics, manufacturers encountered a wave of complaints which accused them of cheapening their products excessively and of deliberately misrepresenting their textiles as having qualities stated by the production ordinances.[98] The government, wavering before these complaints and accusations, asked the General Council of Commerce and Money to undertake a complete study of the problems created by freedom of production.[99] After considering the issue for thirteen years, the Council recommended on April 8, 1808, that independence in production be continued, but sug-

---

[93] ACSV, *loc. cit.;* AHN, *Biblioteca, Colección de Reales Cédulas,* 1789–1790, XX, 910; AHN, *Consejo, Libros de Govierno,* 1789, fols. 976–978; AHMB, *op. cit.,* I, 36; XXXIII, 162; LIX, 164–165.

[94] *Ibid.,* LXXIII, 17–19; Carrera y Pujal, *op. cit.,* IV, 95; V, 313.

[95] AHN, *op. cit.,* 1786, fols. 1340–1342; Carrera y Pujal, *op. cit.,* IV, 130; V, 499. Carrera y Pujal claims that a similar ruling had been issued in 1785 (*Historia Política y Económica de Cataluña,* IV, 96).

[96] AHN, *op. cit.,* 1786, fols. 1340–1342; Carrera y Pujal, *Historia de la Economía Española,* IV, 130; V, 499.

[97] Charles III loosened the bonds from linen producers on December 14, 1784, when he permitted them to modify their loom combs (AHN, *op. cit.,* 1785, II, 387–388; AMH, *op. cit.,* XXVII, 250–253; AHMB, *op. cit.,* XXV; Carrera y Pujal, *op. cit.,* IV, 128.

[98] The ruling of September 21, 1789, required that all textiles not made in accordance with production ordinances carry only the names of the manufacturers and the villages in which they were made. All other cloth carried distinctive seals and markings that indicated that ordinances had been followed. Falsification of these latter symbols was quite simple and frequent.

[99] ACSV, *loc. cit.;* Ventalló Vintró, *op. cit.,* p. 554.

gested that greater care be taken to prevent debasement of textiles and misleading of consumers.[100]

CONCLUSION

The crusade against control of industry by guilds had nearly accomplished its objectives by 1800. In 1813 the Cortes of Cadiz finished the task. Despite the breadth and intensity of the Royal offensive, guilds had not been abolished.[101] They remained as spokesmen for independent artisans, but they no longer controlled the activities of their members. Now any qualified person could become a master without serving an apprenticeship or journeymanship, or without paying excessive fees and tips. The struggle ended with masters free to own and operate any quantity and quality of looms and machines and to hire any number of workers. Women were emancipated from traditional tasks and permitted to enter other occupations. Illegitimacy and past employment in "vile" trades were no longer legal obstacles to crafts, and barriers to the employment of foreign artisans had been removed. The campaign against production ordinances ended with manufacturers free to introduce new methods and to vary the style and quality of their products.

These were extraordinary achievements. And yet, their effects on industrial activity must have disappointed contemporaries. For only in Catalonia and Valencia did sufficient economic motives permit manufacturers to take advantage of the legal demise of guild restrictions. Even here one must not overemphasize the impact of these reforms. Industry in Catalonia and Valencia expanded prior to the major enactments against guilds, upsetting the traditional organization of production and arousing guilds to violent but futile defensive action. Thus it was that changing conditions, not royal legislation, struck the first and deadliest blow at guilds. Their death wails only served to alert the king and instigated legislation which in turn served as their requiem. With the powers of guilds laid to rest, industry in Catalonia and Valencia continued expanding, but at a faster rate.[102]

---

[100] ACSV, *loc. cit.*

[101] An exception occurred on March 17, 1796, when Charles IV abolished all guilds of silk twisters (AHN, *Biblioteca, Colección de Reales Cédulas*, 1793–1794, XXII, 1039; AHMB, *op. cit.*, XLIX, 53–54; Uña Sarthou, *op. cit.*, p. 293).

[102] Events after 1813 denied the expected effects of these liberal measures. Ferdinand VII, in a reactionary move, reëstablished guild ordinances on June 29, 1815. And not until December 6, 1836, did Spanish industry again enjoy freedom from ordinances (*ibid.*, pp. 296–299).

Throughout the rest of Spain, with few exceptions, production activity was so lethargic that pressure against guild restrictions failed to develop in the first place. Even after the major limitations had been removed, industry languished and consequently maintained the traditional organization of the guild.

VII

Provincial Taxes

INTRODUCTION

An oppressive horde of taxes thwarted economic progress in much of Spain when the eighteenth century began. Excises burdened nearly all products, pursuing them through every transaction to their final destinations. Personal wealth and effort also experienced the weight of levies. The confusing variety, the punishingly high rates, the glaringly unequal incidence, and the remorseless fashion of collection of these imposts frightened away investment funds, stunted entrepreneurial initiative, and generally restricted industrial activity. Realizing the harmful consequences of these taxes, the government strove to soften their impact on Spain's economy.

This chapter first describes those taxes that prevailed in 1750; it then demonstrates to what extent they were oppressive, wasteful, and unfair; it thereafter examines the various reforms attempted during the period 1750–1800 and summarizes the influence of these changes on economic growth.

SPANISH TAXES IN 1750

In 1750 Spain possessed a revenue system that had evolved haphazardly through half a millennium. Many of her taxes had their origins in medieval times when the Cortes, or parliaments of nobles, awarded kings temporary levies or services (*servicios*) for financing the reconquest.[1] Although at the outset these taxes were intended to last only during times of financial stress, they often were extended repeatedly until they became permanent. As Spain's ascendancy in world affairs swiftly blossomed in the fifteenth and sixteenth centuries, kings supplemented the old with new sources

---

[1] Manuel Colmeiro y Penido, *Historia de la Economía Política en España*, 2 vols. (Madrid, 1863), II, 540–542; José Canga Argüelles, *Diccionario de Hacienda*, 2 vols. (Madrid, 1833–1834), I, 24; II, 487.

of income.[2] Economic decline in the seventeenth century then reduced the tax base; yet the constant, intensifying struggle to maintain the empire created an even greater need for revenue.[3] Kings therefore continued to multiply taxes and to raise rates.

Spain not only had a wide variety of taxes by 1700, but each region possessed its own unique pattern. In Castile and Leon the most famous, controversial, and lucrative of all taxes were undoubtedly the *alcabala* and *cientos*. Conceded to Alfonso XI by the Cortes in 1342, the *alcabala* evolved into a 10 percent transactions tax levied on all things sold or traded, with the exceptions of arms, horses, and seed.[4] The *cientos*, a 4 percent sales tax likewise imposed on all things sold, traded, or otherwise exchanged, first appeared during the seventeenth century.[5] The *alcabala* and *cientos* together, therefore, amounted to a 14 percent transactions tax levied on all goods each time they were exchanged.[6]

Another basic tax in Castile and Leon was the *servicios de millones*. Like the *cientos*, it first appeared in the seventeenth century.[7] Collected with the *alcabala* and *cientos*, the *millones* em-

---

[2] Colmeiro y Penido, *loc. cit.*

[3] *Ibid.*, 542–543.

[4] BN, MS 10695; Francisco Gallardo Fernandez, *Origen, Progresos y Estado de Rentas de la Corona de España*, 7 vols. (Madrid, 1805–1808), I, 165; Canga Arguëlles, *op. cit.*, I, 24.
The Cortes originally set the rate at 5 percent, but in 1349 increased it to 10. Canga Arguëlles states that this levy existed in some Spanish cities as early as 1341 and that during the reign of Alfonso XI (1310–1350) its use spread throughout Castile and Leon (Canga Arguëlles, *loc. cit.*).

[5] Philip IV imposed the first "one percent" in 1639, the second in 1642, the third in 1656, and the last in 1663. Professor Earl J. Hamilton disagrees with several authors and gives 1664 as the date of origin for the last "one percent." There is, in fact, general disagreement among sources as to the exact dates of creation of many of these taxes (BN, *loc. cit.*; Canga Arguëlles, *op. cit.*, I, 206; Earl J. Hamilton, *War and Prices in Spain, 1651–1800* [Cambridge, 1947], p. 134).

[6] Several taxes similar to the *alcabala* and *cientos* existed by the eighteenth century. The *renta de yerbas* consisted of the *alcabala* and *cientos* on leases of grass and pasturelands belonging to the military orders. The Moors had imposed a tax on sales of roof tile, plaster, brick, and other building materials in Granada. When the Spaniards took Granada, they adopted this tax and called it the *renta de abuela*. Previous to 1785 the king possessed the *alcabala de alta mar*. This tax exacted 14 percent from all sales of foreign merchandise made at sea or in wet and dry ports of Spain. Charles III abolished this levy in 1785 and replaced it with the *derecho de internación* (going inside), a 5 percent impost levied on all foreign products entering the interior of Spain (Gallardo Fernandez, *op. cit.*, III, 250, 292, 329; BN, *loc. cit.*).

[7] *Ibid.*; Gallardo Fernandez, *op. cit.*, I, 187; Canga Arguëlles, *op. cit.*, II, 311.
The Cortes created this levy on July 18, 1650 when they awarded Philip IV a service of 24 million ducats to be paid over a period of six years at the rate of 4 million each year. They extended the *servicio de veinte cuatro millones* every six years until 1813. The second *servicio de millones* also dates from 1650, for in

bodied a cluster of sales taxes levied on a number of items such as meat, wine, vinegar, oil, soap, and candles. In addition, a number of other sales taxes similar to the *millones,* and often collected with them, existed in the eighteenth century.[8]

Kings did not rely solely on excise taxes. The *servicios ordinario y extraordinario,* for example, which yielded 150 million maravedis (about 4,411,764 vellon reals)[9] a year, rested entirely on the wealth of the Third Estate.[10] All persons, excluding the nobility

---

that year the Cortes authorized Philip an additional 8 million ducats with which to pay the salaries of soldiers. It consisted of a levy of one maravedis on every pound of meat weighed and sold in meat markets, one real an animal sold wholesale (*rastreado*), and four reals an arroba of wine sold in taverns or at wineries. This tax became known as the *servicio de ocho millones.* On June 23, 1656, Philip IV received a third service, this one for 3 million ducats. A document presented to Charles III on October 15, 1759, gives the date of origin as July 24, 1658. In any event, an additional sales tax of 32 maravedis an arroba of wine, vinegar, and oil supplied this revenue. Finally, he obtained his fourth service, this time for one million ducats, which consisted of a levy on all meat consumed in Castile and Leon. This last service added four maravedis a pound to the price of meat and four reals a head to the price of sheep.

The combined rates of the *servicios de millones* totaled as follows. On the sale of wine they reached two consecutive one-eighths of the price, plus sixty-four maravedis; on the sale of oil they amounted to two consecutive one-eighths and ninety maravedis; on the sale of vinegar they reached only the two consecutive one-eighths. In addition, the *millones* exacted eight maravedis on each sixteen ounces of meat sold; eight reals on each head of livestock sold at wholesale; four maravedis on each pound of candles sold; and four maravedis on each pound of soap sold (BN, *loc. cit.;* Gallardo Fernandez, *op. cit.,* I, 189; II, 311; Colmeiro y Penido, *op. cit.,* II, 542).

[8] Although some of these imposts might originally have been conceded by the Cortes as part of the *servicios de millones,* they eventually evolved into separate taxes on specific items. The Cortes originated the sugar tax (*renta de azúcar*) in 1632 as a service of 2.5 million ducats. Taxes on the sale of glasswort and saltwort date from 1621 and 1634. Conceded as services, they amounted to six reals a quintal of saltwort and three reals a quintal of glasswort. The provinces of Castile authorized Philip IV in 1642 to collect four maravedis from each arroba of wine, vinegar, and oil gauged, measured, or weighed in the villages. Although Spanish kings first destined the proceeds to the upkeep of the cavalry, they later devoted them to their secret purse (*bolsillo secreto*). Collected with the *millones,* this tax became known as the *fiel medidor.* A tax on ice and snow (*renta de nieve y hielos*) was first imposed during the reign of Philip II as a 2 percent sales tax. Later it became a 20 percent sales tax and was called the *quinto de la nieve.* Kings of Spain collected a duty on wine, vinegar, and oil exported from the ports of Andalusia. Although they recognized it as a species of the *millones,* kings officially called this levy the *renta de cargado y regalia* (BN, *loc. cit.;* Gallardo Fernandez, *op. cit.,* II, 204, 254, 309; III, 146, 246, 309; Canga Argüelles, *op. cit.,* I, 468; II, 365, 580; Colmeiro y Penido, *loc. cit.*).

[9] One vellon real equaled about 20 U.S. cents in the last decade of the century.

[10] This tax has an heritage from medieval times. The *moneda* was a serivce granted by the Cortes for limited periods during the Middle Ages. The Cortes had extended this tax so often that by the reign of Ferdinand and Isabel it was considered a permanent or an ordinary service (*servicio ordinario*). Later,

and the ecclesiastics, contributed amounts arbitrarily set in accordance with their personal financial positions.[11] This impost was a legacy of the Middle Ages.

As a supplement to their tax revenues, kings received profits from monopolies (*estancos*) on the manufacture and sale of strategic products.[12] In this way they artfully camouflaged their exactions. Lacking any such subtlety, however, was the direct taxation of personal services. No import was more direct and more hated than those that compelled villagers to quarter soldiers or provide draft animals and wagons to transport provisions for the army or to aid the royal family in its travels.[13] A particularly painful burden on personal services occurred when kings staffed the army by drafting villagers, casting lots for their service, or by forcing them to enlist.

As kings levied these numerous exactions, so also the municipal governments and the Catholic Church imposed their own.[14] City imposts appeared in medieval times when growing villages taxed the sales, import, and export of merchandise. With the revenue they constructed walls, gates, and bridges and in general provided for the protection and welfare of their inhabitants.[15] To meet its

---

when Philip II needed additional sums to increase the number of ministers in his royal council, the Cortes granted him fifty million maravedis a year. This source of revenue became known as the *servicio extraordinario*. Since the *servicio ordinario* yielded 100 million maravedis annually, the addition of the *extraordinario* made a total of 150 million maravedis. To defray the expense of collection, Philip obtained a surtax that yielded 1½ percent of this revenue (Gallardo Fernandez, *op. cit.*, III, 1–3).

[11] By 1725 the base included foreigners living in Spain. Kings used the proceeds to distinguish the nobility. Charles IV abolished this tax on September 20, 1795 (BN, *loc. cit.*; Gallardo Fernandez, *op. cit.*, III, 9).

[12] These monopolies included tobacco, salt, playing cards, lead, sulphur, gunpowder, quicksilver, vermilion (*piedra cenabria*), corrosive sublimate (*soliman*), powdered vermilion (*bermillon piedra molada y de China*), sealing wax (*lacre encarnado y negro*), and brandy. Although kings of the seventeenth century had leased most of these monopolies to favorites in return for a portion of the profits, Ferdinand VI terminated the contracts, replaced private with government management, and thereby substantially increased revenue (Canga Arguëlles, *op. cit.*, II, 491; Gallardo Fernandez, *op. cit.*, III, 152–154, 215; VI, 234, 305, 467, 479; Colmeiro y Penido, *op. cit.*, II, 543; BN, *loc. cit.*).

[13] Obligatory personal services had been an integral part of Spanish life for many centuries.

[14] Colmeiro y Penido, *op. cit.*, II, 552.

[15] Most cities possessed the *portazgo* in the Middle Ages. With this tax municipalities obtained one-eighth of the value of the merchants' products and used the revenue to build walls and roads. As the centuries passed, they used only about one-third of the revenue for these purposes and destined the remainder to the cities' treasuries (Canga Arguëlles, *op. cit.*, II, 418).

obligations the Church appropriated 10 percent of most agricultural products in the name of the tithe (*diezmo*) and took an additional amount in the name of the *primicias*. The latter yielded one-fourth as much as the tithe.[16] By the fifteenth century Spanish kings had taken from the Church two-ninths of the tithes in many parts of Spain. This revenue became known as the *tercias reales*.[17]

These then—the *alcabala, cientos, millones, servicios ordinario y extraordinario*, monopoly profits, personal services, and *tercias reales*, among others—formed the royal tax structure of Castile and Leon. Some of these taxes were in force throughout Spain, most were limited to the provinces in Castile and Leon. As a natural outcome of the political and economic diversity among regions of the peninsula, Valencia, Aragon, Catalonia, Navarre, and the Basque provinces for centuries had possessed unique tax structures.[18] But in 1700, Valencia, Aragon, and Catalonia rebelled against the crowning of Philip V and thereby forced him to take up arms against them. After defeating each of the three regions, he deprived them of most of their ancient privileges and

---

[16] *Ibid.*, I, 349; II, 435.

[17] The tithe originally belonged to the Spanish kings who probably began to transfer it to the Church in the eleventh century. Two centuries later, the Fourth Lateran Council, held in November, 1215, permanently established it as a payment to the Church. Within a few years, however, Ferdinand III was sharing in the tithe's proceeds, for either in 1219 or 1274 he had obtained the *tercios diezmos*. More concessions of similar nature followed and the impost later became known as the *tercias reales* (Gallardo Fernandez, *op. cit.*, III, 11, 33, 34; BN, *loc. cit.*).

Spanish kings received the entire tithe from some products in certain areas. To cite several examples, Pope Gregory IX in 1248 conceded Ferdinand III the tithe of the terrace and riverbank of Seville (*diezmo del alxarafe y rivera de Sevilla*). This action reserved for the king one-tenth of all the oil, olives, figs, and acorns from these areas. Moreover, in 1567 Philip obtained a brief from Pope Pius V that granted him the tithe from one household, excluding the largest two, in each parish. This tax became known as the *renta del excusado*. On May 21, 1751, another brief gave Ferdinand VI the tithe of the largest contributing household in each parish.

Philip expelled many Moors and Moriscos after they revolted in 1568. Although some historians doubt that Philip forced large numbers to leave Spain, that king apparently succeeded in dislocating a substantial number. He populated their deserted or confiscated villages and lands in southern Spain with Spaniards and imposed taxes on them. Besides taking two tithes, one for the Church and one for himself, Philip exacted one-fifth of all crops of mulberry and olive trees for ten years and thereafter a lesser amount. This tax, called the *renta de población*, existed in a less harsh form until 1797 (Gallardo Fernandez, *op. cit.*, III, 252, 271, 282; Colmeiro y Penido, *op. cit.*, II, 541; Canga Argüelles, *op. cit.*, I, 454; Earl J. Hamilton, "The Decline of Spain," *Economic History Review*, Vol. VIII, no. 2 [May, 1938], pp. 168–179).

[18] Mallorca and the Canaries possessed unique tax systems; however, since this research concentrates on peninsular Spain, it ignores these two areas.

subjected them to taxes that were supposedly equivalent to those in Castile and Leon.[19]

In 1707 Philip selected a tax system for Valencia. Although he first thought of collecting the *alcabala* and *cientos,* he decided instead to impose an "equivalent" from which he would be insured consistent revenue.[20] After charging the kingdom a fixed sum, the king set a quota for each city and village and assessed every inhabitant according to his financial position.[21] To relieve the individuals and guilds at Valencia of part of this burden and to ease the problems of collection in that large city, Philip in 1715 permitted municipal officials to collect part of the quota from an 8 percent duty on selected items entering the city.[22]

Philip imposed a single tax (*única contribución*) in Aragon similar to the one he employed in Valencia. His tax administrators divided the kingdom's quota among the villages on a basis of assessed valuations, and then his justices or magistrates in the villages assigned a share to each individual.[23] Considerable unfairness crept into this system of apportionment (*amillaramiento*), because of either the ignorance, malice, or dishonesty of untrained assessors.

It was in Catalonia where Philip created the most thoroughly refined single tax.[24] Established on December 9, 1715, this impost fell on the values of estates (*haciendas*) and on personal incomes from industry, commerce, and other sources.[25] Trained assessors, working from strict rules, assessed these revenues.[26] Philip then set a 10 percent tax on incomes from houses, buildings, workshops, mills, trust funds, and pensions. Furthermore, he taxed personal earnings from mechanical arts at 8½ percent and taxed the estimated personal income of merchants and masters of most trades at 10 percent.[27]

Although Philip imposed a single tax in Catalonia, he chose

---

[19] Jaime Carrera y Pujal, *Historia de la Economía Española,* 5 vols. Barcelona, 1943–1947), V, 447.

[20] *Ibid.*

[21] *Ibid.,* 448.

[22] So lucrative was this tax that Charles III imposed it on all merchandise entering the city of Valencia (AMH, *Colección de Órdenes Generales de Rentas,* XV, 332–333; Carrera y Pujal, *op. cit.,* V, 457).

[23] Antonio Matilla Tascón, *La Única Contribución y el Catastro de la Ensenada* (Madrid, 1947), p. 57.

[24] Philip set a quota for Catalonia of 3.1 million escudos (*ibid.,* p. 30).

[25] *Ibid.*

[26] *Ibid.*

[27] *Ibid.,* p. 31; Canga Argüelles, *op. cit.,* II, 195; Joseph Townsend, *A Journey Through Spain in the Years 1786 and 1787,* 3 vols. (London, 1792), III, 323.

not to abolish the lucrative *bolla*. Here was one of the most vicious and hated taxes in all Spain. The thirteenth century saw Peter II (1196–1213) first establish it as a light contribution on quilted textiles of wool and silk;[28] but through the centuries the Principality's rulers raised its rate and included more textiles in its base. By the eighteenth century the *bolla* was essentially a 15 percent sales tax on all silks and woolens from which no one, not even kings, escaped.[29] What made it so burdensome were the procedures of collection and enforcement. The Guild of Velveteers and Weavers of Silk of Barcelona complained of these absurdly complicated methods.

They [the producers of textiles] are unable to exercise their arts except in places where the officials of the *bolla* reside. . . . Moreover, producers are aggravated with the repeated bother of having lead seals placed on the piece of cloth when they begin it and then again when they finish it; preceding this, producers must note all new starts [of cloth] in the records of the custom house, a duty which they repeat when they sell the cloth to a merchant or take it from one town to another; in the latter case, they must add another lead seal, besides being required to return with a landing certificate; and if this cloth is sold by varas or palmos, they [the officials of the *bolla*] put a wax seal on each portion sold . . . and affix another lead seal to the end of the piece from which it came.[30]

Because the Basque provinces had supported Philip's succession, they maintained their ancient privileges. They considered the insignificant taxes they paid to Spanish kings as mere donations and certainly not permanent.[31] Custom had so firmly established this unique position that the provinces of Alava, Guipuzcoa, and Vizcaya recognized no sovereign authority other than the Magistrate of Bilbao.[32]

As Spanish taxes were numerous and complex, so they were also oppressive, wasteful, and unfair. Industry in Castile and Leon particularly suffered. Producers staggered under a tower of taxes that had pyramided from the numerous premanufacturing exchanges to the final sale of the finished products. Sevillian manu-

---

[28] Ángel Ruiz y Pablo, *Historia de la Real Junta Particular de Comercio de Barcelona, 1758–1847* (Barcelona, 1919), p. 131.

[29] *Ibid.*, pp. 131–139; Townsend, *op. cit.*, I, 148; Bernardo de Ulloa, *Restablecimiento de las Fábricas y Comercio Español* (Madrid, 1740), pp. 128–129; Gerónimo de Uztáriz, *Theórica, y Práctica de Comercio y de Marina* (Madrid, 1757), p. 358.

[30] Quoted in Uztáriz, *ibid.*

[31] Canga Arguëlles, *op. cit.*, II, 461.

[32] *Ibid.*

facturers, for example, purchased raw silk from Granada for 55 vellon reals and 16 maravedis a pound. Of this price, 28 vellon reals and 16 maravedis consisted of the *alcabala, cientos,* tithe, *arbitrio, tartil, xelix, torres de costas,* and contributions levied on silk as it entered Seville.[33] When these producers sold finished textiles they again incurred the *alcabala* and *cientos.* Manufacturers of woolens in Castile and Leon also paid the *alcabala* and *cientos* when they bought wool that already might have been burdened with tithes of from 12 to 70 percent.[34] Upon purchasing soap and oil, only two of numerous raw materials needed in production, they paid the *alcabala* and *cientos* as well as the *millones,* which by itself exceeded 25 percent. They again paid the *alcabala* and *cientos* when they sold their woolens.

Manufacturers in Valencia, Aragon, and Catalonia were favored by the nature of their provincial taxes, even though they were harassed by obligatory personal services and other exactions. Their moderate tax quotas failed to raise production costs as much as did the pyramiding of excise taxes in Castile and Leon. Herein lies a partial explanation for the expansion of textile production in Valencia and Catalonia.

Since taxpayers in these provinces made payments of definite

---

[33] Uztáriz, *op. cit.,* p. 240; Ulloa, *op. cit.,* p. 24; Townsend, *op. cit.,* III, 72.

During the last quarter of the eighteenth century these taxes on silk were reduced and on November 14, 1801, were abolished (Gallardo Fernandez, *op. cit.,* III, 293, 298, 308).

[34] Canga Arguëlles, *op. cit.,* I, 482.

In 1792 the tithes on summer pasture reached 158 vellon reals and 8 maravedis per one thousand sheep and on winter pasture 495 vellon reals and 6 maravedis per one thousand sheep (*ibid.,* I, 488).

Besides paying the *alcabala, cientos,* and tithes on their wool and flocks, owners of sheep also faced numerous municipal and private taxes. Here are some illustrations: The Duke of Abrantes exacted twenty-four or twenty-six vellon reals a head for passing over his land in Avila. The city of Cadiz charged two vellon reals for each head passing over the bridge of Marzo and three vellon reals a head when embarking for *ranchos.* Owners who took their nomadic flocks across the bridge at Cordova forfeited eight maravedis a head and, later, when their herds passed through the gate of Guzo, they gave up a certain number of sheep to the city. The city of Malaga exacted 3 percent of the value of the flocks and used the proceeds to repair the bridge. In La Mancha the flocks' owners paid the taxes of *las hermandades de Toledo* and *Ciudad Real.* In Salamanca, shepherds paid four vellon reals a head when using the bridges of Alva, Salamanca, Barco de Avila, and Ledesma.

Municipal taxes on wool existed, too. For example, Jaen collected seventeen maravedis on arroba for the tax of *carretaje.* Ubeda and Andujar both exacted seventeen maravedis an arroba of wool. Rioseco taxed each arroba eight maravedis. In Benevente three levies on wool existed: two for the city and one for the Count of Benevente (Gallardo, Fernandez, *op. cit.,* I, 286; Canga Arguëlles, *op. cit.,* I, 484, 485, 486; AMH, *op. cit.,* XXVIII, 527–536).

amounts at specific times, the process of collection was relatively uncomplicated. In Castile and Leon, however, the host of transaction taxes posed a collection problem that kings and municipalities resolved by employing an army of collectors. One author, writing in the last third of the seventeenth century, estimated that in the provinces of Castile and Leon there were 100,000 tax administrators, farmers, guards, inspectors, collectors, commissioners, customs men, and smugglers.[35] According to another writer of that period, the number of tax collectors alone was closer to 150,000.[36] Although these numbers reflect only impressions and undoubtedly exaggerate the truth, they do suggest that activity in gathering taxes was great enough to appall contemporary observers.

Kings often "farmed out" their taxes,[37] in essence selling to private citizens the right to collect levies. They permitted the farmers to post armed guards at city gates, on bridges, and at other strategic places and, to insure success for these entrepreneurs, gave them jurisdiction in civil and criminal tax cases.[38] With these spectacular powers "farmers" became intransigent and abusive.[39] They furthered and protected their positions by advancing money to the king during financial urgencies.

Exorbitant waste was the companion of tax farming.[40] Several chroniclers estimated that in the seventeenth century the royal treasury received only 35 to 60 percent of tax revenues.[41] Other reporters insisted that kings received but one-tenth of the revenue collected on oil, wine, vinegar, and meat.[42] Early in the eighteenth century Philip V knew he received only one million reals from every four million taken in taxes. By midcentury the intendants in Castile and Leon advised that of ten escudos (an escudo was equal to about 37 vellon reals and 22 maravedis) received by the king the villagers had paid sixty or seventy, and not thirty escudos as people commonly supposed.[43] Such diseconomy did not occur in Valencia, Aragon, and Catalonia. In the

---

[35] Matilla Tascón, *op. cit.*, p. 16.

[36] *Ibid.*

[37] In some places the king had transferred (*enajenado*) taxes to individuals in return for large monetary gifts. These individuals collected the taxes and retained all of the revenue.

[38] Colmeiro y Penido, *op. cit.*, II, 555.

[39] Matilla Tascón, *op. cit.*, p. 16.

[40] Colmeiro y Penido, *op. cit.*, II, 556.

[41] *Ibid.*

[42] *Ibid.*

[43] BN, MS 13006, fol. 17.

latter principality, for example, costs of collection were only 10 to 20 percent of gross receipts.[44]

Unfairness also plagued the system in Castile and Leon. For criteria of assessment such as wealth, equity, and justice yielded to the avarice and expediency of tax collectors. Oftentimes, administrators or farmers taxed workers at a rate of 30 percent while they taxed the nobility and ecclesiastics at a rate of only 5 percent.[45] Members of the lower classes in these provinces faced unequal treatment not only in comparison with clergymen and nobles but also when compared to their own kind in other provinces; each Castilian labored under nearly twice the burden carried by each Aragonese.[46] One author states that in the first half of the eighteenth century the average tax payment in Aragon was about seventy-five vellon reals, in Valencia one hundred and thirty-four, in Catalonia one hundred and ninety-five, and in Toledo six hundred and seventy-five.[47] Moreover, a comparison of provincial tax payments with provincial wealth reveals that poorer provinces often paid more taxes in proportion to their wealth than did their more affluent neighbors.[48]

The nature of taxes in Castile and Leon made the overall structure highly regressive. It was a necessary consequence of excises on wine, oil, meat, vinegar, and other staples that the poor contributed a larger portion of their incomes to taxes than did the rich.[49] As the more affluent persons—nobles and ecclesiastics—were exempt from many levies and as they consumed products not burdened with the *millones,* such as poultry, and game birds, so they contributed but little.[50] The poor inevitably supplied most of the tax revenues.[51] In Valencia, Aragon, and Catalonia, however, the single taxes imposed by Philip V, which generally consisted of levies on income and wealth, resulted in less regression.

Now is the time for a summary of taxes in Spain. Rates were higher in Castile and Leon than in Valencia, Aragon, and Cata-

---

[44] *Ibid.*

[45] Canga Arguëlles, *op. cit.,* II, 454.

[46] *Ibid.,* 457.

[47] Colmeiro y Penido, *op. cit.,* II, 549.

[48] Canga Arguëlles, *op. cit.,* II, 455.

[49] As an illustration, witness the taxes of 500 percent that overwhelmed wine sold in Madrid (Matilla Tascón, *loc. cit.*).

[50] Colmeiro y Penido, *op. cit.,* II, 550.

[51] Canga Arguëlles, *loc. cit.*

lonia. Compare the *alcabala* and *cientos* of 14 percent, the *millones* of at least 25 percent and the pyramiding effects of these excises in Castile and Leon with the income taxes of 8½ to 10 percent in Catalonia. Permeating the system in Castile and Leon was incredible inefficiency. Even though collectors in Castile and Leon gathered large sums, kings received only a small portion, the remainder vanishing through a myriad of leakages. By comparison, the collection of taxes in Valencia, Aragon, and Catalonia, although far from perfect, was more efficient. Relative inequality also marred the system in Castile and Leon, for some persons paid little or nothing while others staggered under taxes. Excise taxes levied on consumption goods placed the major burden on the poor. In Valencia, Aragon, and Catalonia, however, where quotas were assessed more or less according to ability to pay, the tax systems were less regressive.

Such fiscal conditions as existed in Castile and Leon bred an atmosphere that smothered industrial expansion. Excise taxes imposed on factors of production raised the prices of those factors and thereby reduced the quantities of finished goods that manufacturers could profitably produce at alternative prices. The wealthy invested their savings where they obtained modest but secure returns independent of industrial success; the talented offered their services to the Church or to the king instead of entering entrepreneurial activities; producers contented themselves with making ordinary products for local markets. The high tax rates, the nature of the taxes, and the methods of imposition and collection thus combined to impede industrial growth and thereby help explain why Castile and Leon lagged behind other Spanish provinces in economic growth.

These words do not mean to suggest that all of the industrial ills of Castile and Leon stemmed from harsh taxes. The existence of economic decadence side by side with oppressive taxes does not prove that the latter caused the former. Other factors, such as developments that created comparative advantages for competing nations, for example, first thrust Spain into decadence. Though her economy sank into ruin, her need for a high level of revenue continued. Thus it was that Spanish kings raised rates, created new taxes, and thereby plunged their country more deeply into trouble. This suggests that harsh taxes were symptoms, not causes, of economic troubles. Nevertheless, their removal was an obvious prerequisite for economic growth in Castile and Leon.

REFORMS AND CONCESSIONS, 1750–1800

As the tempo of his development program quickened, Philip V became increasingly aware of the need for tax reforms in Castile and Leon. The single tax of Catalonia (*catastro de Cataluña*), when compared with the fiscal quagmire in central Spain, intrigued him. Its proportional rates on incomes made the outcome less regressive than excises on basic commodities. Furthermore, assessment carried out by professionals, who were governed by well-defined rules, insured a relatively high degree of equality and justice among taxpayers.[52] The small cost of collection, a result of the taxation of incomes rather than transactions, gave this system a final advantage. For these reasons, Philip V selected Catalonia's single tax as his model when he set out to reform the tax system in Castile and Leon.

He began preliminary studies on February 20, 1736. He never proceeded any further.[53] Thirteen years later, on October 10, 1749, Ferdinand VI, Philip's successor, ordered the complete assessment of the twenty-two provinces of Castile and Leon.[54] Using this information as a basis, he planned to substitute a single tax for the *alcabala, cientos, millones,* and most other royal levies. By November 15, 1757, his tax officials stood ready to inaugurate the new system. But Ferdinand never saw it become a reality, for he himself was in his last, melancholy year; the Marquis de la Ensenada, the driving force behind the reform, had recently fallen from power; and Bartolome de Valencia, the Director of Provincial Taxes and a strong supporter, had died.[55]

Charles III showed active interest in tax reform on June 20, 1760, when he created the Committee of the Single Tax. After permitting the committee to spend four years reassessing the provinces, Charles withheld further action for six additional years.[56] This delay has led Antonio Matilla Tascón to suggest

---

[52] Matilla Tascón, *op. cit.*, p. 58.

[53] Philip requested Pedro de Hontalba y Arce to write a history of the *catastro de Cataluña*. But Hontalba died before completing his assignment and Ceñon de Somodevilla, Marquis de la Ensenada, received the unfinished work (*ibid.*, pp. 52, 53, 54, 62).

[54] Previous to this order, on April 17, 1746, Ferdinand had begun a case study in the province of Guadalaxara to determine the feasibility and workability of a single tax modeled after the *catastro de Cataluña*. After some conflict of opinion, Ferdinand and his ministers accepted the system tried in Guadalaxara (*ibid.*, p. 63).

[55] *Ibid.*, p. 96.

[56] Matilla Tascón classifies the results of the reassessment as catastrophic, for people felt that if they reported less property or income they automatically would

the presence of ". . . certain hidden powers, interested that the idea not be converted into reality." [57]

On July 4, 1770, Charles finally acted. He abolished the tax system of Castile and Leon and substituted in its stead a single contribution, he established tribunals for administering the new system, and he abolished the *alcabala* and *cientos*.[58] But he withheld the launching of these sweeping changes for some future date.[59]

Meanwhile, his intendants pursued the only remaining task—apportionment of quotas to individuals. When all had finally been completed, the Fiscal discovered considerable inequality in assessment within and between provinces.[60] The subsequent postponement doomed the reform, and all future efforts to revive it proved futile.[61] Twenty-five years of work and an outlay of over forty million vellon reals had brought no amelioration for most taxpayers in Castile and Leon.

Not until 1785 did Charles III attempt another general reform.[62] On June 29 of that year he called for a survey of population, land, products, and industrial activity in Castile and Leon.[63] From these data tax administrators and local justices determined a quota for each village and subsequently established rates for the *alcabala*, *cientos*, *millones*, and other taxes, which they imposed on sales of goods in the village markets.[64] If receipts from these taxes in any village failed to satisfy the assigned quota, local officials prorated the deficit among the villagers as a personal tax.[65] In larger towns and in cities, however, the reform made little change. The *alcabala*, *cientos*, and *millones* remained in effect; and regardless of the revenue collected, tax quotas were not assigned to individuals.[66]

Although this reform retained the royal excise taxes, it removed

---

pay less taxes. In some provinces, therefore, one-half less wealth was reported in 1760 than in 1750 (*ibid.*, p. 100).

[57] *Ibid.*, p. 102.

[58] *Ibid.*, p. 107.

[59] *Ibid.*

[60] *Ibid.*, p. 123.

[61] *Ibid.*, p. 124.

[62] AGS, *Secretaria de Hacienda*, leg. 793; Gallardo Fernandez, *op. cit.*, I, 283; Carrera y Pujal, *op. cit.*, I, 338; AMH, *op. cit.*, XXVIII, 342–356.

[63] AGS, *loc. cit.*

[64] Charles did not include the *tercias reales*, *servicios ordinario y extraordinario*, and *cuota de aguardiente* in the new rates; instead, he continued to collect them with no changes (*ibid.*).

[65] *Ibid.*

[66] *Ibid.*

much of their nettle. This it accomplished by exempting all initial sales of domestic merchandise from the *alcabala* and *cientos* and reducing the rate on all succeeding transactions to 2 percent.[67] Sales of foreign merchandise paid at a rate of 10 percent instead of 14. Beyond these measures, the reform set a rate of 2 percent for the sales tax on crude silk[68] and common, ordinary, and coarse wool;[69] it also exacted two reals an arroba (about twenty-five pounds) on sales of unwashed fine and medium-fine wool and fleece of young lambs—all substantial rate reductions. The reform likewise lowered taxes on wine, meat, vinegar, and oil, among other products.[70]

This reduction of tax rates, however, was not nearly as marked as first appears; in most instances it merely reaffirmed decreases that had been granted over the three previous decades.[71] Between 1752 and 1785 Ferdinand VI and Charles III had issued a series of rulings, each succeeding one going further toward freeing industry in Castile and Leon from its burdens, mainly from the *alcabala* and *cientos*. By granting exemptions from selected imposts or else by providing lower rates, these actions benefited the

---

[67] *Ibid.*

[68] This ruling excluded silk from Granada, for silk was taxed according to a ruling given on June 24, 1776 (*ibid.*).

[69] In addition to this tax on wool, the new ruling imposed a 4 percent sales tax on sheep sold at shearing time and a tax of sixty-one vellon reals a hundred sheep in nomadic flocks in Castile and Leon (Gallardo Fernandez, *op. cit.*, I, 286; Canga Arguëlles, *op. cit.*, I, 484; AGS, *loc. cit.*).

[70] The new ruling imposed a levy of three maravedis a pound on meat along with the *alcabala* and *cientos* of 14 percent. It set rates on wine of two consecutive one-eighths of the market price for the *millones*, eight instead of sixty-four maravedis an arroba for a tax called *impuestos*, and, finally, 14 percent for the *alcabala* and *cientos*. Furthermore, it imposed the rates of two consecutive one-eighths for the *millones* and 14 percent for the *alcabala* and *cientos* on sales of vinegar and 102 maravedis on sales of oil. The reform, however, extended the *alcabala* and *cientos* paid on some sales of acorns, grass, and summer pasture to all sales of those items in Castile and Leon (*ibid.*).

[71] The shortcomings of this reform evidently prompted Francisco Cabarrús, the renowned banker, to criticize Pedro de Lerena, Charles's minister, and the reform bitterly. "I shall always feel honored for having had as an enemy the stupid minister who authorized this incomprehensible monument to ignorance and ferocity . . ." (quoted in Carrera y Pujal, *op. cit.*, IV, 343).

Yet, one is disposed to feel that something more than this reform inspired such harsh words, for this revision of taxes certainly improved the chaotic conditions that had previously existed. His anger may have been motivated by the rejection in 1783 of his plan for revising taxes and, at the same time, for retiring the national debt. He wished to abolish the *alcabala* and *cientos* and replace them with a general tax (*imposición general*) on property. He expected the tax to last for twenty years during which time part of the revenue would be used to retire the debt (*ibid.*, IV, 335–338; Matilla Tascón, *op. cit.*, p. 127).

entire textile industry, segments of the industry, and individual artisans.

Ferdinand VI initiated the broad concessions on June 24, 1752, when he exempted producers of all goods in Castile and Leon from certain taxes.[72] This was a reaction to events that had transpired prior to 1752. Ferdinand VI and Philip V had favored five joint-stock companies, which specialized in the production and sale of textiles, and certain private manufacturers with generous concessions, including, among other things, exemption from the *alcabala* and *cientos* on first wholesale and retail sales and from obligatory personal services. Those who had not received corresponding aid suffered competitively as a consequence.

It was to redress this competitive imbalance, that Ferdinand on June 24, 1752, annulled all concessions enjoyed by the companies and independent producers and then awarded general tax reductions to all manufacturers in Spain. Specifically, he exempted their merchandise from the *alcabala* and *cientos* on all first wholesale transactions and freed their raw materials from import duties.[73]

The royal joint-stock companies and individual producers who had been receiving the favor of kings suffered after Ferdinand withdrew their special privileges and gave equal concessions to all.[74] Since most of the companies had been established in areas where industrial activity of any kind faced severe trials, they fell into misfortune almost immediately. Not only the companies felt the impact of the changes. For some manufacturers who had previously been singled out by royal favor withdrew from the industry and others declined to enter, not wishing to compete on a basis of equality. These reactions caused Ferdinand to drift from his policy of equal treatment and on March 30, 1753, again to protect the companies.[75] In this decree, he reaffirmed the nullification of the *alcabala* and *cientos* on first wholesale transactions. In addition, he gave the joint-stock institutions the right of *tanteo* (forced sale)[76] on required raw materials, freedom from obligatory service for their workers, reduction in export duties, and

---

[72] Gallardo Fernandez, *op. cit.*, II, 384; BN, *loc. cit.*; AMH, *Colección de Órdenes Generales de Rentas*, XI, 99–100.

[73] Gallardo Fernandez, *op. cit.*, II, 384; BN, *loc. cit.*; AMH, *op. cit.*, XI, 99–100.

[74] Gallardo Fernandez, *op. cit.*, II, 386–389; ACSV, *Pragmáticas y Reales Cédulas*, no. I; AMH, *op. cit.*, XI, 307–310.

[75] Gallardo Fernandez, *op. cit.*, II, 386–389; ACSV, *Pragmáticas y Reales Cédulas*, no. 1; AMH, *op. cit.*, XI, 307–310.

[76] For a description of the right of *tanteo*, see above, pp. 58–59, n. 35.

complete liberty to vary the quality of textiles destined for export. Remaining at least partially consistent with his stated policy of equality, Ferdinand extended these concessions beyond the companies to all producers in the cities of Toledo, Seville, Granada, and Zaragoza, and the village of Zarza, the seats of the joint-stock firms.

Before any manufacturer could enjoy the concessions embodied in the edicts of June 24, 1752, and March 30, 1753, however, he had to comply with a number of regulations.[77] These complex rules apparently caused disagreement among officials as to whom they should grant tax exemptions. To end the muddle, on October 3, 1753, Ferdinand ordered the General Council of Commerce and Money to recommend for his approval those producers worthy of the special treatment afforded by royal legislation. Essentially, then, only manufacturers who requested and received certification from the General Council of Commerce and Money and subsequently secured royal approval legally enjoyed the privileges.

Yet, during the next several years the General Council of Commerce and Money with or without the king's approval licensed more and more producers to receive exemptions and awarded additional concessions to many others. Tax receipts diminished. Ferdinand attributed this to the

. . . exorbitant privileges and exemptions conceded by individual grants for the aid and promotion of different important producers, and to sustain and increase the factories erected by the companies established in my dominions; but more principally by the generality with which, without such recommended motives, the concessions were extended to the other factories existing in my kingdom . . .[78]

---

[77] Before a manufacturer could enjoy the concessions awarded on June 24, 1752, and March 30, 1753, however, he had to obtain a license from the General Council of Commerce and Money and register it with the officials of his village. Moreover, beginning on March 6, 1753, Ferdinand had required the producer to submit a sworn statement to the magistrate or subdelegate of the General Council of Commerce and Money that specified the exact quantity, quality, dimensions, and destination of his textiles before he shipped them out of the village. With this sworn statement he obtained a certificate (*despacho*) from the tax administrator and when he eventually sold his goods at his final destination he secured the tax concessions only after exhibiting the certificate. Ferdinand instituted this procedure to insure the collection of the *alcabala* and *cientos* on other than first wholesale transactions. On November 27, 1753, he encouraged all those who had not obtained their affidavits to do so immediately, for he would deny exemptions to all but certified producers (Gallardo Fernandez, *op. cit.*, II, 384; BN, *loc. cit.*; AMH, *op. cit.*, XI, 99–100, 288–289; XII, 83–84).

[78] Gallardo Fernandez, *op. cit.*, II, 389.

Responding to his fiscal pressures, the king acted on June 18, 1756, to restrict the granting of special privileges. He informed the joint-stock companies and individual producers that they would not receive supplementary aid after their present concessions expired.[79] Moreover, Ferdinand appointed himself the final arbiter in all future grants of privilege.[80]

In this legislation of June 18, 1756, Ferdinand clarified the general allowances that industry was to receive by setting forth a new slate of concessions. He exempted manufacturers from the *alcabala* and *cientos* on first sales at the factory or shop, from national as well as municipal import duties on needed raw materials, and from taxes on one-half an arroba of oil and six pounds of soap for each new piece of cloth measuring thirty-five to forty varas.[81] Included among those who were to enjoy these aids were producers of narrow and wide silks, wide cotton, painted or stamped linen, and fine woolens. Excluded were makers of all woolens of quality less than fine.[82]

It was to stimulate the output of superior woolens and thus to reduce the importation of the foreign product that Ferdinand embraced the makers of fine woolens with these concessions.[83] Over the next twenty-three years, however, domestic production of high quality woolens did not react to this and other stimuli; only the royal mills and a few private factories wove fine woolens. Nor did the creators of common woolens, slighted by the decree of 1756, expand their outputs significantly. Admitting the weak response of fine woolens and realizing the importance of common woolens, Charles III on November 18, 1779, magnified his assistance to producers of woolens of all qualities.[84]

---

[79] *Ibid.*, 389–392; Carrera y Pujal, *op. cit.*, IV, 99; Eugenio Larruga y Boneta, *Memorias Políticas y Económicas sobre los Frutos, Comercio, Fábricas y Minas de España*, 45 vols. (Madrid, 1787–1800), I, 229; AMH, *op. cit.*, XII, 205–212.

[80] Gallardo Fernandez, *op. cit.*, II, 390.

[81] *Ibid.*, 391.

[82] In the category of silks he included handkerchiefs and stockings. Besides fine stuffs of wool, he included camlet, fine flannel, scarlet or crimson woolens, and a variety of fine serges. Moreover, he included nontextile products such as fine china, fine glass, leather, paper, scissors, and looms (*ibid.*).

[83] Although he recognized that taxes in Valencia, Aragon, and Catalonia supposedly equaled those in Castile and Leon, Ferdinand allowed only producers in Castile and Leon to enjoy the concessions (Carrera y Pujal, *op. cit.*, IV, 142).

[84] AMH, *op. cit.*, XXIII, 501–512; Carrera y Pujal, *op. cit.*, IV, 120. Among the textiles included were: petersham or ratteen (*ratinas*), coating (*bayetones*), red or crimson woolens (*escarlatina*), calamanco (*calamacos*), drugget (*droguetes*), camlet (*barraganes*), flannel (*bayeta*), grosgrain (*cordellates*), tammy cloth (*estameñas*), blankets (*mantas*), rugs (*alfombras*), sackcloth (*sayales*), coarse frieze (*gergas*), crepe (*bu-*

The generosity of these concessions exceeded that of all previous decrees. Charles exempted woolen producers in Castile and Leon from the *alcabala* and *cientos* on retail as well as wholesale sales at the factories.[85] All subsequent sales of woolens he taxed only 2 percent of factory price instead of the regular *alcabala* and *cientos* rate. Reserving the right to levy the traditional 14 percent at any time, he reduced the tax on sales of foreign woolens in Castile and Leon to 10 percent. In cities where he taxed merchandise as it entered, Charles set the *alcabala* and *cientos* at 2 percent on domestic and 10 percent on foreign woolens.[86] He also exempted woolen producers from the *millones* on oil and soap by assigning tax-free quotas, the size of which depended on estimated needs. It was to reduce the extent of arbitrary action and to enable a more uniform and equal operation of the exemptions that Charles enacted a system of quotas.[87]

Perhaps attracted by the burgeoning activity in Valencia and Catalonia,[88] the king gave makers of woolens in these and other

---

ratos), serge fabrics (*sempiternas, anascotes, sargas*), and other fabrics of wool (*coriseas* and *belillas*).

On September 4, 1769, and December 22, 1769, Charles III permitted producers of passementerie, or narrow silk material such as braids and ribbons, to receive tax relief. In addition to the usual concessions, he granted them tax-free purchases of twenty pounds of crude silk a year for each ribbon loom, thirty pounds a year for each passementerie loom, and 150 pounds a year for each machine loom for braids or tapes.

Charles extended some tax relief to the linen industry on October 26, 1779, when he exempted linen and other textiles of hemp and flax from all royal and municipal taxes while being transported by sea from one Spanish port to another. In addition, he exempted producers of linens from the *alcabala* and *cientos* when, in ports certified to trade directly with America, they wholesaled their textiles to merchants who thereafter exported them (AMH, *op. cit.*, XVIII, 241–242; XXIII, 453–456).

[85] *Ibid.*, XXII, 501–512. The wording of this legislation evidently confused some tax officials as to whom they should grant concessions. Charles therefore declared on April 27, 1781, that any person, company, or community that employed its wealth to produce woolens should enjoy absolute exemption from the *alcabala* and *cientos* on the first sales at their factories or warehouses. In addition, he extended this to merchants who, in their public stores, sold woolens made especially for them, provided they offered only these. Then, in order to prevent merchants from escaping the *alcabala* and *cientos* on subsequent sales, Charles levied the tax of 2 percent on all sales if they jointly sold custom-made woolens with others not made at their expense. If a producer put his own goods in a store where merchants sold other woolens, he, too, faced the 2 percent even though he had not consummated the original sale (*ibid.*, XXIV, 554–555; AGS, *loc. cit.*).

[86] This ruling exempted producers in any part of Spain from the *alcabala* and *cientos* while shipping their textiles to certified ports, provided they intended to sell them to merchants who, in turn, intended to export them to America (AMH, *op. cit.*, XXIII, 501, 512).

[87] *Ibid.*

[88] This cedula included producers of woolens in Mallorca and the Canaries.

provinces some consideration in this decree of November 18, 1779. He permitted woolens producers in Aragon, Valencia, and Catalonia, who shipped textiles to Castile or Leon, to contribute only 2 percent on all sales for the *alcabala* and *cientos*.[89] He likewise exempted all producers of woolens in Spain from taxes of transit, transshipment, the port taxes at Barcelona (*puertas de Barcelona*), and similar duties that prevailed on entering or leaving towns in all Spanish provinces.[90] He freed all woolen manufacturers in Spain, Mallorca, and the Canaries from royal and municipal customs duties on ingredients for dyes, machines, and instruments brought in from abroad, provided that manufacturers could not find substitutes of the needed quality in Spain.[91] As a final aid, he gave all makers of woolens in Spain the privilege of *tanteo;* however, he limited its use to wool needed in production and permitted its application only against Spaniards or foreigners who intended to export or resell the wool.[92]

Whether swayed by traditional hostilities or by the superior tax structures in Aragon, Valencia, and Catalonia, Charles did not provide equivalent concessions for woolen producers in these provinces. Only Castile and Leon saw their provincial tax rates fall. It should be noted, however, that Charles had already yielded to pressures from Barcelona when he abolished the *bolla* on January 1, 1770.[93]

Six years after granting the concessions of November 18, 1779, Charles overhauled the provincial tax system in central Spain. By

---

[89] To obtain equality for woolens sent to Valencia from other provinces, Charles lowered the "eight percent" tax at Valencia to 4 percent on all woolens made in the provinces of Castile, Leon, Aragon, Valencia, and Catalonia. He also levied an equivalent of the *alcabala* and *cientos* of 10 percent on all foreign woolens in Valencian ports (*ibid.*).

[90] *Ibid.*

[91] This cedula freed makers of woolens from paying all royal and municipal export duties on raw material and woolens from Spain shipped by land or sea to a foreign nation or just from one Spanish port to another (*ibid.*).

[92] This action of November 18, 1779, abolished all concessions, exemptions, and privileges given to woolen producers by previous cedulas and decrees (*ibid.*).

[93] *Ibid.*, XVIII, 216–239; Ruiz y Pablo, *op. cit.*, p. 139; Townsend, *op. cit.*, I, 152. In place of the *bolla*, Charles imposed an "equivalent" tax on products entering the port of Barcelona and other customs of Catalonia (AMH, *loc. cit.*; Ruiz y Pablo, *op. cit.*, pp. 135–136).
Charles extended the concessions to producers of woolens on May 8, 1781, giving them preference in building dye shops and fulling mills. In addition, he permitted these manufacturers to defend themselves and their goods with defensive arms while on the roads. Finally, to relieve the producers from temporary losses of their draft animals, Charles prohibited the army from taking them, on condition that the producers had planned to ship their goods on the day of the appropriation (AMH, *op. cit.*, XXIV, 562–565; Carrera y Pujal, *op. cit.*, IV, 124).

this action of 1785, he not only confirmed and generalized the tax reductions that textile makers had received in previous years, but he reorganized the methods of levying and collecting taxes in Castile and Leon. Now all products in Castile and Leon, not just textiles, escaped the *alcabala* and *cientos* on their first sales at the factory, and, furthermore, now all products, not just fine woolens, paid only 2 percent on succeeding transactions. But all foreign textiles contributed 10 percent on all sales to satisfy the *alcabala* and *cientos*.[94] The reform embraced all previous tax reductions and exemptions on prime material and machinery, with secondary exceptions and changes.[95] Since this reform made only minor changes in taxes paid by textile makers, its substantive importance for this industry lay more in organization and procedure than in tax reduction.[96]

Before turning to other matters, let us review the refinements of the tax system in Castile and Leon that occurred through 1785.[97] During the decades after 1752 kings promulgated a series of decrees, cedulas, and orders that relieved the textile industry of its heavy tax burdens to some extent. The first, which Ferdinand issued on June 24, 1752, annulled all privileges of royal joint-stock companies and individuals and then exempted producers of all goods from the *alcabala* and *cientos* on first sales of their products and from duties on raw materials. On March 30, 1753, the king restored some privileges to the royal companies, extending these aids to artisans working in the jurisdictions of the companies. On June 18, 1756, however, he again terminated all special

---

[94] Gallardo Fernandez, *op. cit.*, I, 286; AMH, *op. cit.*, XXXVIII, 342–356; AGS, *loc. cit.*

[95] *Ibid.*

[96] Gallardo Fernandez, *op. cit.*, II, 305.

[97] Prior to the reorganization of 1785, Charles had exempted sellers of domestic hemp and flax from the *alcabala* and *cientos* on all sales. Although he issued this concession on May 6 and 29, 1785, he included it in the reorganization of that year. He repeated it on November 19, 1786, and February 18, 1790. On June 8, 1792, Charles IV excused flax dressers, who purchased, processed, and sold foreign hemp and flax to weavers of linen, from the 10 percent normally collected from sales of foreign products. This ruling held that if dressers sold foreign hemp and flax in the same state in which they imported them they would pay the 10 percent. Officials still doubted on February 23, 1795, whether the king had exempted sales of hemp cloth from the *alcabala* and *cientos* and if he had, to what extent. Hence, Charles IV, on that date, exempted first sales of this textile made at the place of production and set a rate of 2 percent on all subsequent transactions. He followed this on April 15, 1797, by freeing sales of thread made of hemp or flax, but stipulated that the buyer had to use the thread in the manufacture of linens (AMH, *op. cit.*, XXVIII, 147; XXXIII, 113, 114; XXXVI, 192–193; XXXIX, 68–70; XLI, 114–115; Gallardo Fernandez, *op. cit.*, II, 224, 249; Carrera y Pujal, *op. cit.*, IV, 129.

privileges upon expiration of their terms. Although Ferdinand ignored makers of common woolens in this action, he exempted manufacturers of most textiles, as well as producers of some other products, from the *alcabala* and *cientos* on first sales, exempted them from import duties on raw materials, and, for each loom, he gave them tax-free quotas of oil and soap. Charles III on November 18, 1779, included producers of common textiles in his exemption of all woolen manufacturers from the *alcabala* and *cientos* on the first transactions and in his levy of only 2 percent on all succeeding sales. He also annulled duties on crucial materials that they imported and, for each loom they possessed, granted a quota of oil and soap on which they paid no taxes. Finally, the reorganization of 1785 generalized the freedom from the *alcabala* and *cientos* on first sales and the reduction to 2 percent on all sales after the original. The provincial tax systems of Valencia, Aragon, and Catalonia remained essentially untouched while all of these changes were occurring in Castile and Leon.

Perhaps Spanish rulers expressed their bias when they openly and vigorously favored industry in Castile and Leon with tax concessions. Nevertheless, they showed no geographical favoritism when they showered manufacturers with individual grants of privilege. Selected makers of textiles throughout Spain received a variety of exemptions, privileges, and honors. Permission to use the royal coat of arms and hence the title of "royal factory" (*fábrica real*) honored numerous establishments.[98] To achieve this distinction, a producer might have developed, for example, a new process for dyeing fast colors, or a unique product, machine, or tool.[99] But those who produced on a large scale and manufactured textiles of fine quality usually commanded this distinction. The title of royal factory therefore awarded past performance and stimulated future effort.[100]

Privileges that accompanied the title of royal factory often gave more advantages than the use of the coat of arms. These prerogatives included exemption from all personal services, such as quartering of soldiers and military service for the producers and their

---

[98] ACA, *Diversorium*, no. 492, fol. 19; AMH, *op. cit.*, XXXV, 111; XLI, 144–148; BCB, *Junta de Comercio*, leg. 12, nos. 10, 14; leg. 53, no. 1; Larruga y Boneta, *op. cit.*, VIII, 12; XII, 273. The royal joint-stock companies, discussed in chapter iv, all received this honor (AGS, *op. cit.*, legs. 852, 856, 857; BN, *op. cit.*, fols. 34–38; Larruga y Boneta, *op. cit.*, VII, 63–71; AMH, *op. cit.*, VII, 412–435).

[99] ACA, *op. cit.*, no. 492, fol. 18; no. 1187, fol. 85; BCB, *op. cit.*, leg. 53, no. 1; Larruga y Boneta, *op. cit*, VIII, 2.

[100] ACA, *op. cit.*, no. 1187, fol. 19; AMH, *op. cit.*, XI, 434–439; XVIII, 299–302; XX, 156–159; XXIX, 289; XLI, 144–148.

employees;[101] permission to use defensive weapons; grants of production monopolies; and quite often the right of *tanteo* on raw
materials and the right of preference in renting houses and buying land.[102] Of course, these privileges yielded special advantages
to recipients only until kings extended them generally to all members of the industry.

In the realm of tax exemptions, kings granted reductions or
exemptions to some producers from duties on machinery, utensils,
and raw materials imported from other provinces as well as from
abroad.[103] Some manufacturers received reductions or even outright freedom from export duties. Kings frequently exempted
textile makers from the *alcabala* and *cientos* on their first sales at
their factories; and they often expanded this concession by allowing producers to construct warehouses at Madrid or other cities
and then defining the warehouses as basing points for pricing
(*pie de la fábrica*).[104] Along with these concessions, privileges, and
honors, kings usually included all benefits previously granted to
other textile producers by general actions.[105]

SUMMARY

In 1750 Castile and Leon possessed a tax system composed principally of transactions taxes, led by the odious *alcabala, cientos,* and
millones. The nature of these levies and the methods of imposition and collection inevitably caused much oppression, waste, and
unfairness. They penalized industrial activity. In contrast, Valencia, Aragon, and Catalonia all possessed single royal taxes that fell
primarily on wealth or incomes. Mainly owing to the nature of
these imposts and to more careful assessment and collection, these

---

[101] ACA, *op. cit.,* no. 492, fol. 19; AMH, *op. cit.,* XI, 434–439; XXVI, 434–436;
AHMB, *Junta General de Comercio,* LXXVIII, 145; BCB, *loc. cit.;* Larruga y Boneta,
op. cit., XIX, 75.

[102] AMH, *op. cit.,* XVIII, 299–302; XXIX, 289; ACA, *op. cit.,* no. 1187, fol. 30.

[103] *Ibid.,* no. 492, fol. 19; AMH, *op. cit.,* XI, 434–439; XXVI, 434–436; XXXV, 111;
XLI, 144–148; Larruga y Boneta, *op. cit.,* XII, 271.

[104] AHMB, *loc. cit.;* BCB, *op. cit.,* leg. 53, no. 7; AMH, *op. cit.,* XX, 156–159;
XXVI, 434–436; XLI, 144–148; Larruga y Boneta, *op. cit.,* XII, 273.

[105] AMH, *op. cit.,* XX, 156–159; XLI, 144–148; Larruga y Boneta, *op. cit.,* VIII,
12; XIX, 75.
One class of manufactory received far greater concessions than all others. Factories owned and operated by the king faced no levies on their final products, on
raw materials and other items purchased for the mill, or on employees. All sales
of royal cloth made by the official agents of the government escaped the *alcabala*
and *cientos;* sales by private merchants contributed the full tax (AMH, *op. cit.,* X,
418–419; XI, 19–26, 442; XIII, 65–66; XX, 615; XXII, 566; XXXI, 547; XXXII, 282–
283; XXXIX, 314; Gallardo Fernandez, *op. cit.,* II, 283, 397–400).

exactions led to less oppression, waste, and unfairness. They favored industrial activity.

During the second half of the eighteenth century, kings studied the tax disadvantages in Castile and Leon and acted to correct them. For several decades they thought of installing a single tax, similar to the Catalonian model. But in 1785 Charles III finally settled for a reorganization of the present system, retaining transaction taxes as his main source of revenue. Previous to 1785, however, they relieved the textile industry of considerable tax burdens. The whole industry, certain branches of the industry, and individual producers were exempted from taxes or were given lower rates to pay. Thus by 1785 the textile makers had received substantial deliverance from harsh taxes in Castile and Leon. During the years 1750 to 1785, however, imposts in Valencia, Aragon, and Catalonia had not been changed, except for abolition of the *bolla* in 1770.

Even though their tax burdens were thus eased from 1750 to 1785, producers of textiles in Castile and Leon continued to languish. The royally supported joint-stock companies failed decisively.[106] Only the king's factories which paid absolutely no taxes showed much growth and they did so despite constant and substantial losses.[107] In contrast, Valencian and Catalonian textile production, not plagued by irksome levies, expanded. The calico industry at Barcelona, for example, spurted forward at a phenomenal pace.[108]

After 1785 the tax payments, including royal and municipal contributions, of many producers in Castile and Leon probably were more in line with those that Catalonian producers had to meet. Yet, as manufacturers in Castile and Leon did not expand their activities commensurately with the concessions they received, Catalonian producers sustained their momentum. Production of silks in Granada, Seville, and Toledo, of woolens in Segovia, Burgos, Valladolid, and Salamanca, for example, expanded slightly, not at all, or even declined.[109] Rare were the cases in which outputs increased. Production of silks at Valencia and of woolens, silks, and calicoes in Catalonia continued to advance after 1785.

As the more favorable tax systems in Valencia and Catalonia clearly supported industrial progress, so central Spain's grievous

---

[106] See above, chapter iv.
[107] See above, chapter iii.
[108] See above, pp. 13–18.
[109] See above, pp. 8–10, 20–21.

system retarded production activity there during the first half of the century. And the gradual lowering of rates and the reforms in methods of assessment and collection that transpired after 1750 obviously were not sufficient to provide a marked expansion of textile manufacture. The *alcabala, cientos, millones,* and other excise taxes still weighed heavily on many factors of production and continued to burden the industry. Though less harsh than previously, confusing methods of imposition and collection survived to form a heavy burden.[110] A bewildering mass of regulations tormented even producers who were exempt from taxes.

But all of Castile's and Leon's ills must not be ascribed to fiscal problems. Other drawbacks hindered industrial growth there. Miles of rugged country through which pathlike roads wound and bandits lurked separated seaports and cities in these regions. Besides the problems of taxes and transporting their goods, manufacturers of silks and woolens faced strong competition from royal mills, the majority of which were situated in Castile. It is possible, therefore, that even had all taxes been abolished, textiles still would not have grown very much. Nor can the prosperity of Valencia and Catalonia be imputed solely to their favorable tax structures, for these regions possessed other advantages, such as fine seaports, adequate, well-situated resources, and populations with commercial and industrial heritages.

---

[110] Canga Arguëlles, writing in the early nineteenth century, offered this strong indictment of tax collecting in Spain: "The method observed in the collection of taxes trades on the respect that propriety merits; it hinders reproduction and enchains the beneficial course of exchanges. Three thousand employees maintain an internal war in the villages to assure payment; and posted on the roads, at the gates of the towns, and in the counting houses, they vex the travelers, carriers, and laborers; they measure the grain, gauge the barrels of wine and oil of harvesters; they register the dispenses of wine shops and wine cellars of taverns in order to identify the inventory and collect the tax; they watch the sales of bread, wine, and others made by the hawkers so that they never sell wholesale; they require guides [customhouse permits] for the muleteers who haul the harvests; and oblige justices to regulate the prices of wine and vinegar each month in order to figure the taxes with more security—steps that yield mortal blows to the internal commerce of the reign" (*op. cit.,* II, 455).

VIII

Spanish Commercial Policy

INTRODUCTION

As Spanish kings turned their reforming zeal on provincial taxes in an attempt to promote domestic production of textiles, so also they manipulated their country's external commerce to this end. Weighty tariffs and embargoes on imports of finished cloth became the chief means of protecting domestic producers from the competition of foreign textiles. In a related fashion kings sought to assist home industry. This they accomplished by reducing duties on critically needed resources and by raising export tariffs on, or by prohibiting exports of, important resources—actions that increased the domestic supply and therefore affected the prices of these resources. Kings also encouraged the dispatching of fabrics abroad when they reduced export duties.

Shadowing the restrictive tariffs and prohibitions, was smuggling, an alarming but predictable specter that inevitably billows up whenever illicit profits attract the adventuresome. Contraband activity increased in direct proportion to the heightened restrictions on commerce. Although kings fought it vigorously, they succeeded only in imposing a mass of controls over the entire economy.

This chapter examines how Spanish kings used customs duties and prohibitions to encourage growth in the textile industry; it thereafter outlines the serious problem of contraband and indicates the measures taken to combat it.

IMPORT AND EXPORT DUTIES

Prior to the eighteenth century, kings of Spain viewed customs duties chiefly as a source of revenue and hence placed in a subordinate position the effects of these imposts on industrial activity. As the eighteenth century progressed, however, Spanish rulers elevated tariffs to a vital role in their struggle to induce economic growth. They reduced import duties on certain factors of production, thus encouraging the manufacture of favored textiles; they raised import duties on other factors of production, thus discouraging the creation of undesirable fabrics. To promote shipments of industrial products to America, kings lowered export duties. But import duties on finished merchandise still retained their primary function as a source of revenue.[1]

Before 1752 kings singled out a few manufacturers and exempted them from duties on imported factors of production,[2] thus allowing the purchase of strategic materials at lower cost. It was to diffuse this advantage throughout the land that Ferdinand VI on June 24, 1752, abolished individual concessions of this nature and excused all Spanish producers from paying import duties on prime materials that were vital in production but unavailable in Spain.[3] Ferdinand essentially repeated this concession on June 18, 1756, but limited it to makers of silks, linens, cottons, and fine

---

[1] Royal import and export duties varied in form and amount between the various regions of Spain. In Andalusia, Granada, and Murcia, whose principal ports were Seville, Puerto de Santa Maria, Cadiz, Malaga, and Cartagena, the tariff was called the *almojarifazgo*, an heritage of Moorish times. This duty, plus a number of "additions" (*agregados*), which first appeared during the seventeenth century, formed a 20 to 25 percent ad valorem tax on imports at the start of the century. By 1750, however, reforms had reduced them to 15 percent.

The king exacted the tithe (*diezmo*), an import-export duty of 10 percent, and "additions" of 5 percent in the ports of Valencia, Asturias, Galicia, Quatro Villas, and Mallorca, and along those frontiers of Aragon and Castile that bordered Navarre, Guipuzcoa, Alava, Vizcaya, and France. A 10 percent duty plus "additions" of 2¾ percent prevailed in the dry ports (*puertos secos*) along most of the Portuguese frontier. In Catalonia the rate of royal customs duties was 3⅓ percent, except at Barcelona where it varied between 7½ and 7¹¹⁄₁₂ percent.

In addition to the royal duties imposed on imports and exports, a number of port taxes prevailed. They consisted of fixed sums levied on ships entering or leaving Spanish ports. The proceeds maintained specific services, such as anchorage and wharf facilities, harbor pilots, quarantine lamps, and security. Although each tax by itself was moderate, when added together they were considerable. A ship of 200 tons, for example, paid 2,515 vellon reals on entering Cadiz.

A few Spanish cities exacted import and export duties on specific products. Alicante taxed rope and esparto grass; Granada taxed exports of wheat, bast fiber (*pleita*), wood, charcoal, and wine; Madrid imposed import duties on sugar, drugs, wines, and porcelain (BN, MS 10695; José Canga Argüelles, *Diccionario de Hacienda*, 2 vols. [Madrid, 1833–1834], II, 496; AMH, *Colección de Órdenes Generales de Rentas*, XXXIII, 77–88, 205–208; XL, 30–37; Jaime Carrera y Pujal, *Historia de la Economía Española*, 5 vols. [Barcelona, 1943–1947], IV, 310–312).

[2] ACA, *Diversorium*, no. 492, fol. 19; AMH, *op. cit.*, XI, 434–439; XXVI, 434–436; XXXV, 111; XLI, 144–148; Eugenio Larruga y Boneta, *Memorias Políticas y Económicas sobre los Frutos, Comercio, Fábricas y Minas de España*, 45 vols. (Madrid, 1787–1800), XII, 271.

[3] Francisco Gallardo Fernandez, *Origen, Progresos y Estado de Rentas de la Corona de España*, 7 vols. (Madrid, 1805–1808), II, 385; BN, MS 13006; AMH, *op. cit.*, XI, 99–100.

woolens.[4] Charles IV expanded it on May 16, 1791, to allow manufacturers to import without paying duties on any instrument, implement, material, or ingredient, even though the item was available in Spain in the desired quality or quantity.[5]

Although these rulings excused manufactures from paying import duties on many prime materials, they did not encompass all factors of production. Selective tariffs fell on imports and exports of commodities such as cotton, hemp, madder, wool, and silk. The nature of these special duties can be illustrated by an inspection of those levied on bulk cotton. Charles III first taxed imports of this item on May 15, 1760.[6] For the remainder of the century, he and Charles IV alternately modified, suspended, and reimposed this duty in response to changing circumstances.

Within a few months after Charles had assessed imports of cotton, he bowed to pressure from producers of calico. He stilled their grumbles on December 20, 1760, with the nullification of duties on 2,500 quintals of Levantine cotton each year for ten years.[7] Supplementing this in May and December, 1761, Charles freed all Maltese cotton from import duties provided it arrived "properly wrapped and sealed."[8] He then excused American cotton from all import duties on October 17 and November 6, 1766, in an attempt to stimulate the cultivation of cotton in America.[9] This bore little fruit in the eighteenth century.

In 1770 Charles provided a temporary and partial extension of

---

[4] Gallardo Fernandez, *op. cit.*, II, 389–392; Carrera y Pujal, *op. cit.*, IV, 99; Larruga y Boneta, *op. cit.*, I, 229; AMH, *op. cit.*, XII, 205–212.

Charles III included all makers of woolens in 1779, but maintained the provision against importing items of the desired quality that were available in Spain (AHN, *Consejo*, leg. 50134; AGS, *Secretaría de Hacienda*, leg. 793; Carrera y Pujal, *op. cit.*, IV, 120; AMH, *op. cit.*, XXIII, 501–512.

[5] Antonio Matilla Tascón, *Catálogo de la Colección de Órdenes Generales de Rentas* (Madrid, 1950), I, 427; Gallardo Fernandez, *op. cit.*, II. 404.

Repeated on June 22, 1791, and January 30, 1796, this ruling required that the items be essential in production and forbade producers to import them for resale. As a precaution, it directed manufacturers to have their imports approved by provincial intendants (AMH, *op. cit.*, XXXV, 228; XL, 21–22; Marcelino Graell, *La Industria Sedera* [Barcelona, 1926], p. 36).

[6] AMH, *op. cit.*, XIII, 272–274; Jaime Carrera y Pujal, *Historia Política y Económica de Cataluña, Siglos XVI al XVIII*, 4 vols. (Barcelona, 1946–1947), IV, 142; Ángel Ruiz y Pablo, *Historia de la Real Junta Particular de Comercio de Barcelona, 1758–1848* (Barcelona, 1919), p. 58.

[7] Carrera y Pujal, *op. cit.*, IV, 143; Ruiz y Pablo, *op. cit.*, p. 62; Juan Pablo Canals, *Colección de lo Perteneciente al Ramo de la Rubia ó Granza de España* (Madrid, 1779), p. 168.

[8] Ruiz y Pablo, *op. cit.*, p. 62.

[9] AMH, *op. cit.*, XV, 628; XVIII, 11–12; BCB, *Junta de Comercio*, leg. 53; no. 2; Ruiz y Pablo, *op. cit.*, p. 103.

the yearly quota of 2,500 quintals; but on September 30, 1771, he again taxed imports of cotton 20 percent.[10] Even though producers of calico had doubled their capacity between 1760 and 1768, they persuaded Charles, on May 12, 1772, to withdraw the duty on Maltese cotton for one year, apply it to one-third of the imports the second year, to two-thirds the third year, and to all imports the fourth year.[11] After that partial exemption, the tariff remained in effect for the remainder of the century, except during brief periods.[12]

Although the motive for imposing the duty on cotton may have been to dampen the growth of calico production, the primary purpose of most import tariffs during the eighteenth century was to provide revenue. And customs revenue ascended rapidly after 1750. Reforms of customs—which unified procedures, took collection away from the tax farmers, and revised rates—help explain this growth in receipts.[13] They reached 33,736,480 vellon reals in 1758, 52,888,523 in 1772, 115,443,930 in 1793, and 182,050,732 in 1796; they fell to 47,773,132 vellon reals during the English blockade in 1798.[14] Far more than an improved system of collection and higher import duties are responsible for these increases. Of much greater importance were a substantial growth in the volume of trade and a rising price level.[15]

Spain's trade with her colonies expanded after 1750, partly in response to a disenthrallment of American commerce. In order to control gold and silver flowing eastward to Europe, Spanish kings had funneled all colonial trade through Seville until 1717 and thereafter through Cadiz; trade in America was similarly limited to certain ports.[16] At midcentury most of Spain's commerce still

[10] AMH, *op. cit.*, XVIII, 444–445.

[11] *Ibid.*, XX, 296–302; Ruiz y Pablo, *op. cit.*, p. 101; Carrera y Pujal, *op. cit.*, IV, 150.

[12] On May 17 and 19, 1782, Charles III exempted imports of cotton during the war with England. The British blockade of America, imposed after 1796, led to a 50 percent reduction of import duties on Levantine cotton (AMH, *op. cit.*, XXV, 128–130; XLIII, 66).

[13] Canga Arguëlles, *op. cit.*, II, 496.

[14] *Ibid.*, 499.

[15] When corrected for changes in the general level of prices, these customs receipts vary less spectacularly. They rise from about 29,723,771 vellon reals in 1758 to 43,818,163 in 1772, to 71,526,599 in 1793, to 98,034,859 in 1796, and then fall to 23,826,998 in 1798. Professor Hamilton's index numbers of nonagricultural prices in New Castile, 1651–1800, with base years of 1726–1750, were used for this correction (Earl J. Hamilton, *War and Prices in Spain, 1651–1800* [Cambridge, Massachusetts, 1947], pp. 172–173).

[16] Clarence Henry Haring, *The Spanish Empire in America* (New York, 1947), p.

originated at Cadiz. Under pressure from other Spanish regions and the pleading of liberal voices, this monopoly slowly eroded away.[17] Charles III applied the *coup de grâce in* 1778 when he permitted all major Spanish ports, except Valencia, Bilbao, and San Sebastian, to trade directly with most ports in America.[18]

Prior to this unfettering of colonial trade, the kings had stimulated trade with America by exempting individual producers from export duties. This was another means for promoting domestic industry. Charles III used it effectively on November 27, 1772, by slashing export duties on all domestic woolens and linens.[19] When he opened American trade to peninsula ports in 1778, Charles exempted Spanish ships from a number of port taxes and excused domestic textiles made from wool, hemp, flax, and cotton from all export duties as well as excise taxes when leaving Spanish ports and entering American ones.[20] He also lowered the duty on silks from 80 to 34 maravedis a pound when shipped to America.[21] These drastic reductions, together with the freedom of colonial trade, stimulated production for export.[22]

321; Roland Dennis Hussey, *The Caracas Company, 1728–1784* (Cambridge, Massachusetts, 1934), p. 5.

[17] In 1728 Philip V chartered the Caracas Company, granting this joint-stock firm a monopoly in trade with Venezuela; he also chartered the Havana Company in 1740 and permitted it to trade in Cuban tobacco; and Ferdinand VI in 1755 chartered the Barcelona Company and gave it the right to trade with the islands of Santo Domingo, Puerto Rico, and La Margarita. Charles III opened the West Indies to the ports of Barcelona, Alicante, Cartagena, Malaga, La Coruña, Gijon, and Santander in 1765 (Richard Herr, *The Eighteenth Century Revolution in Spain* [Princeton, New Jersey, 1958], pp. 121–122; Manuel Colmeiro y Penido, *Historia de la Economia Política en España*, 2 vols. [Madrid, 1863], II, 460; Hussey, *op. cit.*, p. 60).

[18] *Almanaque Mercantil ó Guía de Comerciante para el Año de 1804* (Madrid, 1804), pp. 223–224; AMH, *op. cit.*, XXIII, 137–140.

[19] ACSV, *Reales Cédulas*, no. 2; AMH, *op. cit.*, XX, 391–394.

[20] *Almanaque de 1804, loc. cit.;* AMH, *op. cit.*, XXIII, 137–140.

[21] Ferdinand VI had lowered this duty to eighty maravedis a pound on December 26, 1749, and later, on January 27, 1750, included in it all municipal duties (Matilla Tascón, *op. cit.*, I, 105; AMH, *op. cit.*, X, 23).

[22] Besides those already mentioned, other reductions of export duties occurred. For example, Charles III ruled on October 26, 1779, November 18, 1779, November 17, 1780, and July 5, 1783, that textiles made from hemp, flax, and wool were not to pay duties when exported to any destination, including from one Spanish port to another. On March 6, 1794, Charles IV ordered that cottons, woolens, and linens, which had been partly processed in foreign nations, be considered as domestic and thus exempt from export duties. He did not include calicoes made from Maltese cotton; instead, he placed the burden on producers to prove that their textiles contained only American cotton. If any doubts existed, customs was to levy a 3 percent duty (*ibid.*, XXIII, 453–456, 501–512; XXVI, 210–211; XXXVIII, 50–53; Carrera y Pujal, *Historia de la Economia Española*, IV, 120; AHN, *Consejo*, leg. 50134; AGS, *loc. cit.*).

IMPORT AND EXPORT RESTRICTIONS

Because kings depended upon tariffs to provide much of their income, they rarely boosted rates so high that imports stopped. Import duties were thus a source of much income, and the protection they offered Spanish textile makers was incomplete. When a king felt strongly about shielding an industry, he simply prohibited the importation of competing products. Throughout the period 1750–1800 Spain's rulers forbade the import of numerous types of textiles as they strove to create a market for domestic products; they also barred the exportation of raw materials which they considered strategic to favored segments of the textile industry. Prohibitions became a powerful tool in the kings' possession.

Kings employed this device effectively when, as part of their program to stimulate the output of silk fabrics, they forbade exports of raw silk. Despite a relatively large domestic supply, the kings, as well as the weavers, wished to stop the export of raw silk;[23] they realized that this would increase the domestic supply and force a lower price than that which would have obtained in the absence of any restrictions. Even though kings adopted prohibitions, the flow of raw silk from Spain continued. For, in the wake of the embargoes, price differentials between nations widened swiftly and assured clandestine exports. Prices of silk in Spain were nevertheless lower than if no bans had existed, and that difference reflected the expenses and risks of smuggling.

Charles II originated the embargoes that marked the eighteenth century when, on June 23, 1699, he blocked all exports of silk.[24] This was a prohibition in name only, for 200,000 pounds a year illegally entered foreign commerce from Valencia and Murcia alone.[25] Charles swelled that quantity by granting many export licenses. Thus it was that Philip V merely acknowledged reality on January 4, 1738, when he permitted export of raw silk; however, to protect manufacturers of silk textiles, he conceded the right of *tanteo,* or the prerogative for producers legally to confiscate silk destined for export.[26] Within two years, pressure from textile makers forced him to reimpose the prohibition.[27]

---

[23] Carrera y Pujal, *op. cit.,* V, 459–460.

[24] Matilla Tascón, *op. cit.,* I, 18.

[25] Carrera y Pujal, *op. cit.,* V, 459.

[26] Matilla Tascón, *op. cit.,* I, 58; Carrera y Pujal, *op. cit.,* V, 459–460. For an explanation of *tanteo,* see above, pp. 58–59, n. 35.

[27] Matilla Tascón, *op. cit.,* 60; Rosario Alcazde Miranda (unpublished and un-

Growers of silk then complained of low prices and unsold harvests, and much raw silk filtered into foreign countries through the defenses of Spain. Silk exports nevertheless remained prohibited for twenty additional years. Charles III finally removed the ban on May 15, 1760, as part of his sweeping liberalization of Spain's economy.[28] Still, he placed restraints on the silk trade, limiting shipments to the period May 15–November 15, and then only from the ports if Alicante, Cartagena, and Barcelona.[29] He also maintained rigorous controls over domestic sale and transport of silk.[30]

Merchants and producers ignored Charles' edict that silk be exported only from May 15 to November 15 and continued their shipments abroad throughout the year.[31] After receiving reports of "excessive prices" and the "insatiable greediness" of silk merchants, Charles prohibited the exportation of silk at any time on August 12, 1774.[32] Four years later, he repeated the embargo and expressed the belief that his recent liberalization of colonial trade would stimulate the demand of Spanish manufacturers for raw silk.[33]

His expectations failed to materialize at first, for several consecutive bumper harvests depressed the price and forced him to permit the export of silk from November 15, 1781, to May 15, 1782, through designated ports.[34] During the last two decades of the century, however, the domestic demand increased markedly and Spain imported silk. Charles III even permitted manufacturers to import free of duty 200,000 pounds of silk from August 19,

titled dissertation for the degree of Doctor of Philosophy and Letters, University of Valencia, February, 1949), p. 67; Carrera y Pujal, *op. cit.*, 467.

He extended this prohibition to waste silk on November 28, 1739 (Matilla Tascón, *op. cit.*, I, 61; Carrera y Pujal, *op. cit.*, V, 467).

[28] AMH, *op. cit.*, XIII, 276–279.

[29] On January 8, 1764, Charles III opened the port of Grao, serving Valencia, to the exportation of silk (*ibid.*, XV, 3–4).

[30] *Ibid.*, XIV, 124–127.

[31] Due to an abnormally large harvest of silk, Charles permitted exports throughout the year in 1762. On June 28, 1771, he stopped exports during all months because of a harvest failure (*ibid.*, XIV, 333–334; XX, 150–153; Carrera y Pujal, *op. cit.*, V, 323).

[32] AMH, *op. cit.*, XXI, 123–124.

[33] *Ibid.*, XXII, 582–587.

A crop failure caused a shortage of silk in 1774. To aid the industry, Charles III permitted duty-free importation of 100,000 pounds of silk, provided it was carried by Spanish ships and was landed at Cartagena or Alicante (*ibid.*, XXI, 157–158).

[34] *Ibid.*, XXIV, 592–597.

1784, until May 31, 1785.[35] He later extended this period until January 1, 1786,[36] but exacted one-half the normal duty on twisted silk for one year beginning July 1, 1791.[37]

Charles III's prediction that domestic industry would expand and thus consume more silk came true during the decade of the eighties. While the liberalization of American commerce was an important factor in this expansion of silk weaving, so also was the prohibition on raw silk exports. When free commerce in silk prevailed in 1738, for example, Valencia possessed 1,419 looms; twelve years later, after the prohibition had been imposed, 1,765 looms existed.[38] Free exports were occurring in 1767 and concurrently 1,519 looms were active while 1,915 were idle. Under protection of the export prohibition the number of active looms rose to 3,186 in 1785.[39]

Partial credit for this expansion must also be awarded import prohibitions. They filled an even greater role in the commercial policies of the kings than did embargoes on exports. By shutting out foreign textiles, Spanish rulers protected the peninsular market for domestic producers, sometimes purposely, other times unintentionally.

Ferdinand VI and Charles III imposed numerous bans on foreign merchandise between 1750 and 1785. One of the first important prohibitions began on September 12, 1752, when Ferdinand VI stopped all imports of cloth containing threads of false silver or gold.[40] He permitted their importation on August 1, 1774, only to ban them again on June 25 and November 27, 1778, unless they possessed all the physical characteristics set forth by Spanish law.[41] Additional import restrictions imposed by Ferdinand and Charles III embraced nearly all clothes: Ferdinand prohibited used clothes on December 31, 1753, and January 7, 1754;[42] Charles stopped imports of all "smaller articles" made of

[35] *Ibid.*, XXVII, 145.
Charles raised the import duty from six to nine vellon reals a pound.
[36] *Ibid.*, XXVIII, 298.
Charles allowed weavers at Malaga to import silk without paying duties from February 22, 1786, until July 10, 1786.
[37] *Ibid.*, XXXV, 234–236.
[38] Carrera y Pujal, *op. cit.*, V, 460; Eduard Martinez Ferrando, *La Industria Valenciana de la Seda* (Valencia, 1933), p. 14.
[39] ACSV, *Mano de Anotaciones . . . Reyno de Valencia;* Carrera y Pujal, *op. cit.*, V, 516.
[40] AMH, *op. cit.*, XI, 182–183.
The king repeated this prohibition on September 13, 1759 (*ibid.*, XIII, 138–139).
[41] *Ibid.*, XXI, 116; XXII, 609–617; ACSV, *Reales Cédulas*, no. 2.
[42] AMH, op. cit., XI, 321, 416.

flax, hemp, and cotton, such as mittens, embroidered-cuff wrist-bands, and all knitted stockings, on July 14, 1778, and December 21, 1779;[43] and he prohibited imports of all types of interior or exterior clothing made for women or men that contained silk, linen, wool, or cotton, on May 24, 1799.[44]

Continuing to swell the number of forbidden textiles, Charles thwarted the import of all fabrics on November 27, 1778, unless they conformed to production standards as stated by Spanish law.[45] On December 23, 1782, he published a list of prohibited goods that contained, for example, textiles woven completely or partly of silk whose widths were not at least two-thirds of a vara, linen thread whose value was less than twenty vellon reals a pound, and linen lace whose value was less than ten vellon reals a vara.[46] For the remainder of the century, kings did not basically

---

[43] AHN, *Biblioteca, Colección de Reales Cédulas,* 1788, XI, 482; AMH, *op. cit.,* XXII, 351–356.
Some other *manufacturas menores* were: linen, woolen, and cotton buttons for shirts; silk and linen braid for interior decoration; all types of ribbon or tape of linen, colored or white, embroidered or plain; all types of plain lace, wide or narrow; all kinds of chenille made of cotton, wool, linen, or silk; tassels for coiffeurs; all styles of frogs and braid trimmings; bullion fringe and epaulettes; net purses; plain mesh for every use; tablecloths and aprons of mesh; all similar goods of prime material such as hemp, wool, linen, or cotton (ACA, *Acordadas,* no. 577, fol. 11; AHN, *Consejo, Libros de Govierno,* 1779, fols. 795–796; AMH, *op. cit.,* XXIII, 542–545).
Charles placed shawls and women's capes made of silk or wool on the list of banned textiles on July 31, 1778 (*ibid.,* XXII, 371–375).
[44] *Ibid.,* XXIII, 195–198.
[45] *Ibid.,* XXII, 609–617.
[46] Other textiles included on the list of prohibited goods were: lace, rugs, saddlebags, and knapsacks; manufactured or woven cotton, excepting spun and bulk; all types of pillows and pads; dressing gowns; broad or narrow silk strip lace; plumes and flounces; all purses; buttons of fur, linen, gold, wool, or bristle; silk shirts with any edging; other shirts; ribbon tape of cotton, silk, wool, fur, or horsehair; ribbon or sash of any type; bedspreads, necklace card; scarves and neckties; twine, cord; and silk lace whose value was not five vellon reals a vara; spun worsted; mats of silk, linen, or wool; bands and plush velvets; all fringe except gold and silver; all bonnets; gloves; any decoration made of wool, linen, hemp, or fur; yarn less than twenty vellon reals a pound; yarn or thread of twisted silver; coarse wool garters, mufflers, shawls, woolen traveling rugs, mantillas, and short jackets; wool, fur, linen, cotton, or leather stockings; mittens less than a vara wide; mosquito netting; puppets with fabric clothing; church ormnaments of cloth; silk fan decorations; netting and hairnets; sheets; sacking of linen or wool; bed linen and tablecloths; greatcoats; silk or net for fans; woven or manufactured silk, wool, or linen, or any other material mixed with silver, false or real, or gold, false or real; stamped or printed linen; clothing—exterior or interior—for men or women, made of gold, silver, silk, linen, wool, cotton, fur, hemp, or a mixture of any of these, or of lace, or adornment (*ibid.,* XXV, 391–401).

change these prohibitions, they merely enlarged upon and clarified them in response to new textiles from abroad.[47]

With most embargoes, the kings purposely sheltered manufacturers of specific fabrics. Thus it was with a series of prohibitions against imports of cottons. They were designed to shield the traditional silks, woolens, and linens from the relatively cheap and attractive calicoes and muslins from Asia, China, and Europe. Although creation of a domestic cotton industry was far from the intentions of the kings and their ministers, a nucleus of calico production developed in Barcelona under this indirect protection and became Spain's most important textile center by 1785.

The first assault on foreign cottons in the eighteenth century occurred on April 20 and June 20, 1718, when Philip V banned the import as well as the use of cottons from China and Asia.[48] Merchants and consumers paid little heed to this embargo. For this reason, Philip repeated the prohibition on June 4, 1728, June 14, 1728, April 5, 1734, and August 30, 1734;[49] throughout his reign he maintained his position against, and consumers maintained theirs for, foreign cottons.[50]

Ferdinand VI revoked the ban on muslins and fine fustians on October 8, 1748, replacing it with a 35 percent import duty.[51] Eight years later, however, he prohibited all imports of textiles from China, printed cotton and linen from Asia and Africa, and imitations from Europe, under the shallow pretext that they threatened public health.[52]

By 1760 a bustling center of calico production with 353 looms and 10,000 workers had taken root in Barcelona under this unintentional protection. But on May 15 of that year, Charles III suddenly withdrew his favor and opened Spain to silks, cottons, and printed linens manufactured in Asia, Africa, or Europe.[53] A

---

[47] For example, see *ibid.*, XXVI, 125, 186, 202, 254, 462; XXVIII, 197–199; XXIX, 15, 206, 633, 672–673; XXX, 424–426; XXXII, 231–232, 248; XXXIII, 3, 22; XXXIV, 255–257; XXXV, 85, 292–293, 346; XXXVI, 16, 127, 146–147; XLI, 103–104, 132, 351; XLII, 317; XLIV, 446.

[48] Matilla Tascón, *op. cit.*, I, 33.

[49] Carrera y Pujal, *op. cit.*, V, 306; AMH, *op. cit.*, XIII, 184–186; Matilla Tascón, *op. cit.*, I, 47, 54, 55.

[50] Philip made an exception of fabrics called *blavetes* or *blahuetes*. He banned them in January, 1742, admitted them on payment of a 30 percent duty ten months later, prohibited their import again in December, 1743, and readmitted them in January, 1744 (Carrera y Pujal, *op cit.*, V, 329; Matilla Tascón, *op. cit.*, I, 70).

[51] AMH, *op. cit.*, VIII, 192.

[52] *Ibid.*, XII, 203–204.

On July 13, 1752, Ferdinand had prohibited the importation of all printed linen (*ibid.*, XI, 105–106).

[53] *Ibid.*, XIII, 272–274.

duty of 20 percent awaited these imports. During the next decade, Charles struggled with several developments that eventually forced him to reconsider this portion of his program to emancipate Spain's commerce. Producers of calicoes complained persistently and bitterly.[54] So did manufacturers of silks, for imported muslins and similar fabrics displaced domestic taffeta and other silks; the 20 percent duty on foreign cottons made smuggling still profitable; and expanding imports of cottons, legal as well as illegal, increased Spain's unfavorable balance of trade.

Surrendering to these circumstances, Charles issued a pragmatic sanction on June 24, 1770, that prohibited imports of muslins.[55] But he realized the folly of banning imports of a popular good and then hoping to control the contraband, so he also prohibited his subjects from using muslin.[56] He issued another pragmatic sanction on June 28, 1770, forbidding the use of shawls and women's capes other than those of silk and wool.[57] Charles expanded the embargo on cottons on November 14, 1771, to include all textiles containing any cotton fibers, as he considered them formidable substitutes for domestic woolens and silks.[58] In none of his legislation did Charles mention any intention of protecting makers of cottons.

Consumers flaunted the ban on using imported cottons and continued to demand and obtain them from smugglers.[59] Muslin,

---

[54] Charles tried to placate the Catalonians on July 8, 1768, by prohibiting imports of painted or printed handkerchiefs and linens containing flax or cotton. On January 19, 1770, he went a little further and banned imports of *cotonadas, blavetes,* and *biones en blanco y azul* (*ibid.,* XVII, 228; Ruiz y Pablo, *op. cit.,* pp. 98–99).

[55] AHN, *Consejo, Libros de Govierno,* 1770, fols. 334–337; AHN, *Biblioteca, Colección de Reales Cédulas,* 1770, VI, 270; Carrera y Pujal, *op. cit.,* IV, 109; AMH, *op. cit.,* XIX, 97–104; Ruiz y Pablo, *op. cit.,* p. 99; Juan Sempere y Guarinos, *Historia del Luxo, y de las Leyes Suntuarios de España,* 2 vols. (Madrid, 1788), II, 172.

[56] AHN, *Consejo, Libros de Govierno,* 1770, fol. 336; Carrera y Pujal, *op. cit.,* IV, 109; AMH, *op. cit.,* XIX, 97–104.
He permitted citizens to wear existing muslin for two years and gave merchants six months in which to sell their stock of muslin.

[57] *Ibid.,* XIX, 105–108; AHN, op. cit., fols. 339–341; AHN, *Biblioteca, Colección de Reales Cédulas,* 1770, VI, 273.

[58] AMH, *op. cit.,* XX, 247–252; AHN, *Consejo, Libros de Govierno,* 1771, 498–501; AHN, *Biblioteca, Colección de Reales Cédulas,* 1771, VII, 318.

[59] Gaspar Melchor Jovellanos, a critic of the prohibition, argued that such controls were futile. "The present measure, whose solution is being dealt with here, offers an irrefutable proof of this [inevitability of smuggling]. This contravention of the laws was the most scandalous that history offers, for neither the repeated prohibitions, nor the compliance of government, nor the advantages offered in the uses of other goods were enough to banish the use of muslins. All had been scorned, all had been useless, and all had demonstrated with a very sad example

a substitute for silk in shawls and capes, became the favorite of Madrid's sophisticates. Resigned to the inevitability of contraband, Charles IV decided on September 7, 1789, to permit imports of bleached muslin and thereby to collect at least some import duties.[60] He amended this on February 19, 1791, by allowing only imports of muslin whose price was at least thirty vellon reals a vara, expecting in this way to exclude cheaper cottons.[61] By September 23, 1793, however, the cotton industry in Catalonia, mushrooming into national prominence, had readily persuaded Charles to reimpose the ban on all muslin except that imported by the Company of the Philippines.[62]

Thus it was that kings unintentionally stimulated an amazing growth of calicoes at Barcelona when they protected manufacturers of silks and woolens from foreign cottons. This is not to say that Barcelona would have lacked production of calicoes without the prohibition. Catalonia held an obvious comparative advantage in calicoes. During the period 1760–1770 that industry enjoyed only the protection of a 20 percent import duty, yet the number of producers increased nearly threefold and the number of active looms grew more than twofold.[63] Nevertheless, the prohibition of foreign cottons aided and abetted that advantage. After the embargo of 1770, the industry's rate of expansion quickened as the number of manufacturers and looms expanded more than threefold from 1771 to 1784.[64] By 1804 the industry in Catalonia possessed more than 100 producers, 4,000 looms, and 100,000 employees.[65]

---

that the remedies adopted up to now were insufficient for the cure of an evil originated by opinion and caprice, always more powerful than the laws when combated face to face" (*Biblioteca de Autores Españoles* [Madrid, 1859], L, 47).

[60] AMH, *op. cit.*, XXXII, 348–351; AHN, *Biblioteca, Colección de Reales Cédulas,* 1789–1790, XX, 907; AHN, *Consejo, Libros de Govierno,* 1789, fols. 691–693; Carrera y Pujal, *op cit.*, V, 340.

[61] Archivo Histórico Municipal de Barcelona, *Depósito Santa Cruz* [hereafter cited as AHMB *Santa Cruz*] *Judicial Corregidor;* AMH, *op. cit.*, XXXV, 75–76.

[62] AHMB *Santa Cruz, op. cit.;* AMH, *op. cit.*, XXXVII, 353–356; AHN, *Consejo, Libros de Govierno,* 1793, 825–827; AHN, *Biblioteca, Colección de Reales Cédulas,* 1793–1794, XXII, 1066.

The kings made no further changes during the remainder of the century other than to enforce existing prohibitions. For examples of this, see: AMH, *op. cit.*, XXXVII, 361–365, 424; XL, 71; XLI, 292, 312; XLII, 3, 78–79, 108, 231–232.

[63] BCB, *op. cit.*, leg. 53, nos. 4, 40.

[64] *Ibid.*, leg. 53, no. 29.

[65] *Almanaque de 1804, op. cit.*, p. 320; Federico Rahola y Tremols, *Cámara Official de Comercio y Navagación de Barcelona* (Barcelona, 1931), p. 151.

CONTRABAND AND CONTROLS

Contraband inevitably accompanied prohibitions and high customs duties. Because these curbs on imports reduced the supply of textiles on the peninsula and thus raised prices of cloth, they tempted many persons to spirit less expensive fabrics into Spain and sell them for handsome profits. Drawn into the dangerous profession by this lure of gain, smugglers operated along the many miles of Spain's coasts, on the isolated frontiers of Portugal and France, and especially in major seaports. They came from all walks of life—members of the ecclesiastical estate, high government officials, lowly *bandidos* from the rugged mountains, and noblemen.[66]

Some of the most active participants were textile producers who, using their workshops as fronts for receiving contraband, placed their registered seals on textiles so as to give them a legitimate appearance. Jean Francois de Bourgoing claimed that about twenty looms for narrow silks at Cadiz wove very little, yet their products were in great demand. He was certain that these looms served mainly as camouflage for placing Spanish marks on foreign textiles.[67] This and other indications of widespread and vigorous contraband impressed Bourgoing.

Smuggling, a word which is alone sufficient to make the Spanish government shudder, has not a more brilliant theatre than the port of Cadiz. It cannot fail to be naturalized wherever prohibitions are numerous, and the temptations to infringe them frequent and highly alluring. . . .[68]

This deep and ubiquitous disorder appalled and infuriated kings of Spain, arousing them to a fury of defensive measures.[69]

---

[66] From reading legislation aimed at destroying illicit trade, one gets the feeling that smuggling pervaded all Spanish society (AMH, *op. cit.*, XI, 311–315, 484; XIII, 83–91, 148–149, 478–479; XXX, 133; XXXI, 217–219; XXXIII, 251–254; Gallardo Fernandez, *op. cit.*, II, 48; IV, 19, 24).

[67] Jean Francois de Bourgoing, *Modern State of Spain*, translated from the 1807 edition, 4 vols. (London, 1808), III, 189.
Enough similar instances occurred to indicate that Bourgoing was not witnessing an isolated event. For the case of the village of Lluvia, for example, see *AHMB, Junta General de Comercio*, XXIII, 109, 116.

[68] Bourgoing, *op. cit.*, III, 182.

[69] Matilla Tascón, *op. cit.*, I, 114; AMH, op. cit., X, 358–359. The usual sentence was several years in a closed penitentiary. On July 26, 1751, however, Ferdinand VI drafted into the army or the naval yards all contrabandists whose crimes were not "too bad" (*ibid.*).

Charles III published on July 22, 1761, these penalties for contraband violations:[70] loss of merchandise, carts, carriages, mules,
baggage, and all other items used in transporting the goods; three
years in a presidio for first convictions, six years for second convictions, and eight for third convictions. If contrabandists resisted
arrest with arms, they received four additional years; if they were
noblemen, they received six more. He also decreed the death penalty if the severity of resistance warranted it.[71]

Forewarnings such as these deterred only timid souls, not rov-
ing bands of professional thieves who found the contraband trade
lucrative. These men carried offensive arms, which they used most
efficiently at the slightest provocation during their pillaging and
smuggling forays. Charles consequently ordered the death penalty
on April 2, 1783, for smugglers who resisted arrest with steel arms
(*armas blancas*) and sentenced them to ten years in the penitentiary if they surrendered peacefully.[72]

All such threats were fanciful. Instead of diminishing, smuggling kept pace with increases in tariffs and prohibitions. Determined to crush this illicit trade, Charles III formed three
companies of mountain musketeers (*compañias de fusileros de
montaña*) on April 29, 1761, to support customs guards on the
Aragon frontier.[73] He formed another company on May 8, 1761,
to serve in Extremadura.[74] By the summer of 1787, customs agents
in Catalonia asked for and received two night patrols of fifteen
men each.[75] Despite these and other efforts, smuggling became
so intensive by 1796 that Charles IV dispatched army units to aid
the customs guards and musketeers.[76]

Through this web of customs guards, musketeers, night patrols,
and army, poured an endless stream of illicit textiles.[77] Once in

---

[70] Gallardo Fernandez, *op. cit.*, IV, 21; *ibid.*, XIV, 164–173.

[71] To reduce smuggling along the coasts, Charles IV prohibited construction of
warehouses and country houses near the sea, for they might have served as
entrepôts for illicit goods (*ibid.*, XL, 361).

[72] *Ibid.*, XXVI, 97–98.

[73] *Ibid.*, XIV, 90–97.
Each company consisted of a captain, two lieutenants, three sublieutenants,
six sergeants, twelve corporals, two drummers, and one hundred musketeers.

[74] *Ibid.*, XIV, 102.

[75] Charles III invited smugglers to join, provided they retire from their present
occupation (*ibid.*, XXX, 248–249).

[76] *Ibid.*, XL, 262.

[77] Since the king knew that his customs officials and guards accepted bribes from
smugglers, he offered them a share in the confiscated merchandise, hoping thereby
to maintain their loyalty. The amount they received depended upon the region,
whether they caught the smuggler, who tried the case, and the type of goods. In
most cases they received one-fourth of the receipts from the sale of the contraband.

Spain contraband fabrics passed into the hands of merchants and producers who then attempted to dispose of them along with licit merchandise. All textiles in transit through Spain, therefore, were suspect. In order to differentiate domestically produced and legally imported goods from contraband, Spanish rulers developed a complex system of stamps and customs receipts.

Philip V laid down basic rules for customs receipts on July 8, 1717, when he commanded that a merchant must obtain a customs receipt or paper guide when his merchandise passed through customs.[78] At his final destination, the merchant presented the guide to a proper official [79] who compared the items on the guide with those in the merchant's possession. If they coincided, the official gave the merchant his guide and sent a copy to Madrid where it was compared with the original. Before the merchant could send these same goods on to, say, a fair he had to acquire another guide and observe the same regulations;[80] if he failed to sell all his goods at that fair, he had to obtain an extension for his guide before returning home. He transported textiles without proper credentials at the risk of a heavy fine and having his goods, his horse, and his cart confiscated.[81]

The system worked imperfectly. For merchants easily obtained guides by counterfeiting them or by bribing actuaries to falsify the documents.[82] This led Ferdinand VI on March 17, 1753, to strengthen procedures for issuing guides.[83] By 1753 merchants and producers needed them to accompany domestic as well as foreign merchandise.

In further efforts to segregate domestic fabrics and contraband, the kings required producers to stamp their textiles with lead or wax identification seals. As the flow of illicit fabrics into Spain increased, the reliance on stamps also increased. The General Council of Commerce and Money on November 27, 1774, ordered manufacturers of calicoes, handkerchiefs, and other cotton goods

---

On June 29, 1784, Charles III offered a reward of sixty vellon reals for each smuggler captured, one hundred if he resisted (*ibid.*, X, 86; XII, 257; XIII, 78; XXXI, 528; XXXVIII, 262–263).

[78] *Ibid.*, III, 126–129.

[79] The official designated to accept the guide was either the administrator of customs or the tax farmer. If neither of these functionaries lived in the locality, the king appointed the subdelegate or superintendent of royal taxes, the magistrate, the governor, or the justice of the peace (*ibid*).

[80] *Ibid.*

[81] *Ibid.*

[82] *Ibid.*, XI, 297–298.

[83] *Ibid.*

to stamp both ends of their cloth so that customs could recognize their origin even when sold by half pieces.[84] Charles III instructed producers on June 22, 1778, to have their imported linens stamped by customs before processing them. At the same time he directed these fabricators to place their own stamps, which acted as personal trademarks, on the ends of each piece of their textiles.[85] Rules created to govern commerce with America in 1778 required that manufacturers stamp each piece of fabric with their personal mark, the name of the village in which the cloth was made, and the quality and quantity of the fabric.[86] Repeating this instruction on March 15, 1779, Charles extended it to all textiles, not just those going to America, and gave producers fifteen days in which to send samples of their stamps to Madrid.[87]

Smugglers soon developed sophisticated means of counterfeiting seals, especially in Catalonia and Valencia. To meet this challenge, Charles created three counterstamps on July 11, 1786; a large one for woolens, a medium-sized one for silks, linens, and cotton, and a small one for stockings. He decreed that all producers place them, besides the stamps indicating their names and villages, on all textiles that might be shipped to America.[88]

The counterstamp increased the burdens already placed on producers by the government.[89] Manufacturers sometimes had to travel miles with their textiles just to obtain the necessary credentials and stamps. Fees, transportation expenses, wasted time, and other annoyances caused by this regulation turned it into a ridiculous hindrance. Gaspar Melchor de Jovellanos led a debate against these controls in the General Council of Commerce and Money, arguing in the following manner.

On the other hand, ponder the distractions, the expense, and the loss of time a producer will be exposed to when obligated to observe these formalities. The sworn relation completed, first he will go to obtain the counter-mark, which might be located not only out of his house, but, in many cases, out of the village and in a distant one; then he will have to pay transportation expenses for his woolens, and stamp fees; then he will look for the administrator who is to give him the

---

[84] BCB, *op. cit.*, leg. 51, no. 5.

[85] AMH, *op. cit.*, XXII, 377–383; BCB, *op. cit.*, leg. 53, no. 23.

[86] *Almanaque de 1804*, *op. cit.*, p. 224; ACSV, *loc. cit.*

[87] AHN, *Consejo, Libros de Govierno*, 1779, fol. 292.

[88] AMH, *op. cit.*, XXIX, 338–347; ACSV, *loc. cit.*

[89] Charles III issued additional instructions for using the counterstamp on October 30, 1786 (AMH, *op. cit.*, XXIX, 559–565).

certification, for the administrator does not always live in the same house or village as the counter-stamper; forthwith he will look for the subdelegate or intendant to give approval, and for this, another trip; he will solicit the witness of actuaries, which he perhaps will have to have duplicated or triplicated, for two actuaries will be needed for witness of the sworn statement, the certification, and the approval, since all three may not be in the same but in different villages; after other trips and fees the woolens will finally pass to the port of departure; they will suffer new inspections, and even then, no matter who possesses them, the producer will not yet be free of defending the legitimacy of the goods and their stamps. . . .[90]

Finally convinced that counterstamps unduly burdened industry and were easily counterfeited, Charles IV on August 13, 1790, abolished the requirement that seals be placed on textiles destined for America.[91] He entirely repealed the royal counterseal on November 13, 1790, and stated that manufacturers need only use those stamps that revealed their names, locations of the villages in which they produced the textiles, and their personal marks.[92]

Since the purpose of prohibitions and protective tariffs was either to reduce or increase the supply of certain items in Spain, controls against smuggling were imperative. Duties and embargoes retarded merchandise from entering or leaving by normal channels; customs guards, musketeers, customs guides, and stamps retarded merchandise from entering or leaving by illicit channels. Even though Spanish rulers struggled vigorously against smuggling, they could not adequately guard the hundreds of miles of frontier and coast nor carefully police the activities of their own employees. Contraband was inevitable. Nevertheless, the defensive efforts of kings were effective enough to maintain either a higher or a lower price, whichever the case may be, than if unencumbered commerce had prevailed.

The cost of defending against contraband, however, must be set against the gains of textile manufacturers. Salaries of customs employees, musketeers, soldiers, judges, among others, came from tax receipts; and since regression characterized Spain's tax system,

---

[90] Jovellanos, *op. cit.,* 73.

[91] Matilla Tascón, *op. cit.,* I, 412.

[92] AMH, *op. cit.,* XXXIV, 353–354; ACSV, *loc. cit.*

Nevertheless, customs guides, private and customs stamps, inspections, and other formalities continued to hinder Spanish producers. For examples, see: AMH, *op. cit.,* XXXIV, 360; XXXV, 79, 139–140; XXXVI, 12, XXXIX, 249, 315; XL, 87–90; XLI, 50; XLII, 122, 271, 272; XLIII, 89, 95; XLIV, 440; Gallardo Fernandez, *op. cit.,* II, 183, 207.

producers escaped much of that burden at the expense of peasants, laborers, and lowly craftsmen. They bore some of the costs directly, of course, when they paid fees, bought lead stamps, and consumed hours of their time. But their gains were undoubtedly greater than their expenses. It is doubtful that the majority of Spaniards benefited, for they not only provided resources to oppose smuggling but also paid higher prices for protected goods.

IX

General Factors Affecting Growth

Kings of Spain labored throughout the eighteenth century to awaken industry from its dismally long slumber. Textile production received the major share of their concern and efforts, especially during the period 1750–1800. By constructing and operating manufactories for woolens, silks, calicoes, and linens and by chartering joint-stock companies, whose purpose it was to stimulate textile manufacture and commerce, Spanish rulers hoped to provide momentum and example for individual entrepreneurs. Moreover, kings fostered the private sector with tax concessions and removed obstacles in its way by reforming provincial imposts; similarly, they reduced export duties on textiles, raised them on essential raw materials, reduced import duties on essential raw materials, and raised them on foreign fabrics. Import and export prohibitions and reforms of the colonial trading policy were employed in parallel fashion. Immobility of labor and barriers against technological advances received equal attention: kings revoked the traditional prerogatives of guilds and directly and indirectly promoted immigration of foreign artisans and importation of new technology.

While textiles received this massive and diversified assistance, other segments of Spanish industry also drew the concern of kings, albeit to a lesser extent. Much of the legislation enacted primarily for textiles, such as circumventing the power of guilds and promoting the immigration of foreigners, served equally as stimulants to producers of other products. But in separate provisions, kings bestowed special concessions on nontextile industries.

Paper manufacturing was one of the beneficiaries. Though already exempted from taxes and favored with grants of privilege by a series of decrees, this industry received additional assistance when Charles III prohibited the export of hides (*carnaza*) and rags, two important raw materials, in 1767 and then lowered provincial taxes on rags in 1768.[1] To stimulate further the making of paper, Charles III on October 26, 1780, exempted first sales of all paper from the *alcabala* and *cientos,* set a 2 percent rate on subsequent transactions, and taxed all sales of the foreign product 10 percent.[2] As a prime purchaser of paper, the printing industry viewed these actions favorably. With even more approval it accepted concessions on June 2 and July 9, 1778, that forbade the import of foreign books, abolished taxes on domestic books, and protected the copyright privileges of authors' heirs.[3]

In like fashion, manufacturers of porcelain obtained important concessions on July 7, 1778, May 23, 1780, and August 12, 1792;[4] makers of crystal received privileges on March 16, 1788;[5] and producers of glass received some on April 10, 1788.[6] Charles III and Charles IV generously assisted the leather industry a number of times between 1765 and 1793;[7] Charles III likewise aided makers of hats in 1769, 1773, 1780, 1783, and 1786.[8] As the century progressed, kings extended similar grants of privileges throughout nearly the entire industrial sector, embracing producers of many items, such as buttons, hardware, boxes, cards, rugs, tapestry, soap, and corks.[9]

While emphasizing manufacture, the kings nevertheless gave goodly consideration to agriculture. Cultivation of madder, for

---

[1] Jaime Carrera y Pujal, *Historia de la Economía Española,* 5 vols. (Barcelona, 1943–1947), IV, 107; Jaime Carrera y Pujal, *Historia Política y Económica de Cataluña, Siglos XVI al XVIII,* 4 vols. (Barcelona, 1946–1947). IV, 186.

[2] *Ibid.,* IV, 190; Carrera y Pujal, *Historia de la Economía Española,* IV, 123; Francisco Gallardo Fernandez, *Origen, Progresos y Estado de Rentas de la Corona de España,* 7 vols. (Madrid, 1805–1808), II, 395; Antonio Perez Rioja, "La Protección del Libro Bajo Carlos III," *Revista de Archivos, Bibliotecas y Museos,* Vol. LIX, nos. 1–3 (1953), p. 248; Antonio Matilla Tascón, *Catálogo de la Collección de Órdenes Generales de Rentas* (Madrid, 1950), I, 285.

[3] Perez Rioja, *op. cit.,* pp. 243–245; Carrera y Pujal, *Historia de la Economía Española,* IV, 119; Matilla Tascón, op. cit., 256–257.

[4] *Ibid.,* 257, 280, 446.

[5] *Ibid.,* 373.

[6] Gallardo Fernandez, *op. cit.,* II, 399; Matilla Tascón, *op. cit.,* I, 374.

[7] This industry received significant aid in 1765, 1768, 1779, 1781, 1783, 1786, and 1793 (*ibid.,* 200, 241, 270, 290, 345, 456; Carrera y Pujal, *op. cit.,* IV, 106, 107; Gallardo Fernandez, *op. cit.,* II, 374, 397).

[8] Carrera y Pujal, *Historia Política y Económica de Cataluña,* IV, 201; AMH, *Colección de Órdenes Generales de Rentas,* XXIV, 406–413; XXIX, 273–280; Gallardo Fernandez, *op. cit.,* II, 405; Matilla Tascón, *op. cit.,* I, 208, 231, 285, 311, 345.

[9] See: AHN, *Biblioteca, Colección de Reales Cédulas,* 1768–1769, V, 209; *Memorias de la Sociedad Económica de Madrid* (Madrid, 1780), II, 229–235; Gallardo Fernandez, *op. cit.,* II, 395, 396, 406, 407; Joseph Townsend, *A Journey Through Spain in the Years 1786 and 1787,* 3 vols. (London, 1792), I, 268; II, 328, 329; III, 39, 87, 177.

example, received more than passing concern, for red textile dye came from the root of this plant. Before 1730 all madder used by Spanish dyers originated principally in Holland, even though it grew wild in Castile; and as textile production on the peninsula began to revive, the price of madder rose precipitously.[10] First stimulated by Philip V in 1742, this industry received assistance in 1763, 1768, 1772, and 1776.[11]

The extractive industries likewise came by the patronage of kings. Expanding industry and growing population burdened the sparse forests on the peninsula. Thus it was that wood's best substitute, coal, attracted the kings' attention and industry's demand in the decades after 1750.[12] Consequently, Charles III on August 15, 1780, exempted operators of coal mines from all royal, municipal, and private taxes, customs, and tributes levied on their outputs as well as on their necessary machinery, equipment, and supplies.[13] Other privileges, such as the use of the royal coat of arms, permission to build warehouses anyplace, pasture rights, and use of royal forests, were included. Extensive legislation followed in 1789, 1790, 1792, 1793, and 1794, strengthening and expanding these concessions.[14] Similar but less ambitious measures promoted the mining and smelting of iron, copper, brass, and other metals.[15]

The conscious efforts of kings doubtless proved a powerful economic force prodding Spanish industry into motion during 1750–1800. But reënforcing these royal actions were several parallel and independent developments. These were times of enlightenment during which the Bourbon kings nurtured speculation in economic ideas and liberal institutions blossomed; resistance to change and to industrial growth weakened before these events. Concurrent with this ascending intellectual horizon, the last half of the cen-

[10] Eugenio Larruga y Boneta, *Memorias Políticas y Económicas sobre los Frutos, Comercio, Fábricas y Minas de España*, 45 vols. (Madrid, 1787–1800), I, 48.

[11] Juan Pablo Canals, *Colección de lo Perteneciente al Ramo de la Rubia ó Granza de España* (Madrid, 1779), pp. 41, 61, 143–148; AMH, *op. cit.*, XXI, 474–476; Carrera y Pujal, *Historia de la Economía Española*, IV, 132–135.

[12] Carrera y Pujal, *Historia Política y Económica de Cataluña*, IV, 178; Larruga y Boneta, *op. cit.*, XXVII, 126; Gallardo Fernandez, *op. cit.*, VI, 205.

[13] Gallardo Fernandez, *op. cit.*, VI, 194–200; Carrera y Pujal, *Historia de la Economía Española*, IV, 122; Carrera y Pujal, *Historia Política y Económica de Cataluña*, IV, 178; Larruga y Boneta, *op. cit.*, XXVII, 127.

[14] Gallardo Fernandez, *op. cit.*, II, 42, 280, 376; VI, 201, 203, 205–210, 211, 214; Matilla Tascón, *op. cit.*, I, 399, 412, 413, 447, 460.

[15] For example, see: Gallardo Fernandez, *op. cit.*, II, 222, 223, 373, 393, 401, 406, 408, 411, 412; Carrera y Pujal, *Historia de la Economía Española*, IV, 180; Carrera y Pujal, *Historia Política y Económica de Cataluña*, IV, 175; Matilla Tascón, *op. cit.*, I, 147, 195, 222, 266, 273, 275, 310, 361, 371, 373, 399, 406, 459, 460.

tury saw improvements in the crude, awkward coinage of the nation. And of importance to economic advancement were the rising population as well as the redistribution of Spain's inhabitants from rural to urban regions. Spanish America also began to be a crucial influence by providing markets for the rapidly growing industrial centers of Valencia and Barcelona. Such were the factors that complemented the royal program of industrial expansion.

Despite these friendly conditions, profound and formidable obstacles lay in the path of economic growth. Since history began, Spain had been divided geographically, politically, and economically; and the last half of the eighteenth century saw these divisions impede economic integration of the peninsula. The Catholic Church, with its vast landholdings and policy of almsgiving, perpetuated the inefficient use of wealth. Agricultural tenure, the Mesta (or sheepherders' guild), inadequate communications, inferior resource endowments, and international conflicts all counteracted the forces at work building industry.

The next section of this chapter examines those influences that complemented the king's policies of industrial development; the last section concerns those influences that opposed economic growth.

FACTORS FAVORING GROWTH

Enlightened despotism arrived in Spain with Philip V and his French entourage. Holding that "public welfare must be fostered, but the public must be given no participation in government," this political philosophy proved more efficient and effective than the irresolute policies of government in the seventeenth century.[16] Philip V employed French ministers, reorganized the government of his new land, and applied economic policies that struck at the core of Spain's economic problems.[17] Even though French influence waned and Italian prominence grew when the widowed Philip married Isabel Farnese in 1714, the Spanish monarchy remained relatively strong and informed.[18] With the passing years, Ferdinand VI and Charles III adopted, enlarged, and refined this enlightened central control. Moreover, they replaced

[16] Rafael Altamira y Crevea, *A History of Spain from the Beginning to the Present Day,* translated by Mina Lee (New York, 1958), p. 438.

[17] Charles E. Chapman, *A History of Spain* (New York, 1938), p. 434; Altamira y Crevea, *op. cit.,* 427; Robert Jones Shafer, *The Economic Societies in the Modern World, 1763–1821* (Syracuse, 1958), p. 7.

[18] Altamira y Crevea, *loc. cit.;* Chapman, *op. cit.,* pp. 382, 387.

the ministers of foreign origin with many able Spaniards, including the Marquis de la Ensenada, the counts of Valparaiso and Campomanes, and Gaspar Melchor de Jovellanos.

One of the first significant consequences of the reign of Philip V was a rush of French scholarly works into Spain. From these words and thoughts came a rekindling of Spanish intellectual curiosity.[19] Publication of books and newspapers increased markedly, especially after 1750, even though the king licensed and censured printing.[20] Often the government subsidized literature. Charles III, for example, published and distributed Campomanes' major writings; and the General Council of Commerce and Money assisted Antonio de Capmany y de Montpalau and Eugenio Larruga y Boneta with their important works.[21]

Spanish writers debated the causes of their homeland's economic dilemma. Their discourses aroused the public's interest, formed an atmosphere acceptable to change, and influenced the policies of kings. Ranging from hard and fast mercantilists to Smithian liberals, they spoke critically of conditions on the peninsula: they blamed economic backwardness on the poor governmental organization, the lack of protection of industry, and oppressive taxation.[22] All offered solutions. Some argued for freedom of internal and external commerce, better roads and more canals, and a reduction in the power of guilds; others suggested forbidding the import of foreign goods and export of raw materials, abolishing the *censos* (purchase of annuities), and employing the idle.[23]

The words of a few rang out above all others. Francisco Romá y Rosell, one of the most distinguished economists of the century, blamed the destruction of Spain's economy on the influx of specie in the sixteenth and seventeenth centuries: a subsequent rise of prices, followed by the introduction of foreign goods, had hobbled domestic industry.[24] He consequently feared an increase in

---

[19] Shafer, *op. cit.*, p. 17; Carrera y Pujal, *Historia de la Economía Española, III,* 455; Richard Herr, *The Eighteenth Century Revolution in Spain* (New Jersey, 1958), pp. 52–57.

[20] Carrera y Pujal, *op. cit.*, III, 456. Of censorship, Shafer says ". . . the censorship was somewhat relaxed, especially under Charles III. Much restrictive law remained in force, of course, and the Index continued to expand its lists, in the middle and later century especially anathematizing the works of the enlightenment" (*op. cit.*, p. 19).

[21] Carrera y Pujal, *op. cit.*, III, 457.

[22] For a presentation of these writers and their thoughts, see *ibid.*, 458–650.

[23] *Ibid.*

[24] *Ibid.*, p. 483.

the money supply without an associated increase in production. Romá y Rosell's program for economic regeneration included development of adequate communications, reorganization of guilds, prohibitions of the export of wool, and freedom of trade in grain.[25]

Pedro Rodriquez, Count of Campomanes, probably influenced Spanish economic thought of his time more than any other writer. His merit lay not in his ideas, for they were not new, but rather in his attempt to create an atmosphere favorable to the study of the problems and to the growth of industry.[26] Campomanes campaigned during the last quarter of the century for household industry—the integration of agricultural and industrial tasks. If a farmer devoted his idle time to weaving, reasoned Campomanes, production costs of weaving should fall. To implement this and other programs, he urged Spaniards to form economic societies and initiate economic revival on the local level.[27]

Although he fiercely attacked guilds, Campomanes wished to reform, not suppress, them: reduce the exorbitant expenses of examination, destroy their monopoly over output and employment, and prohibit them from restricting anyone from producing or selling goods or from using new methods.[28] Contrasted to this liberal position, he defended the prohibition of exports of raw materials needed in domestic industry, and he considered it preferable to introduce foreign artisans and thereafter to produce goods rather than to allow foreign merchandise into Spain.[29]

Campomanes argued for a free internal commerce but for a controlled external commerce. His philosophy therefore ultimately demanded a powerful yet gifted king who would exercise final control over the economic system. In contrast to this quasi mercantilism, Francisco Cabarrús, Gaspar Melchor de Jovellanos, and Valentin Foranda forcefully spoke for political and economic liberalism. Cabarrús, Frenchman by birth, Spaniard by choice, financier by profession, combined his vocation with a literary avocation and influenced the course of economic history during the final two decades of the century. Spain's first paper money and national bank owe much to him.[30]

---

[25] *Ibid.*

[26] *Ibid.*, p. 518.

[27] *Ibid.*, p. 523; Altamira y Crevea, *op. cit.*, p. 465.

[28] For his position on guilds, see Pedro Rodriguez, Conde de Campomanes, *Apéndice a la Educación Popular*, 4 vols. (Madrid, 1775–1777), III, iii-ccix.

[29] Carrera y Pujal, *op. cit.*, III, 534.

[30] *Ibid.*, 615–621. For Cabarrús' part in founding the Bank of Spain, see Earl

Gaspar Melchor de Jovellanos, an eloquent and articulate member of the Economic Society at Madrid and minister under Charles III, authored various papers that illustrated the closeness of his ideas to those of the physiocrats and Adam Smith. With a style both elegant and simple, he argued before the General Council of Commerce and Money for, among other issues, the suppression of guilds and unrestricted import of muslins.[31] Removing all obstructions from the market and thereby liberalizing the economy was the purpose of Jovellanos' efforts.

The breadth of Valentin Foranda's liberalism, in contrast, embraced all human activities, not just those of the market. His thoughts on economic matters show a complete confidence in the price system as a regulator of economic activity. On taxes, tariffs, grants of privilege, and guilds he strikingly approximates Adam Smith. A foe of the mercantilist doctrine of a favorable balance of trade, Foranda reasoned that even if one nation did corner all the world's silver, its prices would rise, foreign goods would rush in, and the precious silver would stream away.[32] He criticized grants of privilege to industry by asserting that such aid was useless if a business could survive without it, while if it was needed this was proof of inefficiency.[33] Consistent with his repugnance for any interference with the market, Foranda envisioned guild ordinances as a "complex of statutes, extravagant and tyrannical, dictated by avarice, without respect for the unfortunate luck of the poor. . . ."[34]

Although Foranda, Jovellanos, and other liberals influenced economic discussion and policy in their time, they presented a philosophy more acceptable to the early nineteenth than late eighteenth century. Royal absolutism rejected laissez-faire and embraced the liberalized mercantilism of moderate economists such as Campomanes and Floridablanca.[35] Instructed by this tem-

---

J. Hamilton, "The Foundation of the Bank of Spain," *Journal of Political Economy,* LIII (1945), 97–114; "The First Twenty Years of the Bank of Spain," *Journal of Political Economy,* LIV (1946), 17–37, 116–140.

[31] A number of his papers appear in *Biblioteca de Autores Españoles* (Madrid, 1859), L.

[32] Valentin Foronda, *Cartas sobre los Asuntos mas Esquisitos de la Económica y Leyes Criminales,* 2 vols. (Madrid, 1789), I, letter dated August 3, 1788.

[33] Foronda also believed that subsidies raised the price of the subsidized product (*ibid.,* May 29, 1788).

[34] *Ibid.,* June 14, 1788. When speaking against restrictions placed on guildsmen by ordinances, Foronda declared, "What would you say to one of the statutes that excludes women from the function most appropriate to their sex? Is this not the same as inciting them to prostitution?" (*ibid.,* June 14, 1788).

[35] The acceptance of liberalized mercantilism was nevertheless an important

perate counsel, kings swept away many impediments to individual enterprise, but at the same time enlarged their control over the direction of economic activity.

One other result of this resurgence in speculation on economic matters was that men of influence became fired with enthusiasm and formed economic societies.[36] Privately organized and financed, but actively promoted by the king, these societies encouraged agriculture, industry, commerce, and arts and sciences.[37] They sprang up during the last fifty years of the century in numerous cities and towns where, among other activities, they translated and published foreign books, supervised instruction in many fields of thought and activity, encouraged new methods of production, experimented with new processes and products, and provided work for the unemployed.[38]

Of all the economic societies formed during the century, one of the most important as well as the first to appear was the Basque Society of the Friends of the Country.[39] Created in 1765, it, among many other activities, established a school at Vergara in which primary letters, religion, humanities, mathematics, physical sciences, chemistry, and mineralogy were taught.[40] In his *Discurso Sobre el Fomento de la Industria Popular*, Campomanes enthusiastically supported the Basque society and proposed that noblemen and other influential persons form similar organizations throughout the land.[41] The Royal Economic Society of Madrid received its license in June, 1775;[42] fifty-six societies existed in 1789; seventy-two in 1804.[43]

---

change, for the bulk of Spaniards "remained conservative and traditionalist" (Shafer, *op. cit.*, p. 23).

[36] *Ibid.*, pp. 17–23.

[37] Herr, *op. cit.*, pp. 154–155; Shafer, *op. cit.*, pp. 64–68, 75–110; Carrera y Pujal, *op. cit.*, IV, 9, 141.

[38] Shafer, *op. cit.*, pp. 64, 88.

[39] Carrera y Pujal, *op. cit.*, IV, 9; Altamira y Crevea, *op. cit.*, p. 455; Herr, *op. cit.*, p. 154; Shafer, *op. cit.*, pp. 29, 30.

[40] The Basque Society named its school the Real Seminario Patriótico Bascongado (Herr, *op. cit.*, p. 157; Shafer, *op. cit.*, p. 38). Of this school, Shafer writes, "In 1768 Society members were teaching mathematics, algebra, geometry, geography, history, Latin, French, dancing, and fencing" (Shafer, *loc. cit.*).

[41] Herr, *op. cit.*, p. 155; Shafer, *op. cit.*, p. 49; Carrera y Pujal, *loc. cit.*; Campomanes, *Discurso sobre el Fomento de la Industria Popular* (Madrid, 1774), pp. 141–157.

[42] Herr, *op. cit.*, p. 156; Carrera y Pujal, *loc. cit.*; Shafer, *op. cit.*, pp. 51, 52.

[43] Herr, *loc. cit.*; Altamira y Crevea, *loc. cit.* Shafer states that "some seventy Economic Societies of Friends of the Country were formed in Spain between 1770 and 1820. . . ." He cites the economic societies of Tudela and Baeza as the only ones formed between 1764 and 1775. Carrera y Pujal adds the Conferencia de Física at Barcelona and the Academia de Agricultura at Lerida as societies formed

Despite this large number of economic societies, only a minority actively promoted education and industry. For either a lack of funds or interest doomed many in small towns and cities;[44] and others withered before a hostile rural oligarchy and the Church.[45] The former saw the societies as rivals for the king's favor, while the latter objected to their liberal teachings. Even though many failed to contribute much, the few active societies in general furthered the dissemination of technical knowledge and skill and thus promoted economic growth.[46]

It was in education that economic societies contributed most significantly to Spain's economic revival during the period 1750–1800.[47] Through these years Spanish kings also realized the importance of education and hence assisted in establishing numerous trade schools and led the reorganization of higher education. Prominent among such efforts were the schools for spinning wool. As a means of ensuring an adequate supply of yarn, the royal factories at Guadalaxara, Brihuega, and San Fernando, established many schools in adjacent villages, beginning in the third quarter of the century.[48] A large supply of yarn as well as a supply of trained spinners resulted. Noting this success, Charles III on May 21, 1786, charged his provincial officials with establishing, conserving, and promoting similar spinning schools throughout Spain.[49] He hoped to provide yarn for weaving and employment for many idle persons. Other trade schools for dyeing, design, printing on cloth, and similar tasks came about in parallel fashion, thereby adding to Spain's supply of skills.[50]

Higher education, which had been free from royal influence and subject only to the Church, especially the Society of Jesus,

---

during those eleven years (Shafer, *op. cit.*, p. 48; Carrera y Pujal, *loc. cit.*). Shafer estimates the total membership of the societies at less than five thousand in 1800, only a part of which actively took part (Shafer, *op. cit.*, p. 115).

[44] Herr, *op. cit.*, p. 159; Shafer, *op. cit.*, p. 56.

[45] Herr, *op. cit.*, p. 160; Shafer, *op. cit.*, p. 57.

[46] *Ibid.*, p. 117.

[47] Herr, *op. cit.*, p. 157; Shafer, *op. cit.*, pp. 55, 84–88; Carrera y Pujal, *op. cit.*, IV, 13; Altamira y Crevea, *loc. cit.*

[48] AGS, *Secretaría de Hacienda*, legs. 765, 776, 780.

[49] AHN, *Biblioteca, Colección de Reales Cédulas*, 1786, XVII, 753; AMH, *op. cit.*, XXIX, 216–224. Charles III stipulated that private manufacturers should have precedence over governmental authorities in establishing spinning schools; moreover, he imposed a tax of $\frac{1}{2}$ real an arroba of washed wool and $\frac{1}{4}$ real an arroba of dirty wool exported from Spain, the receipts from which should aid these new institutions (AHN, *Biblioteca, Colección de Reales Cédulas*, 1786, XVII, 753).

[50] For example, see: Gallardo Fernandez, *op. cit.*, II, 396; Carrera y Pujal, *Historia Política y Económica de Cataluña*, IV, 221; Matilla Tascón, *op. cit.*, I, 393, 441, 514, 542.

underwent substantial changes during the last third of the century.[51] Scholasticism in 1750 still dominated the curricula; neglected were mathematics, physics, and modern philosophy. But after Charles III expelled the Jesuits in 1767, he resolutely moved into the vacuum and reorganized the universities of Spain.[52] The Imperial College of Madrid opened again in 1771 as the Royal College of Sciences and Letters of San Isidro. Its faculty, now minus regular clergy, taught experimental physics, the laws of nature and nations, and logic.[53] Reorganized in 1769, the University of Seville received a revamped curricula, new professors, and buildings taken from the Jesuits.[54]

The Council of Castile took a significant step in modernizing higher education when in 1770 it commanded all universities to develop new curricula and to include in them moral philosophy, elementary mathematics, and experimental physics.[55] The University of Salamanca, Spain's leading intellectual center, balked at the proposed changes; however, many of the twenty or so other universities on the peninsula more readily accepted change. Valencia, with 2,400 students, for example, progressed most impressively.[56] Still, perhaps a majority of teachers in Spain steadfastly refused to abandon Scholasticism, and the role of innovator fell to a minority of professors who adopted modern texts on philosophy and advanced the instruction of mathematics and medicine.[57] This "new spirit of education" aided the growth of industry by graduating persons with more fundamental knowledge of the arts and sciences and with more enlightened attitudes toward progress.

While the economic societies and the kings created, aided, and reorganized schools and universities, still another institution, the councils of commerce, assisted education in the arts and crafts as part of their mission to promote trade and industry.[58] The Gen-

---

[51] Herr, *op. cit.*, p. 24.

[52] *Ibid.*, p. 163.

[53] *Ibid.*, pp. 163–164.

[54] *Ibid.*, p. 165.

[55] *Ibid.*

[56] *Ibid.*, p. 166.

[57] Specialized institutions appeared during this century, bypassing the traditional colleges and universities and teaching progressive knowledge—the Royal Spanish Academy in 1713, the Academy of History in 1738, the Academy of Fine Arts of Saint Ferdinand in 1774, special colleges of surgery and pharmacy, the School of Mines at Almadén, and a Museum and Garden of Botany at Madrid (Shafer, *op. cit.*, p. 20).

[58] Herr, *op. cit.*, p. 156; Shafer, *op. cit.*, p. 25; Carrera y Pujal, *Historia de la Economía Española*, V, 485. See also: Ángel Ruiz y Pablo, *Historia de la Real*

eral Council of Commerce and Money first appeared on January 29, 1679, when Charles II asked the Duke of Medinaceli to form a council and study means by which to reëstablish industry.[59] Extinguished in 1680, reëstablished in 1682, and reorganized and enlarged several times thereafter, the Council assumed ever increasingly important functions throughout the eighteenth century.[60] It had jurisdiction over commercial and industrial disputes in Spain, formulated many of the king's economic policies, and in general administered the programs of economic development.[61] Local councils of commerce, under the jurisdiction of the General Council of Commerce and Money, were created in important cities, including Valencia and Barcelona.[62] The General Council and the local councils opposed interference from local officials and thereby gave a more consistent and continuous application to royal economic policies.

Thus it was that with the arrival of Bourbon kings, Spain awoke intellectually; an energetic, widespread debate of economic matters erupted and influenced political action. Economic societies were born of this atmosphere and entered the field of action, applying modern ideas to specific problems. New Schools were a major contribution. Kings also created, promoted, and reorganized schools and universities. Economic societies, modern education, and councils of commerce acted as vehicles and catalysts for the economic reforms of the period 1750–1800.

These beneficial happenings were joined by still others. Among them were monetary factors. Though Ferdinand VI adopted the "prudent policies" of Philip V and thereby maintained the integrity of Spain's coinage, he passed on to Charles III an heterogeneous money supply, which one observer classed as more similar to the money of a barbarous people than to a great nation.[63] Copper coins abounded so that they "circulated in large bags" instead of being counted.[64] For twelve years, Charles III ignored these and other defects of the monetary system. Then on

Junta Particular de Comercio de Barcelona, 1758–1847 (Barcelona, 1919), and Larruga y Boneta, *op. cit.*, IV, 229.

[59] *Ibid.*

[60] *Ibid.*, 230–258.

[61] AHMB, *Junta General de Comercio*, LIX, 159; Larruga y Boneta, *op. cit.*, IV, 240–242.

[62] Carrera y Pujal, *loc. cit.*; Herr, *loc. cit.*

[63] Edward Clarke, *Letters Concerning the Spanish Nation, Written at Madrid during the Years 1760 and 1761* (London, 1763), p. 271; also quoted in Earl J. Hamilton, *War and Prices in Spain, 1651–1800* (Cambridge, 1947), p. 63, n. 31.

[64] Clarke, *loc. cit.*; Hamilton, *loc. cit.*

Christmas Day, 1771, he ordered the mint at Segovia to strike new coins of pure copper; the old copper coins could remain in circulation for six years.[65] Since the mint coined a total of 8,172,440 vellon reals but retired only about 1 million vellon reals of old coins by April 27, 1787, fractional coinage increased by more than 7 million vellon reals.[66]

On May 29, 1772, Charles initiated the only other major change in coinage during the century by calling in all gold and silver coins and by ordering the mints at Seville and Madrid to strike new ones.[67] His purpose was to change the design of these coins to make it more difficult to counterfeit, file, and clip them; however, unbeknown to his subjects, Charles ordered the gold content of the new coins reduced.[68]

Despite this instance of underhandedness, Charles improved Spain's coinage and in so doing facilitated the exchange of goods and services. He also introduced his subjects to paper money, but here the aftermath is not so clear. Soon after hostilities with England began in 1779, the royal treasury stood empty and Charles searched for revenue.[69] Either he would not or could not tax to raise sufficient revenue; and since he was unable to borrow large sums, he accepted the offer of a syndicate of Dutch, French, and Spanish merchants in the summer of 1780 to provide funds in return for interest-bearing paper currency (*vales reales*) which would circulate as legal tender.[70] The first issue consisted of 16,500 vales of 600 pesos each or a total of 9.9 million vellon pesos.[71] Continued financial pressure forced an issue of 17,677 vales of 300 vellon pesos (*medios vales*) on March 20, 1781, and 49,333 vales also of 300 vellon pesos on June 20, 1782. To pass this last group of vales and to make foreign remittances, Charles on June 2, 1782, chartered the Bank of Spain.[72]

[65] *Ibid.*, p. 63.

[66] Vellon remained at par in spite of the large increase in supply, according to Professor Hamilton, because of rapid population increase, increase in wealth, rise in prices, and wholesale expulsion of silver by the adverse bimetallic ratio after 1779 (*ibid.*, p. 65).

[67] *Ibid.*, p. 66.

[68] *Ibid.*, pp. 66–67.

[69] *Ibid.*, p. 78.

[70] *Ibid.*, pp. 78–79.

[71] A vellon peso was an accounting unit worth 15 reals and 2 maravedis. Each vale bore 4 percent interest annually and was to pass at face value plus accrued interest. Vales were not legal tender for retail transactions nor for wholesale transactions of less than 600 pesos; they could not be forced on employees for wages, salaries, or pensions (*ibid.*, p. 79).

[72] Hamilton, "The Foundations of the Bank of Spain," and "The First Twenty Years of the Bank of Spain."

Only several minor issues of vales occurred during the peaceful years of 1784 to 1793.[73] By 1791, 35,565,808 vellon pesos worth of vales still circulated in Spain.[74] But future events assured the increase of this sum. War broke out with France in March, 1793; in the next twenty-eight months Charles IV ordered consecutive issues of vales of 16.2 million, 18 million, and 30 million vellon pesos and thereby trebled Spain's paper currency.[75] Then war with England flared in the summer of 1796; after financing the first three years of hostilities with the sale of bonds and with mercantile credit, Charles issued 53,109,300 vellon pesos worth of vales on April 6, 1799.[76]

These outpourings of paper currency merged with rising imports of specie from America and swelled the money supply in Spain during the period 1750–1800. Professor Earl J. Hamilton claims that commodity prices rose by nearly 100 percent,[77] wages by less than 20 percent. And since wages amounted to about two-thirds of the cost of most items, Professor Hamilton hypothesizes that the substantial lag of wages behind commodity prices raised business profits enormously and thereby provided extra motivation, as well as funds, for capital investment.[78] It is to this phenomenon of profit inflation that Professor Hamilton ascribes the growth of Spanish industry.[79] But this intriguingly simple explanation of economic development has been vigorously challenged by economists in recent years. So telling has been their criticism, that the wage-lag hypothesis in its present state must be abandoned and the effect of price inflation on Spanish industrial

---

[73] The exceptions were that Charles III issued 11,000 vales of 600 pesos each in July, 1785, and December, 1788, for completion of the Imperial Canal of Aragon and work on the Tauste Canal, and the Philippine Company on March 3, 1791, issued 3,990,000 pesos worth (Hamilton, *War and Prices in Spain*, p. 81).

[74] Although vales circulated near par when first issued, they dropped to a low of 22 percent in October, 1782, in response to military defeats and more issues of vales. Soon after the war, however, they recovered and from 1786 to 1792 circulated at a premium of 1 to 2 percent in terms of specie (*ibid.*, pp. 81–82).

[75] *Ibid.*, p. 83.

[76] *Ibid.* By 1794 vales had fallen below par as new issues were ordered and outstanding vales were not being redeemed. The discount reached 22 percent in the summer of 1795, then recovered to about 5 percent after conclusion of peace with France and before war with England in 1796, and thenceforth declined rapidly until it stood at 75 percent in 1802 (*ibid.*, pp. 84–85).

[77] *Ibid.*, p. 220.

[78] Earl J. Hamilton, "Profit Inflation and the Industrial Revolution, 1751–1800," *Quarterly Journal of Economics*, LVI (1942), 256–273; reprinted in Frederic C. Lane and Jelle C. Riemersma, eds., *Enterprise and Secular Change* (Homewood, Illinois, 1953), pp. 328, 332; Hamilton, *War and Prices in Spain*, p. 220.

[79] *Ibid.*, pp. 220–222.

growth during the years 1750 to 1800 must be considered inde-
terminate.[80]

More intelligible were the consequences of Spain's increasing
population. The number of inhabitants on the peninsula prob-

[80] R. A. Kessel and A. A. Alchian argue that "unwarranted validity has been
assigned to the wage-lag hypothesis, given the character of the evidence that has
been used to support it." They deny that inflation brings about a negative correlation between real wages on the one hand and money wages and prices on the
other, i.e., that wages must lag behind prices during inflation. To use this idea
as a basis for explaining time series of wages and prices, they claim, is extremely
difficult, for the level of real wages can be affected by any number of real forces,
such as, for example, changes in the size of the labor force relative to the stock
of capital. "Furthermore, increases in the general price level can be produced by
changes in the real stock of goods, e.g., by droughts, plagues, wars, etc., even
with a fixed money stock." Thus, when one observes any time series of real wages
one faces a virtually impossible task of determining whether changes in the level
of real wages occurred because of either real or monetary forces.
   Although Hamilton is aware of this problem of imputation, he ignores it,
according to Kessel and Alchian, when he directly discusses his wage-lag hypothesis
and thereby implicitly attributes any fall in real wages to monetary forces. But
a close examination of the historical evidence turns up real forces that explain the
variation in real wages. On top of this criticism, Alchian and Kessel point out that
Hamilton's data do not always unambiguously show a fall in real wages during
selected inflations.
   David Felix states his major objection to the wage-lag, or profit inflation,
hypothesis in the following manner: "The most obvious criticism of the profit
inflation thesis is that there is no correlation either between the degree of price
inflation and the degree of profit inflation, or between the rates of profit inflation
and the apparent rates of industrial growth. Spain, undergoing the greatest price
inflation during the 150 to 200 years of the Price Revolution, had the least
profit inflation. . . . France, with the least price inflation, had the greatest profit
inflation. England with less profit inflation than France had a greater rate of
industrial growth. Moreover, during the seventeenth century English wages rose
more rapidly than prices with no apparent retarding effect on the rate of industrial
growth. Clearly, price inflation was not synonymous with profit inflation, and a
widening spread between wage and price indices did not necessarily mean a more
rapid rate of growth." Before Felix had voiced these doubts, a noted economic
historian, John U. Nef, had taken issue with Hamilton's hypothesis when he
compared the degree of profit inflation (or lag of wages behind prices) in France
and England with the rates of industrial growth in these two countries. The
comparison did not support the wage-lag thesis.
   Focusing on Hamilton's explanation for the growth of Spanish industry during
the eighteenth century, Felix again suggests that Hamilton may have misread the
evidence. "Did the industrial growth, after all," asks Felix, "depend on profit inflation from rising prices or on independent institutional factors and the increased
inflow of specie?"
   Even if one were to ignore these damaging criticisms, still other difficulties
remain to becloud this explanation for Spain's economic growth. Professor Hamilton's most reliable and abundant price and wage data for the eighteenth century
are for New Castile; those for Old Castile, Andalusia, and Valencia act as checks
on the former's reliability. In all four regions he discovered profit inflation. But
there is no unambiguous evidence that any significant growth in industry (at least
not in the important textile field) developed in New Castile. The same is true for
Old Castile and New Castile. For Catalonia, however, where surely the most

ably rose by about 42 percent from 1750 to 1800.[81] Of greater importance than mere size, however, was the redistribution that transpired. Born in rural areas and unable or unwilling to earn their sustenance there, many thousands of persons migrated to cities where they swelled the supply of labor.[82] Barcelona, for example, grew from 37,000 in 1715 to 130,000 in 1800.[83] This urbanization exerted a downward pressure on wage rates. In at least two other interrelated ways the growing population and the increasing density may have favorably influenced industrial growth. First, accompanying the enlarging centers of population were the economies of a more refined specialization of labor. Second, with a larger population and more densely populated cities entrepreneurs could increase the size of their plants and thus enjoy the advantages of increasing returns to scale.

A similar growth in the population of Spain's American colonies enlarged her overseas markets. By the end of the eighteenth century between 14 million and 18,802,000 individuals lived under Spanish rule in America; more than 8 million of them were *mestizos* and whites.[84] Guided by mercantilistic dogma, kings of Spain for several centuries had attempted to control closely the commerce between homeland and foreign possessions. To obtain gold and silver was the overwhelming aim. But as population grew and cities expanded, thus becoming more than foreign out-

---

dramatic industrial ascent in all Spain occurred, particularly in cotton textiles, Professor Hamilton did not develop wage and price indices. But he relates economic expansion in Catalonia with profit inflation in New Castile. Only in Valencia did considerable industrial expansion concur with a lag of wages behind prices (R. A. Kessel and A. A. Alchian, "The Meaning and Validity of the Inflation-Induced Lag of Wages Behind Prices," *The American Economic Review,* L [March, 1960], 43, 44, 49, 50, 64; David Felix, "Profit Inflation and Industrial Growth: The Historical Record and Contemporary Analogies," *The Quarterly Journal of Economics,* LXX [August, 1956], 444, 453–454; John U. Nef, "Prices and Industrial Capitalism in France and England, 1540–1640," *Economic History Review,* VII [1936–1937], 155–185; Hamilton, *War and Prices in Spain,* pp. 5, 211, 221–222).

[81] Supposedly the population of Spain at about midcentury reached 7,423,590 and by 1797 it stood at 10,541,221 (Herr, *op. cit.,* p. 86; José Canga Argüelles, *Diccionario de Hacienda,* 2 vols. [Madrid, 1833–1834], II, 409; *Censo Español Ejecutado de Orden del Rey Comunicada por el Excelentisimo Señor Conde de Floridablanca, Primer Secretario de Estado y del Despacho, en el Año de 1787; Censo de la Población de España de el Año de 1797* [Madrid, 1787], *Executado de Orden del Rey;* Manuel Escudé Bartoli, *La Producción Española en el Siglo XIX* [Barcelona, 1895], p. 12).

[82] Altamira y Crevea, *op. cit.,* p. 468; AHN, *Consejo,* leg. 51501 (1); Shafer, *op. cit.,* p. 91.

[83] Canga Argüelles, *op. cit.,* I, 130.

[84] Altamira y Crevea, *op. cit.,* p. 479; Artiñano y de Galdacano, *La Producción Español en la Edad Moderna* (Madrid, 1914), p. 60.

posts, Spanish colonial policy began to shift ground, and the importance of America as a market for home production rose in the scale of royal considerations. To promote the exploitation of this huge market, kings of Spain insisted that Spanish ships carry all merchandise entering American ports, placed tariffs on foreign goods entering the colonies, and gradually permitted any Spaniard to trade directly from any part of Spain with any part of the Indies.[85] The crown also tried desperately to stem the flow of contraband arriving in America and hence to provide a more protected market for Spanish industry.

INFLUENCES BLOCKING ECONOMIC GROWTH

Set against these complementary factors were a number of influences that adversely affected economic progress. It is to these conditions that lack of growth in most areas of Spain can be traced. Industrial advance suffered from the geographical, political, and economic division of the peninsula; social divisions and attitudes also aligned against industry; the Catholic Church dampened economic progress by giving alms and holding much land idle; agricultural tenure limited the mobility of private and municipal lands; the Mesta restricted the progress of enclosures; inadequate transportation facilities hindered the movement of merchandise and people; a poor endowment of natural resources damned most regions to poverty; and several harsh wars drained resources from Spain and separated her industry from its markets. Such impediments strongly counteracted those factors working to build Spanish industry. This section examines these obstacles to economic growth.

Mountain ranges crisscross the peninsula and divide Spain into a number of regions. Running along the Atlantic coast to the north in an extension of the Pyrenees, the Cantabrian range isolates Spain's northern seashore from the interior; a series of ranges slashes the peninsula from Portugal to the Mediterranean, separating Old Castile, Leon, and Aragon from New Castile and southern Spain; the Iberian range further separates the northern half of the peninsula as it shields Old Castile from Navarre and Aragon; to the south, the Sierra Morena runs from east to west and divides New Castile from Andalusia; and the Betique mountain range dominates the southern Mediterranean coast. Between

---

[85] Clarence Henry Haring, *The Spanish Empire in America* (New York, 1947), p. 341.

these strings of mountains lie a few fertile valleys and vast expanses of windswept, arid plateau lands.

Spanish history bears the mark of this geographical dismemberment. Each geographically contained region developed along unique lines through the centuries. Isolated from one another by mountain barriers, separate kingdoms emerged with distinct laws, taxes, customs, and languages.[86] Gradually over the centuries political unity began to appear. It was with the marriage of Ferdinand and Isabel that the kingdoms of Castile, Leon, and Aragon finally became one.[87] Nevertheless, Aragon, Catalonia, Valencia, Navarre, and the Basque provinces retained substantial political and economic autonomy. So nearly independent were Navarre and the Basque provinces during the eighteenth century that their borders with other Spanish provinces were treated by Spain as customs frontiers. Catalonia, Aragon, and Valencia, however, supported Archduke Charles in 1700 for the throne of Spain and lost. Philip V penalized them by revoking most of their prerogatives: perhaps of most importance, he imposed tax systems supposedly equivalent to the one in Castile and Leon, and he no longer convened the Cortes of these mutinous regions. Cities there could only send representatives to the Cortes of Castile.[88]

Despite this imposition of royal absolutism, a sentiment of separatism remained, especially in Catalonia. Animosity, suspicion, contempt, and jealousy marred the relations between Madrid and these areas. More often than not, kings concentrated their programs of development in Castile and Leon, slighting Catalonia, Aragon, and Valencia.[89] Moreover, Castilians usually received the important governmental posts. This lack of political homogeneity affected the coördination of the king's policies and slowed the rate of growth in some provinces.

---

[86] C. Perez-Bustamente, *Compendio de Historia de España* (Madrid, 1957), pp. 169–170.

[87] *Ibid.*, pp. 204–206.

[88] Herr, *op. cit.*, p. 11.

[89] For example, kings erected their manufactories for fine woolens, silks, cottons, and linens in central Spain; moreover, they openly favored Castilian producers and often ignored the pleas for assistance from Catalonian merchants. Charles III, a most enlightened king, banned the import of cotton fabrics on June 24, 1770, and November 4, 1771, not because he wished to aid the calico industry at Barcelona but because foreign cottons substituted for woolens, linens, and silks made elsewhere on the peninsula (AMH, *op. cit.*, XVII, 228; XIX, 97–104, 105–108; XX, 247–252; AHN, *Consejo, Libros de Govierno*, 1770, fols. 334–337, 339–341; 1771, fols., 498–501; AHN, *Biblioteca, Colección de Reales Cédulas*, 1770, VI, 270, 273; 1771, VII, 318; Carrera y Pujal, *op. cit.*, V, 333; Ruiz y Pablo, *op. cit.*, p. 99).

Physical barriers likewise affected Spain's economy. Rugged mountains, treacherous gorges, swift, unpredictable streams, and harsh weather hindered the free flow of commodities and knowledge of prices from one area to another. Internal customs barriers, though modified by Philip V, further splintered Spain into regional markets. Merchandise nevertheless laboriously moved from province to province as arbitragers sought profits whenever price differentials exceeded transportation costs and risk factors.[90]

Besides Spain's geographical, political, and economic cleavages, a structure of social classes existed that also retarded industrial growth. Of the nobility, the grandees of Spain and titles of Castile ranked highest. In 1787 there were 119 grandees and 535 titles, and ownership of the large seigniories and entailed estates rested with these two groups.[91] Next in rank came the caballeros —men whom the king had named to life membership in one of four military orders.[92] The caballeros shared the income from landholdings obtained during the reconquest.[93] Below these nobles were the lower aristocracy, most of whom lived in Asturias, the Basque provinces, and Navarre. Although they enjoyed the title of nobility, they could hardly be distinguished from commoners. Many were poor, some even begged.[94] All nobles, however, enjoyed legal privileges: they could not be arrested for debts nor forced to quarter soldiers, and they had the right to display their coats of arms and be called "don." [95]

Industrialists, merchants, landowners, and professional literary men formed a middle class that held a position below the nobility. Their wealth or well-being distinguished them from the lower classes, and their lack of title from the nobility.[96] Workingmen, neither wealthy nor titled, filled out the population. As wage earners in towns and cities and as wage earners, tenant farmers, sharecroppers, or small landowners in rural areas, they supplied Spain with its manpower.

---

[90] This is one reason why Professor Hamilton's price indexes for different regions in Spain correlate so closely year by year. Apparently arbitragers acted swiftly enough to overcome price differentials that might have existed from one year to the next. However, monthly time series for these regions, for example, would probably correlate less closely and thus support the existence of regional markets.

[91] Herr, *op. cit.*, p. 96.

[92] *Ibid.*

[93] Those holdings consisted of 3 cities and 783 other places (*ibid.*).

[94] *Ibid.*, p. 97.

[95] Altamira y Crevea, *op. cit.*, p. 458; Herr, *loc. cit.*

[96] Altamira y Crevea, *op. cit.*, p. 460.

Members of the middle and lower classes envied and respected the nobility; many imagined themselves attaining rank some day.[97] Even though they had little chance of achieving their dreams, at least they could emulate the ways of life of nobles. The traditional repugnance felt by nobles for an industrial or commercial occupation therefore became also a trait of commoners. Middle-class merchants and industrialists, for example, once they became wealthy, purchased country estates, retired, and urged their sons to enter honorable professions such as government service or the clergy.[98] Eugenio Larruga decried this practice, stating that it harmed Spain's economy.

The Spanish producers who, by the good fortune of their business or by some event, become rich are considered disgraced if their sons enter their business, and so they put them in other careers which are honorable: this damage is grave and is indefensible whenever the arts are undervalued.[99]

Hence, the stigma of being a merchant or a producer restricted entry into the entrepreneurial ranks; a similar psychology existed among laborers. They looked upon certain crafts as degrading.[100] Carding wool was one of those. So general had the contempt for the trade become that when a person spoke ill of another he might use the expression "send him to card."[101] Examples of ridicule and mistreatment of persons exercising this and other trades abound in contemporary manuscripts and clearly suggest the seriousness of such intolerance.[102] Manuel Colmeiro correlated these "vile trades" with the worship of nobility.

------

[97] As shown by their coats of arms and titles of "don," an obsessive sense of rank marked Spanish nobility in the eighteenth century. From 1750 to 1800 kings stimulated this pride by creating several new orders. With rank often came vast wealth; nobles with seigniorial estates and large entailed estates received enormous incomes—in 1787, seigniorial rights were held over 17 cities, 2,358 villas, and 8,818 villages and towns. The Duke of Medinaceli received 1 million vellon reals annually from his fisheries alone; while the Count of Aranda had a yearly income of 1 million vellon reals (Antonio Dominguez Ortiz, "El Ocaso del Régimen Señorial en la España del Siglo XVIII," *Revista Internacional de Sociologia*, X:2 [1952], 180; Altamira y Crevea, *op. cit.*, pp. 458, 459; Herr, *loc. cit.*).

[98] Altamira y Crevea, *op. cit.*, p. 461; Larruga y Boneta, *op. cit.*, XL, 254; Artiñano y de Galdacano, *op. cit.*, p. 40; AHN, *Consejo*, leg. 51501 (1).

[99] Larruga y Boneta, *loc. cit.*

[100] AHN, *loc. cit.*; Shafer, *op. cit.*, p. 5; Larruga y Boneta, *op. cit.*, V, 515; IX, 139; XXXIV, 266; Manuel Comeiro y Penido, *Historia de la Economia Política en España*, 2 vols. (Madrid, 1863), II, 222; AHN *Consejo, Libros de Govierno*, 1783, fols. 521–522; Carrera y Pujal, *op. cit.*, IV, 126, 179.

[101] AHN, *Consejo*, leg. 51501 (1).

[102] For an extended discussion of "vile trades," see *ibid.*

One of the first necessities of the Spanish people in the eighteenth century was to honor and ennoble the mechanical arts, in general little respected and some persecuted with a note of infamy, remains of that ancient, idiotic, and common preoccupation that the white hands of an *hidalgo* or *caballero* should not be stained nor cut with plebeian labors.[103]

Although most young Spaniards longed for a title of nobility and along with it honor and wealth, they yearned in vain. Many of them turned, therefore, to the clergy as a profession more honored than industry or commerce. During the seventeenth century the Catholic Church in Spain had grown more powerful in wealth and numbers. By 1788, 2,000 convents and monasteries for men and over 1,000 for women, housing 68,000 monks and 33,000 nuns, dotted the peninsula.[104] Elsewhere in Spain about 90,000 secular clergy and other religious officials resided. Landed property held by the Church grew through the power of mortmain: by 1756 the Church held about one-sixth of the land in Castile and Leon, and in 1797 it had jurisdiction over 2,592 cities, towns, and villages.[105]

Since the Church's primary motive was not profit maximization, it left idle much land that could have been productive; and churchmen diverted part of the income from their holdings to almsgiving,[106] but permitted only a trifling amount to be used in building up the nation's industrial capacity. Cathedrals and churches across the land became congregating places for the unemployed, beggars, and ne'er-do-wells. Contemporary economists bitterly opposed this form of charity, for they felt it encouraged idleness and perpetuated Spain's growing population of mendicants.[107]

[103] Colmeiro y Penido, *loc. cit.*

[104] Herr, *op. cit.*, p. 29.

[105] Antonio Matilla Tascón, *La Única Contribución y el Catastro de la Ensenada* (Madrid, 1947), *apendice* xxxiv; Herr, *op. cit.*, p. 89. The distribution of income from the wealth of the twenty-two provinces of Castile and Leon, however, indicated that the Church either held much valuable land, used its one-sixth more efficiently than other landowners, or received income other than from its own lands. In about 1756 this total income was 1,076,321,207 vellon reals of which 259,654,410 vellon reals went to the Church, leaving 816,666,797 vellon reals to the lay property owners. Thus while the Church owned only $\frac{1}{6}$ of the land, it received nearly $\frac{1}{4}$ of the income (Matilla Tascón, *op. cit.*, p. 91; *apendice* xxxv).

[106] Herr, *op. cit.*, pp. 30–33.

[107] In light of Spain's exploding population and lagging production, this almsgiving could have served a useful purpose. Charity supplied the unemployed with income, most of which was undoubtedly spent on consumption goods; a withdrawal of these funds by the Church would have caused a multiple contraction in total spending, unless the Church diverted the money to investment areas. The

Kings weakened the Church's power by gaining the right to appoint church officials and to tax church lands in 1753, by expelling the Jesuits from Spanish dominions in 1767, and by gradually nullifying the Inquisition's power.[108] Nevertheless, through the eighteenth and into the nineteenth century the Church continued to retard progress, mainly by its control over vast areas of productive land.

While the Church's hold on natural resources was considerable, that of the cities, towns, and villages was apparently greater, for they owned more land than the Church. Originally obtained by municipalities during the reconquest, common lands were rented or leased, the proceeds from which provided, along with local tax receipts, the incomes of towns.[109] Private land in entail rivaled town land in extent. By and large only about 10 to 25 percent of private land could be sold, though this varied from a high of 50 percent in Aragon, Navarre, Vizcaya, and Galicia, to a low of 3 to 7 percent in Andalusia.[110]

Because such a large percentage of land in Spain was entailed and thus not marketable, farmers leased their land either from the Church, municipalities, or private landowners. The types of leases varied from hereditary to short-term. Short-term leases generally predominated in the southern half of Spain; subleasing also became common.[111] Through this system of tenure a rural oligarchy emerged: since municipal offices had become hereditary and wealthy families inherited these positions, wealthy families therefore controlled municipal lands.[112] Essentially then, in much of Castile and Andalusia, private lands of wealthy nobles and vast tracts of city lands became indistinguishable.[113]

With so much land controlled by the Church, municipalities, and the nobility, large portions of productive land lay idle or was inefficiently used. For apparently none of these institutions showed an unusual inclination or aptitude for maximizing the income from their holdings.[114] Philip V and Ferdinand VI did little to change the situation. Charles III, however, came to believe that a prosperous industry required a thriving peasantry. In 1760 he

---

alternative to investment, and the probable choice, would have been hoarding. In that event, unemployment would have grown and output fallen.

[108] Herr, *op. cit.*, pp. 13–14, 28–29, 35.

[109] *Ibid.*, p. 90.

[110] *Ibid.*, p. 98.

[111] *Ibid.*, pp. 106–107.

[112] *Ibid.*, p. 109.

[113] *Ibid.*

[114] Shafer, *op. cit.*, pp. 4, 14; Herr, *op. cit.*, p. 30.

intervened in municipal finances and ordered that all common lands be auctioned regularly; and in 1770, he commanded all Spanish municipalities to enclose and allot their commons not then cultivated. Private and Church entails also came under attack during the last half of the century.[115] Such laudable attempts to reform land tenure and to provide a more equitable and efficient division of land failed—the character of rural Spain remained essentially unchanged.[116]

Banded together for centuries in the Mesta, owners of flocks of Merino sheep benefited from the prevailing land tenure and thus joined the rural oligarchy to fight the enclosing of common land in many parts of Spain.[117] Each autumn they drove their flocks south from their summer pastures in the sierras of Castile and Leon to their winter pastures in Extremadura and Andalusia. Because the wool from these Merino sheep brought dear prices in foreign markets, the Mesta had secured valuable rights from kings; one of them was the right of *posesión*—the prerogative to use for perpetuity and at fixed rentals pastureland it had once used.[118] Enforcing this right with its own judges, the Mesta gained virtual entail of miles of pasture along a corridor running nearly the length of the peninsula. Much land thereby remained out of cultivation.

Recognizing the harm done to farming by migrating sheep, Philip V in 1712 permitted towns in Castile and Andalusia to enclose and sell part of their commons; he extended this privilege to all Spain in 1738.[119] In Castile alone 173 towns had received and used such permission by 1747. Nevertheless, the Mesta convinced Philip's successor, Ferdinand VI, of the great injury done the migratory sheep industry by such enclosures; consequently, in 1748 that king reconfirmed the right of *posesión* by ordering municipalities to return all land taken from pasturage during the last twenty years.[120]

When Charles III moved against the traditional patterns of land

---

[115] For discussions of the legislation concerning land tenure, see: Altamira y Crevea, *op. cit.*, p. 472; AHN, *Biblioteca, Colección de Reales Cédulas*, 1788, XIX, 857; Gallardo Fernandez, *op. cit.*, II, 349, 373; Carrera y Pujal, *op. cit.*, IV, 316–321; Chapman, *op. cit.*, pp. 415–416; Herr, *op. cit.*, pp. 112–115.

[116] Chapman, *op. cit.*, 416; Herr, *op. cit.*, p. 118; Shafer, *op. cit.*, p. 98.

[117] Julius Klein, *The Mesta, A Study in Spanish Economic History, 1273–1836* (Cambridge, Massachusetts, 1920), p. 97; Herr, *op. cit.*, pp. 111–112.

[118] Klein, *op. cit.*, p. 346; Herr, *op. cit.*, p. 111.

[119] Klein, *op. cit.*, p. 344; Herr, *op. cit.*, p. 112.

[120] *Ibid.*

tenancy in 1760, he also fell upon the Mesta. And as senior member of Charles's royal council, Campomanes concurrently held the presidency of the Mesta, a position that he used after 1779 also to attack the Mesta.[121] Charles and Campomanes succeeded by 1788 essentially to undermine the sheepowners: Charles in 1786 abolished the privilege of *posesión;* in 1788 he permitted all Spanish landlords to enclose their lands and use them in any way they wished;[122] and Campomanes ordered all judges of the Mesta to give preference to local interests.[123]

Thus it was that Spanish agriculture gained its independence from the sheepowners. The weakening of the Mesta benefited wool production directly, for sheepowners traditionally had repressed the domestic woolen industry in favor of the profitable international market for wool. But the Mesta's emasculation had taken at least eighty-eight years of the century; and even then, though shorn of its power, the Mesta continued on as a political and economic force.

As these sheepowners stood in the way of economic progress, so the medieval system of transportation in Spain also obstructed growth of industry. "Degenerating into paths for pack and saddle animals" under the last Hapsburgs, Spanish roads offered a sad picture for Philip V.[124] That king began a feeble effort at road construction in 1718.[125] Nevertheless, not until the reign of Charles III and the ministry of Floridablanca did road building occur. On June 10, 1761, in a royal decree, Charles unveiled an ambitious project for uniting Madrid with Andalusia, Valencia, Catalonia, and Galicia by a network of highways.[126] By 1780, however, only five leagues of road had been built from Aranjuez toward Valencia and five leagues from Valencia toward Madrid; the same had occurred at Barcelona and La Coruña; and in Andalusia only one league had been completed.[127] In the meantime, other roads as well as the mountain passes of Guadarrama and Santander, among others, had fallen to abandon. Nevertheless, from 1780 to 1788 some progress occurred, for the minister Florida-

---

[121] Klein, *op. cit.,* p. 53.

[122] *Ibid.,* pp. 345–346; Herr, *op. cit.,* pp. 113–114, 117.

[123] *Ibid.,* p. 117.

[124] Hamilton, *op. cit.,* p. 100.

[125] Jaime Vicens Vives, *Historia Social y Económica de España y América,* 4 vols. (Barcelona, 1957–1959), IV, 202.

[126] AMH, *op. cit.,* XIV, 132–133; Carrera y Pujal, *op. cit.,* IV, 279; Vicens Vives, *loc. cit.*

[127] Carrera y Pujal, *op. cit.,* IV, 280.

blanca claimed that he had repaired and built nearly 400 leagues of roads, constructed bridges and sign posts, and had established tollhouses, inns, lodging houses, and brigades of laborers for maintaining the roads.[128]

Such favorable progress evidently changed the state of Spain's roads from impossible to possible but appalling. The peninsula definitely lacked an efficient system of highways in the waning years of the eighteenth century. Eugenio Larruga in 1793, speaking of the depressed state of Rioja, declared:

Another very grave (and in my concept the principal) calamity that oppresses us is the pitiful state of all the roads of Rioja . . . from November to May droves of beasts of burden (*recuas, requas*) cannot travel without great danger and delays, and even in summer the few carriages that travel the road, which here we call royal, are overtaxed.[129]

Larruga's complaints joined a chorus of others. By 1800, Hendaye was the only city on the frontier connected with Madrid by a continuous road for wheeled vehicles. One observer even claimed that in most provinces mules and donkeys still transported nearly everything.[130]

Only inadequate alternatives to this crude form of land transportation could be found. Rivers navigable by oceangoing vessels scarcely existed; the Ebro to Tortosa and the Guadalquivir to Seville were the only ones.[131] Rivers in Spain failed to offer a means of transportation either because of swift currents, rapids, or insufficient volumes of water during most of the year.[132] Although Spain had no important canals at the start of the century, a number had their origin during the period 1750–1800. Planned on a grandiose scale, the Canal of Aragon was to connect the Mediterranean with the Bay of Biscay and to facilitate commerce between Catalonia, Aragon, and Navarre; the Canal of Castile was to join Madrid with Santander and to serve as a means for shipping products from Castile to that northern port; and another canal was to open a waterway south from Madrid to the

---

[128] *Ibid.*, Vicens Vives, *loc. cit.*

[129] Larruga y Boneta, *op. cit.*, XXVII, 208.

[130] Hamilton, *op. cit.*, p. 100, n. 18. For other descriptions of roads in Spain late in the century, see; Larruga y Boneta, *op. cit.*, XXVII, 96, 221, 222; Antonio Joseph Cavanilles, *Observaciones sobre la Historia Natural, Geografía, Agricultura, Población y Frutos del Reyno de Valencia*, 2 vols. (Madrid, 1795–1797), I, 126; Townsend, *op. cit.*, I, 104.

[131] Hamilton, *op. cit.*, p. 99.

[132] *Ibid.*

Guadalquivir and the Atlantic. Several shorter canals were projected for New Castile and Murcia.[133]

The immensity of these watercourses matched their proposed lengths; the Canal of Aragon, for example, was 9 feet deep, 20 feet wide at the bottom, and 56 feet wide at the top.[134] To build 12 leagues cost 60 million vellon reals.[135] Ignoring the terrain, engineers constructed the Canal of Castile straight, wide, and deep. Perhaps more than anything else, the expenses of digging these ribbon-like trenches across the rugged, hard-crusted peninsula explain why none of them was completed. Of the proposed 100 leagues of the Canal of Aragon, only 28 had been completed by 1833;[136] the Canal of Castile, according to Joseph Townsend, contained 20 leagues in 1787;[137] but according to Eugenio Larruga, it was behind schedule in 1793.[138] After ostentatious beginnings, the canals of Guadarrama and Manzanares were abandoned; others were not even begun.[139] Although the network of canals failed to remedy substantially the transportation bottleneck between and within provinces, they did provide much needed irrigation for parts of rain-starved Old Castile and Aragon.

But the flow of water from these canals hardly began to overcome the insufficient rainfall that characterizes extensive areas of Spain—much of Aragon, La Mancha, southern Andalusia, Old and New Castile, and Leon resemble deserts.[140] Rainfall, however, makes Galicia, Asturias, the Basque provinces, parts of Extremadura and Leon, and the southern slopes of the Pyrenees in Navarre, Aragon, and Catalonia a picture of greenery where trees and grass abound. Nevertheless, arid Spain enclosed most of the important political, social, and economic segments of the peninsula.

Where rain fell only sparsely, the position of agriculture was precarious. Old Castile, for example, poor, dry, and treeless, specialized in growing wheat, yet its output often fell short of feeding its own population.[141] The humid regions and the fertile river valleys of other sections of the peninsula, however, pro-

---

[133] Canga Arguëlles, *op. cit.*, I, 439; II, 180–181; Carrera y Pujal, *op. cit.*, IV, 281–283; Hamilton, *op. cit.*, p. 100; Herr, *op. cit.*, pp. 132–133.
[134] Townsend, *op. cit.*, I, 213.
[135] *Ibid.*, I, 212.
[136] Canga Arguëlles, *op. cit.*, I, 439.
[137] Townsend, *op. cit.*, I, 368.
[138] Larruga y Boneta, *op. cit.*, XXXII, 279.
[139] Canga Arguëlles, *op. cit.*, I, 181; II, 439.
[140] Herr, *op. cit.*, p. 99; Altamira y Crevea, *op. cit.*, p. 467.
[141] *Ibid.*

duced agricultural products for export to the rest of Spain. Regional specialization thus characterized some provinces: Valencia, Murcia, and Aragon led the peninsula in silk cultivation, while the two Castiles and Extremadura, over which huge flocks of sheep migrated, produced the fine wool of Spain.

As nature withheld rain from large parts of Spain, so she also scantily endowed the country with other resources. Because of insufficient moisture, only a few forests existed on the peninsula and thereby made fuel relatively scarce, especially when population and industrial activity ascended. With the price of logs and charcoal rising, industrialists at Barcelona, among other places, turned to coal. But limited outcroppings of high-grade coal near the city restricted the extent of that substitution.[142] Steep mountains, long distances, and a lack of navigable rivers, canals, or highways kept the price of coal high in most of Spain.[143] Only in the Basque provinces did forests and deposits of coal and iron ore exist in quantities and qualities sufficient to support a metals industry.[144] Deposits of other metals, such as lead, copper, and quicksilver, were either exploited by the king or by independent Spaniards on an insignificant scale.

Although an arid climate, lack of forests, inaccessible coal mines, few deposits of iron ore, and shortages of other resources moderated the expansion of some industries and prevented the establishment or growth of others, international hostilities also

---

[142] Carrera y Pujal discusses the use of coal at Barcelona. In 1786 Tomas Perez obtained a design for a glass furnace that used coal instead of charcoal; soon thereafter coal was used for producing glass at Barcelona. Apparently the city government feared the effects of coal dust and smoke on the population's health and hence tried to limit coal's use within the city walls. However, Carrera y Pujal does not feel that coal appeared in great quantities (*Historia Política y Económica de Cataluña*, IV, 182, 182, 232).

[143] Professor Hamilton (*op. cit.*, pp. 179–180) notes that the price of firewood and charcoal "lagged behind the rising general commodity indices" from 1751–1800. He has no index of coal prices. He concludes: "Hence neither the feverish efforts to discover and exploit coal mines nor the sensational advance of Spanish industry can be attributed to extraordinary scarcity or increasing dearness of organic fuel." Several other interpretations can be placed on the phenomenon of lagging prices of firewood and charcoal. First, the production of coal could have grown considerably in response to the king's stimulation and thereby increased the total supply of fuel, causing firewood, charcoal, and coal prices to rise less precipitiously. Second, the expansion of industry might have been far less than assumed and hence the demand for fuel would not have risen as much as assumed. A moderate increase in the supply of coal would then explain why the price of firewood and charcoal lagged behind other commodities.

[144] Shafer, *op. cit.*, p. 35; Canga Arguëlles, *op. cit.*, I, 466, 467; *Censo de Frutos y Manufacturas de España é Islas Adyacentes . . . Don Juan Polo y Catalina* (Madrid, 1803), p. 55.

exerted their influence on the fate of Spanish industry. Spain lost men, equipment, ships, and buildings fighting either England or France during the century. Of more importance to industrial growth, however, were the periodic blockades of Spanish ports and colonial markets.

War engrossed Spain two out of every three years during 1700–1750; but it took up only about one out of every four years from 1750–1800.[145] The cautious, peace-loving Ferdinand VI kept Spain out of conflicts from 1748 to 1759.[146] Charles III, however, entered the Seven Years' War in 1762 on the side of France. After little more than a year of fighting, Spain had lost Minorca and Florida, but had gained Louisiana. Again in June, 1779, Charles joined France to fight England; in slightly over four years of war Spain neither gained nor lost much.[147] But for these years of fighting the reign of Charles III was one of comparative peace, and, it should be noted, this era witnessed the greatest economic advancement of the seventeenth and eighteenth centuries.

It was during Charles IV's reign that warfare significantly deterred economic expansion in Spain. Charles joined the first coalition against France after the execution of Louis XVI on January 21, 1793; but after invading Roussillon, his army was driven back to the Ebro and his colonial markets put in jeopardy.[148] He sued for peace in 1795. Within a year Charles had allied with France and another war began, lasting until 1802.[149] During this conflict England's seapower overwhelmed Spain; English ships completely blockaded Cadiz from 1797 until 1800 and effectively besieged other ports, including Barcelona.[150] By cutting off Spanish manufacturers from their major markets in America, industry at Barcelona and Valencia, among other places, came to a virtual halt.[151]

SUMMARY

Now is the time to restate the various circumstances that influenced industrial expansion in Spain during the period 1750–1800.

---

[145] William L. Langer, ed., *An Encyclopedia of World History* (Cambridge, Massachusetts, 1960), pp. 450–452.

[146] Altamira y, Crevea *op. cit.*, p. 437.

[147] Langer, *op. cit.*, p. 452; Altamira y, Crevea, *op. cit.*, pp. 441–442.

[148] *Ibid.*, p. 515.

[149] *Ibid.*, pp. 516, 521; Langer, *op. cit.*, p. 452.

[150] Herr, *op. cit.*, pp. 388–389.

[151] ACSV. *Varios*, leg. 1, no. 6; AHMB, *op. cit.*, XXVI, 93; Censo de Frutos, *op. cit.*, p. 16; Canga Arguëlles, *op. cit.*, I, 29; Jean Francois de Bourgoing, *Modern State of Spain*, translated from the 1807 edition (London, 1808), III, 306; Herr, *op. cit.*, p. 389.

First were those that complemented the economic programs of kings. When Philip V assumed the throne in 1700, he introduced Spain to the ways of Louis XIV; as one consequence, French ministers in the tradition of Colbert reorganized the government and centralized the royal powers. As Spain received these efficient methods of government from France, so she also benefited from the intellectual influence then flowing down from north of the Pyrenees. Awakened by this influx of scholarly works, Spaniards began to debate the peninsula's economic condition and to offer points of view that varied from mercantilism to extreme liberalism.

These authors stimulated the formation of economic societies, besides affecting the king's economic policies. Economic societies fostered industrial growth at the local levels with their educational efforts. From 1750 to 1800, the crown also addressed the problem of education. It promoted a number of schools for training individuals in specific skills, such as spinning, dyeing, and designing; moreover, it did much to rid universities of Scholasticism and to include in its place modern disciplines. Another institution of major importance became prominent during this time: the General Council of Commerce and Money and several local councils of commerce were formed to give meaning and continuity to the king's economic reforms.

Monetary improvements by Charles III also favored industry. Domestic population expanded and shifted toward cities. An enlarging supply of labor for industry thus appeared. Besides creating an expanding market, the larger and more dense population made possible a deeper division of labor and opened up the possibilities of increasing returns to scale. Moreover, a rising population in the colonies conveniently offered Spanish producers a market for their merchandise.

These helpful conditions supported the efforts of kings to promote industry; but only Valencia and Catalonia responded markedly. Most other areas still wallowed in idleness or made agonizingly slow advances, for powerful impediments smothered the forces of progress there. Divided into geographical regions by a number of mountain ranges, Spain was late developing a political unity. When the eighteenth century began, the Basque provinces, Navarre, Aragon, Catalonia, and Valencia still possessed some autonomy. Philip V then did much to gain control over these provinces; yet, where autonomy was crushed, a strong sentiment of separatism remained.

Reverence for the ways of nobility so pervaded the mentality of Spaniards that rich merchants and industrialists urged their sons to seek honorable employment in the clergy or government service; common laborers even refused to accept employment in certain trades which they considered below their dignity. The Catholic Church, after growing in power during the seventeenth century, held more than 15 percent of the land in most provinces, allocated it inefficiently, and used its income in ways that did not promote industrial growth.

Land in entail owned by private individuals and by municipalities included a majority of all acreage in most provinces. Here, too, as with the Church, a poor allocation of land often resulted— fertile fields lay idle or were used in relatively unproductive ways. The Mesta controlled much land, reserving it for pasturage. Although kings attempted to reform land tenure, they failed essentially to improve existing conditions.

While they were seeking a solution to land problems, kings also grappled with the wretched communications system on the peninsula. But they did little to make rivers navigable, failed at canal building, and improved the network of roads only slightly. This lack of canals and roads could have been overcome, but the poor endowment of many natural resources could never be surmounted. Water supplies, forests, coal deposits, and other resources existed in relatively small quantities and often of mediocre qualities. However, there was no shortage of wars during the first fifty years of the century. The first four decades of the period 1750–1800, in contrast, witnessed only light hostilities and thus little disruption of economic activity. Then, drawn into the wars of the French Revolution after 1789, Spain suffered severely in resources, markets, and pride.

In areas where these hindrances to economic expansion touched lightest—Catalonia, Valencia, and the Basque provinces—industrial growth marched forward. Textile producers in Catalonia, for example, benefited from fine port facilities, swift, clear streams, local and Aragonese wool and silk, Maltese cotton, a moderate climate, and a large population that was willing to accept new ideas and methods from France and, most important, was eager to work. Furthermore, Catalonia and Valencia were little bothered by unsound royal policies. In most parts of Spain, however, obstacles to growth plus the king's ignorance of market forces nullified the royal programs for economic development and the other complementary forces.

X

Summary

In 1700 Philip V gave to Spain a program of economic development reminiscent of the one Colbert had created in France much
earlier. Over the ensuing decades this Spanish variety of economic
statism evolved, reaching its highest and most sophisticated form
during the last fifty years of the eighteenth century. It was in this
decisive period that Ferdinand VI, Charles III, and Charles IV
used the power, prestige, and wealth of the Spanish crown in an
effort to dislodge their country's economy from its backward state
and to make it competitive with other nations of Western Europe.
Their methods varied from direct intervention in the productive
process to subtle encouragement of private enterprise.

Even though textiles received more royal attention than any
other sector of the economy from 1750 to 1800, the output of
cloth expanded unevenly. Mushrooming around Barcelona, cotton production far outdistanced other segments of the industry;
a spectacular rate of ascent, emergence of large-scale producing
units, and a revolutionary change in technology characterized this
industry during these years. The last half of the century also saw
a marked expansion of silks in Valencia and Catalonia. But the
rate of growth fell short of that sustained in cottons, and the essential techniques of production improved less dramatically. The
manufacture of woolens and linens increased in Catalonia, Valencia, and in a few other regions. Meager growth, stagnation, or
decline typified textiles in the remaining provinces. The forces
of development set in motion by the crown therefore did not
sweep through Spain and transform the traditional characteristics
of textile production. They touched the Mediterranean littoral
at Valencia and Barcelona. They failed to penetrate into the interior despite the energetic beckoning of Spanish kings and ministers. Ironically, Valencia and Catalonia, infrequent recipients
of royal favor, enjoyed the greatest industrial success.

In a burst of activity after 1750, royal legislation opened all doors to influences that might have aided industry, especially in Castile and Leon. Central Spain received the royal factories. These institutions acted as centers for training artisans and diffusing technology. They also turned out large quantities of fine woolens, silks, cottons, and linens, and sold them in the major cities of Spain and Spanish America. Kings likewise chartered joint-stock companies in central Spain. After amassing funds by selling shares and borrowing, these firms constructed textile mills and engaged in domestic and international trade.

The need of industry for finer skills and modern technology also occupied the attention of government. It was in overcoming this deficiency that kings succeeded most admirably. They enticed many foreign artisans with wide varieties of skills to immigrate, and new techniques of production and advanced machinery concurrently arrived in Spain. When aliens entered the country and sought employment, however, they frequently ran headlong into the ubiquitous hostility of guilds. Kings set out to remove this obstacle to labor's mobility and to producer's freedom.

In the realm of tax reforms, kings focused their attention almost exclusively on Castile and Leon. It is well they should have, for the tax system there violated reason. As Spanish kings used tax reforms to assist industry in central Spain, so they manipulated tariffs and prohibitions to stimulate the production of textiles, particularly of woolens and silks. Perhaps the single most important modification in the regulation of Spain's external commerce was the disenthrallment of colonial trading: by 1778 most of the important peninsular ports could ship merchandise directly to Spanish America.

A vigorous, enlightened crown thus created textile mills, chartered joint-stock companies, obtained foreign skills and technology, and reformed guilds, provincial taxes, and commercial policy. Along with these royal actions there appeared a number of independent influences that supported industrial development. The arrival of the Enlightenment, the improvement of currency, and the expansion of population in Spain and her colonies, all affected textile manufacturing favorably. But the shackles binding industry in most of Spain held tight, despite all these attempts to remove them.

Responsibility for industry's continued impoverishment over large parts of the peninsula must rest partly on certain basic errors in the government's economic policies. The kings were frequently unaware of market forces and hence unwittingly over-emphasized the technical or engineering aspects of their projects. For example, some royal mills were monuments to modern technology, yet they were all economically inefficient. The larger factories suffered from internal diseconomies, for kings constructed them on abnormally large scales and with much vertical integration. In contrast to these diseconomies, the smaller royal mills suffered from a lack of division of labor. Moreover, kings obliged most of their manufactories to weave fine cloth, even though Spanish markets demanded mostly common fabrics.

Royal manufactories did not clearly benefit the textile industry. Nor did the joint-stock companies achieve their intended goals: their factories were small, inefficient, and complete failures. The absence of most characteristics that yield a comparative advantage plagued the impoverished regions in which the companies were formed, and the government's failure to realize this fact condemned the undertakings from the outset.

One of the most successful of all royal economic projects was the importation of foreign artisans and technology. Nevertheless, even here the crown's ignorance of market forces stands out. Kings emphasized the need for artisans and techniques for making fine fabrics, yet Spanish industry was turning from the smaller market for fine cloth to the larger one for common textiles where its advantage in production clearly lay. For this reason, producers refused much of the knowledge and tools associated with the creation of fine cloth.

What the kings accomplished in reforming the guild system, although substantial, actually had little effect throughout most of Spain. At Barcelona, the bursting forth of industrial progress had already emasculated the important prerogatives of guilds by the time the reforms were enacted. In other parts of Spain the antiguild legislation was of little consequence, for industry there did not challenge the guild's authority. The status quo remained.

While an overemphasis on technical considerations thus weakened the king's program of economic development, other influences, independent of the government, also undermined royal efforts. An adverse climate, an inept transportation system, poor resource endowment, and institutions that were inimical to economic change, among other factors, militated against industrialization and nullified those measures of kings that were economically sound. Perhaps no amount of effort could have overcome the absolute disadvantage that most of Spain had in textiles.

Although Catalonia and Valencia received only slight attention from kings, these two regions benefited directly and indirectly from royal economic policies. All Spain received foreign workers and knowledge, but only parts of the country benefited substantially. Imported technology triumphed at Barcelona. The introduction and diffusion of such machines as the spinning jenny, the water frame, and the steam engine transformed that city into one of Europe's busiest industrial centers. Even though taxes in Catalonia and Valencia remained basically unchanged from 1750 to 1800, at the outset they were less restrictive of industry than were taxes in Castile and Leon. Moreover, merchants in Catalonia and Valencia benefited especially from the freedom given them in 1778 to ship their goods directly to America without first having to transport them to Cadiz. With this new opportunity, merchants swiftly exploited the vast, rich colonial market. It was no coincidence that the rate of expansion of textiles in Valencia and Catalonia thereafter quickened.

Besides these encouraging deeds of government, Catalonia and Valencia possessed a comparative advantage in textiles. Excellent port facilities, nearness to raw materials, and large cities with populous hinterlands help explain this economic ability. In Valencia, for example, laborers harvested silk in the fertile countryside, made thread of it, and then carried it into the nearby city. Working within an extensive division of labor and the putting-out system, artisans transformed this thread into finished merchandise. Specialization in production thus brought forth economies external to the individual workshops. Similar conditions existed at Barcelona. They rarely appeared elsewhere on the peninsula.

Although industry in Catalonia and Valencia might have expanded without any royal support, it clearly benefited from the assistance it received. Surely it would have benefited more had it received a greater share of the government's economically sound programs. But kings focused their efforts on Castile and Leon, where natural barriers would have blocked industrial progress even had all the measures been wise.

BIBLIOGRAPHY

Bibliography

The material for this study came mostly from various archives in Spain. The General Archives of Simancas, a rich depository of state papers, contain many bundles relating to royal factories, royal joint-stock companies, and foreign artisans. Unfortunately, during the summer and fall of 1958 and the winter and spring of 1959, several sections of the archives were walled up in cellar storerooms while workmen repaired a leaky roof. One of those sections contained papers of the General Council of Commerce and Money. Although no inventory existed for this material, a staff member reported that it related mostly to nineteenth-century matters. The bulk of the papers of the General Council of Commerce and Money, though supposedly at Simancas, has disappeared. Fortunately, Eugenio Larruga y Boneta, the Council's archivist in the eighteenth century, filled forty-five volumes with material taken in large part from those lost papers. Strangely enough, his last volume ends at about the date at which the material that remains at Simancas begins.

Valuable information covering, among other topics, the royal cotton factory at Avila, the economic society at Madrid, foreigners in Spain, and legal proceedings against guilds, exists in the National Archives at Madrid. The Archives of the Ministry of Hacienda, also at Madrid, contain one of the most complete collections of royal orders, decrees, and cedulas in all Spain.

Important material telling of the silk industry at Valencia was found at the private archives of the College of the Greater Art of Silk of that city. The Archives of the City of Barcelona hold the most important documents detailing industry in Catalonia. Tax rolls for most of Barcelona's craft guilds and a collection of documents relevant to the activities of the Council of Commerce of that city are kept there. The Archives of the Kingdom of Aragon (Real Audiencia) enclose documents pertinent to the changing status of guilds. And the Central Library of Barcelona also contains a number of bundles of importance to the industry in Catalonia.

In addition to archival material, numerous monographs and other printed works authored by contemporary economists, royal ministers,

[187]

pamphleteers, and itinerant travelers were consulted. The works of several Spanish economic historians of the present generation (Jaime Carrera y Pujal and J. Vicens Vives) proved useful for supporting evidence as well as for supplementary data. Professor Earl J. Hamilton's research was, of course, indispensable.

PUBLISHED

Books

Addison, Joseph. *Charles the Third of Spain*. Oxford, 1900.
Almanaque Mercantil ó Guía de Comerciante. Madrid, 1795–1807.
Almanaque Mercantil ó Guía de Comerciante para el Año de 1804. Madrid, 1804.
Altamira y Crevea, Rafael. *A History of Spain from the Beginning to the Present Day*. Translated by Mina Lee. New York: Van Nostrand Company, 1958.
———. *Historia de España y de la Civilización Española*. 4 vols. 2d ed. Barcelona: J. Gili, 1909–1911.
Anzano, Tomás de. *Discursos sobre los Medios que Pueden Facilitar la Restauración de Aragón*. Zaragoza, 1768.
Argenti y Leis, Felipe. *Discursos Políticos y Económicos sobre el Estado Actual de España*. Madrid, 1777.
Artiñano y de Galdacano. *La Producción Español en la Edad Moderna*. Madrid, 1914.
Asso del Río, Ignacio Jordán de. *Historia de la Economía Política de Aragón*. Zaragoza, 1798.
Balanza del Comercio de España con los Dominios de S. M. en America y en las Indias en el Año de 1792. Madrid, 1805.
Balanza del Comercio de España con las Potencias Extrangeras en al Año de 1792. Madrid, 1803.
Barcelo de la Mora, José Luis. *Historia Económica de España*. Madrid: A. Aguado, 1952.
Beawes, Wyndham. *A Civil, Commercial, Political and Literary History of Spain and Portugal*. 2 vols. London, 1793.
———. *Lex Mercatoria Rediviva*. London, 1783.
Beramendi, Carlos. *Memoria sobre la Naturaleza é Importe de las Necesidades Ordinarios y Extraordinarios de la Nación Española en la Época Presente*. Madrid, 1812.
Bourgoing, Jean Francois de. *Modern State of Spain*. Translated from the 1807 edition. London, 1808.
Cabarrús, Francisco, Conde de. *Cartas del Conde de Caburrús sobre los Obstáculos que la Naturaleza, la Opinión y las Leyes Oponen a la Felicidad Pública, Dirigidas al Sr. D. Gaspar de Jovellanos*. Havana, 1814.
———. *Cartas Político-Económicos Dedicadas al Conde de Lerena, Obra Inedita*. Madrid, 1841.

———. *Elogio de Carlos III, Rey de España y de las Indias.* Madrid, 1789.

———. *Memoria que d. Francisco Caburrús Presentó a su Majestad para la Formación de un Banco Nacional.* Madrid, 1782.

Campomanes, Pedro Rodriguez, Conde de. *Apéndice a la Educación Popular.* 4 vols. Madrid, 1775–1777.

———. *Cartas Político-Económicas.* Edited by Antonio Rodriguez Villa. Madrid, 1878.

———. *Collección de las Alegaciones Fiscales del.* Edited by José Alonso. 4 vols. Madrid, 1841–1842.

———. *Discurso sobre la Educación Popular de los Artesanos y su Fomento.* 6 vols. Madrid, 1775.

———. *Discurso sobre el Fomento de la Industria Popular.* Madrid, 1774.

———. *Repuesta Fiscal sobre Abolir la Tasa y Establecer el Comercio de Granos.* Madrid, 1764.

———. *Tratado de la Regalía de Amortización.* Madrid, 1765.

Canals, Juan Pablo. *Colección de lo Perteneciente al Ramo de la Rubia ó Granza de España.* Madrid, 1779.

Canga Arguëlles, José. *Diccionario de Hacienda.* 2 vols. Madrid, 1833–1834.

Capella, Miguel, and Antonio Matilla Tascón. *Los Cinco Gremios Mayores de Madrid.* Madrid: Imprenta Saez, 1957.

Capmany y de Montpalau, Antonio de. *Memorias Históricas sobre la Marina, Comercio y Artes de la Antigua Ciudad de Barcelona.* Madrid, 1792.

Carrera y Pujal, Jaime. *Historia de la Economía Española.* 5 vols. Barcelona: Bosch, 1943–1947.

———. *Historia Política y Económica de Cataluña, Siglos XVI al XVIII.* 4 vols. Barcelona: Bosch, 1946–1947.

———. *La Lonja del Mar y los Cuerpos de Comercio de Barcelona.* Barcelona: Bosch, 1953.

Cavanilles, Antonio Joseph. *Observaciones sobre la Historia Natural, Geografía, Agricultura, Población, y Frutos del Reyno de Valencia.* Madrid, 1795–1797.

Censo de Frutos y Manufacturas de España é Islas Adyacentes, Ordenado sobre los Datos Dirigidos por los Intendentes, por el Oficial Don Juan Polo y Catalina. Madrid, 1803.

Censo de la Población de España de el Año de 1797, Executado de Orden del Rey. Madrid, 1797.

Censo Español Executado de Orden del Rey Comunicada por el Excelentísimo Señor Conde de Floridablanca, Primer Secretario de Estado y del Despacho, en el Año de 1787. Madrid, 1787.

Chapman, Charles E. *A History of Spain.* New York: The MacMillan Company, 1938.

Clarke, Edward, *Letters Concerning the Spanish Nation, Written at Madrid During the Years 1760 and 1761*. London, 1763.

Colmeiro y Penido, Manuel. *Historia de la Economía Política en España*. 2 vols. Madrid, 1863.

Coxe, William. *Memoirs of the Kings of Spain of the House of Bourbon, From the Accession of Philip to the Death of Charles III, 1700–1788*. 5 vols. 2d ed. London, 1815.

Cruilles, Marques de. *Los Gremios de Valencia*. Valencia, 1883.

Desdevises du Dezert, Georges Nicolas. *L'Espagne de L'Ancien Régime*. 3 vols. Paris: Societe Française d'imprimerie et de libraire, 1904.

Dillon, John Talbot. *Viaje de España*. Dublin, 1781.

Escudé Bartoli, Manuel. *La Producción Española en el Siglo XIX*. Barcelona, 1895.

Farinelli, A. *Viajes por España y Portugal*. 2d ed. Vol. II. Roma: Real Accademia d'Italia, 1942.

Ferrer del Río, Antonio. *Historia del Reinado de Carlos III en España*. 4 vols. Madrid, 1856.

Foquet Marsal, José. *Cofradias-Gremios, Especialmente Fluviales de la Ribera del Ebro en Tortosa*. Madrid, 1923.

Foronda, Valentin. *Cartas sobre los Asuntos mas Esquisitos de la Económica y Leyes Criminales*. 2 vols. Madrid, 1789.

Fos, Joaquín Manuel. *Instrucción Metódica sobre los Mueres*. Madrid, 1790.

Gallardo Fernandez, Francisco. *Origen, Progresos y Estado de Rentas de la Corona de España*. 7 vols. Madrid, 1805–1808.

Gassó, Antonio Buenaventura. *España con Industria, Fuerte y Rica*. Barcelona, 1816.

Geoffrey, W. Ribbons. *Catalunza i Valencia Vistes pels Viatgers Anglesos del Siglo XVIII*. Barcelona, 1955.

Graell, Guillermo. *La Cuestión Catalana*. Barcelona, 1902.

———. *Historia del Fomento del Trabajo Nacional*. Barcelona, 1911.

Graell, Marcelino. *La Industria Sedera*. Barcelona, 1926.

Hamilton, Earl J. *War and Prices in Spain, 1651–1800*. Cambridge: Harvard University Press, 1947.

Haring, Clarence Henry. *The Spanish Empire in America*. New York: Oxford University Press, 1947.

Herr, Richard. *The Eighteenth Century Revolution in Spain*. New Jersey: Princeton University Press, 1958.

Herrera Oria, Enrique. *La Real Fábrica de Tejidos de Algodón Estampados, de Ávila y la Reorganización Nacional de esta Industria en el Siglo XVIII*. Valladolid, 1922.

Hussey, Roland Dennis. *The Caracas Company, 1728–1784*. Cambridge: Harvard University Press, 1934.

Ionnes, Moreau de. *Estadística de España*. Barcelona, 1835.

Jovellanos, Gaspar Melchor de. "Inform Dado a la Junta General de

Comercio y Moneda sobre el Libre Ejercicio de las Artes" in *Biblioteca de Autores Españoles*. Vol. L. Madrid, 1859.

————. *Informe de la Sociedad Económica de Madrid al Real y Supremo Consejo de Castilla en el Expediente de la Ley Agraria*. Madrid, 1820.

Kany, Charles E. *Life and Manners in Madrid, 1750–1800*. Berkeley: University of California Press, 1932.

Klein, Julius. *The Mesta, A Study in Spanish Economic History, 1273–1836*. Cambridge: Harvard University Press, 1920.

Labrada, José Lucas. *Descripción del Reino de Galicia*. La Coruña, 1803.

Laborde, Alexandre de. *Itinéraire Descriptif de L'Espagne*. 5 vols. Paris, 1808.

Lane, Frederic C., and Jelle C. Riemersma, eds. *Enterprise and Secular Change*. Homewood, Illinois: Richard D. Irwin, Inc., 1953.

Langer, William L., ed. *An Encyclopedia of World History*. Cambridge, Massachusetts: Houghton Mifflin, 1960.

Lansola, Pascual Vicente. *Extracto de las Actas de la Real Academia Económica de Amigos del Pais de Valencia, 1786*. Valencia, 1786.

Larruga y Boneta, Eugenio. *Memorias Políticas y Económicas sobre los Frutos, Comercio, Fábricas y Minas de España*. 45 vols. Madrid, 1787–1800.

Marquez y Pérez, Manuel. *Vicisitudes del Régimen Aduanero Reinados de Carlos III a Alfonso XIII*. Vigo, 1895.

Martinez Ferrando, Eduard. *La Industria Valenciana de la Seda*. Valencia, 1933.

Matilla Tascón, Antonio. *Catálogo de la Colección de Órdenes Generales de Rentas*. Madrid: Sucesores de Peña Cruz, 1950.

————. *La Única Contribución y el Catastro de la Ensenada*. Madrid: Sucesores de Sánchez Ocaña, 1947.

Memorias de la Sociedad Económica de Madrid. 2 vols. Madrid, 1780.

Moñino, José (Floridablanca). *Representación Hecha al Sr. D. Carlos III*. Murcia, 1809.

Mounier, André. *Les Faits et la Doctrine Économiques en Espagne sous Philip V, Gerónimo de Uztáriz*. Bordeaux: Imprimerie de L'Université, 1919.

Ortiz, José Alonso. *Ensayo Económico sobre el Sistema de la Moneda-Papel y sobre el Crédito Pública*. Madrid, 1796.

Pi Suñer, Carlos. *Estudios sobre la Exportación Textil Algodonera*. Barcelona, 1929.

Ponz, Antonio. *Viaje de España*. Madrid: M. Aguilar, 1947.

Rahola y Tremols, Federico. *Cámara Oficial de Comercio y Navagación de Barcelona*. Barcelona: Artes Gráficas, S. A., 1931.

Romá y Rosell, Francisco. *Las Señales de la Felicidad de España y Medios de Hacerlas Eficaces*. Madrid, 1768.

Romeva Ferrer, Pau. *Historia de la Industria Catalana.* 2 vols. Barcelona: Bas d'Igualada, 1952.

Rumeu de Armas, Antonio. *Historia de la Previsión Social de España.* Madrid: Editorial Revista de Derecho Privado, 1944.

Ruiz y Pablo, Ángel. *Historia de la Real Junta Particular de Comercio de Barcelona, 1758–1847.* Barcelona, 1919.

Sánchez, Santos. *Extracto Puntual de Todas las Pragmáticas, Cédulas, Provisiones, Circulares, Autos Acordados y Otras Providencias Publicados en el Reinado del Señor Don Carlos III.* 3 vols. Madrid, 1792–1793.

Santillan, Ramón. *Memoria Histórica de los Bancos Nacional de San Carlos, Español de San Fernando, Isabel II, Nuevo de San Fernando y de España.* 2 vols. Madrid, 1865.

Sarrailh, Jean. *L'Espagne Éclairée de la Seconde Moitié du XVIIIᵉ Siecle.* Paris: Imprimerie Nationale, 1954.

Scott, William Robert. *The Constitution and Finance of English, Scottish and Irish Joint-Stock Companies to 1720.* 3 vols. Cambridge, London: The University Press, 1910–1912.

Sempere y Guarinos, Juan. *Biblioteca Española Económica Política.* 4 vols. Madrid, 1801–1821.

———. *Ensayo de una Biblioteca Española de los Mejores Escritores del Reynado del Carlos III.* 6 vols. Madrid, 1785–1789.

———. *Historia del Luxo, y de las Leyes Suntuarias de España.* 2 vols. Madrid, 1788.

Shafer, Robert Jones. *The Economic Societies in the Modern World, 1763–1821.* Syracuse: Syracuse University Press, 1958.

Soler, Miguel Cayetano. *Memoria sobre el Estado Actual de la Real Hacienda y sobre Recursos para Urgencias.* N.p., 1779.

Thicknesse, Philip. *A Year's Journey through France and Part of Spain.* 2 vols. 2d ed. London, 1788.

Townsend, Joseph. *A Journey Through Spain in the Years 1786 and 1787.* 3 vols. London, 1792.

Ulloa, Bernardo de. *Restablecimiento de las Fábricas y Comercio Español.* 2 vols. Madrid, 1740.

Uña Sarthou, Juan. *Las Asociaciones Obreras en España.* Madrid, 1900.

Uztáriz, Gerónimo de. *Theórica y Práctica de Comercio y de Marina.* 3d ed. Madrid, 1757.

Ventalló Vintró, José. *Historia de la Industria Lanera Catalana.* Tarrasa, 1904.

Vicens Vives, Jaime. *Historia Social y Económica de España y America.* 4 vols. Barcelona: Editorial Teide, 1957–1959.

———. *Manual de Historia Económica de España.* Barcelona: Editorial Teide, 1959.

Vizcaino Pérez, Vicente. *Discursos Políticos sobre los Estragos que Cau-*

san los Censos, Felicidades y Medios de su Extención. Madrid, 1766.

La Vuelta Por España, Un Sociedad de Literatos. Barcelona, 1872.

Walton, Perry. *The Story of Textiles.* New York: Tudor Publishing Co., 1925.

Ward, Bernardo. *Proyecto Económico.* Madrid, 1779.

Young, Arthur. *Travels during the Years 1787, 1788 and 1789 in France, to which is Added the Register of a Tour into Spain.* Dublin, 1793.

ARTICLES

Alcázar, Cayetano. "España en 1792: Floridablanca: Su Derrumbamiento del Gobierno y sus Procesos de Responsibilidad Política," *Revista de Estudios Políticos,* 71 (1953), 93–138.

Artola, Miguel. "Campillo y las Reformas de Carlos III," *Revista de Indias,* XII (1952), 685–714.

Brown, Vera Lee. "Studies in the History of Spain in the Second Half of the 18th Century," *Smith College Studies in History,* XV (1920–1930), pp. 7–92.

Carande, Ramón. "Colección de Manuscritos é Impresos de Juan Sempere Guarinos," *Boletín de la Real Academia de la Historia,* Vol. CXXXVII, no. 2 (1955), pp. 247–313.

Christelow, Allan. "Great Britain and the Trade from Cadiz and Lisbon to Spanish America and Brazil: 1759–1783," *Hispanic American Historical Review,* XXVII (February, 1947), pp. 2–29.

Cobos Cárdenas, Eduardo. "Joseph Gabriel de Mora: Una Nota para el Estudio de las Ideas sobre Política Industrial en el Siglo XVIII," *Anales de Economía* (January–March, 1947).

Dominguez Ortiz, Antonio. "El Ocaso del Régimen Señorial en la España del Siglo XVIII," *Revista Internacional de Sociología,* X (1952), 139–180.

Echegary, Julia María. "Los Talleres Reales de Ebanistería, Bronces y Bordados," *Archivo Español de Arte,* Vol. XXVIII, no. 111 (1955), pp. 237–259.

Felix, David. "Profit Inflation and Industrial Growth: The Historical Record and Contemporary Analogies," *Quarterly Journal of Economics,* LXX (August, 1956), 441–463.

Hamilton, Earl J. "The Decline of Spain," *Economic History Review,* VIII (1937–1938), 168–179.

———. "The First Twenty Years of the Bank of Spain," *Journal of Political Economy,* LIV (1946), 17–37, 116–140.

———. "The Foundations of the Bank of Spain," *Journal of Political Economy,* LIII (1945), 97–114.

———. "Monetary Disorders and Economic Decadence in Spain: 1651–1700," *Journal of Political Science,* LI (1943), 477–493.

———. "Monetary Problems in Spain and South America: 1751–1800," *Journal of Economic History*, IV–V (1944–1945), 21–48.

———. "Recovery in Spain Under the First Bourbon: 1701–1746," *Journal of Modern History*, XV (1943), 192–206.

———. "War and Inflation in Spain: 1780–1800," *Quarterly Journal of Economics*, LIX (1944–1945), 36–77.

Kessel, R. A., and A. A. Alchian. "The Meaning and Validity of the Inflation-Induced Lag of Wages Behind Prices," *American Economic Review*, Vol. L, no. 1 (March, 1960), pp. 43–66.

Nef, John U. "Prices and Industrial Capitalism in France and England, 1540–1640," *Economic History Review*, VII (1936–1937), 155–185.

Pérez Rioja, Antonio. "La Protección del Libro Bajo Carlos III: Dos Reales Cédulas de 1778 y otra de 1780," *Revista de Archivos, Bibliotecas y Museos*, Vol. LIX, nos. 1–3 (1953), pp. 248–249.

"Sobre la Decadencia Económica de España," *De Economía*, Vol. VI, no. 11 (1952), pp. 483–816.

Viaje de Campomanes a Extremadura," *Revista de Estudios Extremeños* (September–December, 1949), 199–246.

Vigil Alvárez, Fausto. "La Minería en Siero," *Boletín del Instituto de Estudios Asturianos*, Vol. VIII, no. 22 (1954), 236–252.

Vilar, Pierre. "Dans Barcelone, au XVIIIᵉ Siecle: Transformations Économiques, Élan Urbain et Mouvement des Salaires dans de Bâtiment," *Estudios Históricos y Documentos de los Archivos de Protocolos, Colegio Notarial de Barcelona*, II (1950), 47–48.

Viñas Mey, Carmelo. "Las Compañías de Comercio y el Resurgimiento Industrial de España en el Siglo XVIII," *Revista Nacional de Economía*, Vol. XII (1922).

UNPUBLISHED

ARCHIVES

Archivo del Colegio del Arte Mayor de la Seda de Valencia [cited as ACSV]
> *Libros de Cuenta y Razón (Mayorales)*: nos. 20, 21, 22, 23, 24. *Libros de Bolla*: no. 6. *Varios*: legs. 1, nos. 1, 3, 6; 3, no. 3. *Mano de Anotaciónes. Manuscritos Sobrantes*: no. 11. *Valeros y Pregones*: no. 13. *Pragmáticas y Reales Cédulas*: no. 1. *Reales Cédulas*: no. 2. *Memoriales*. Alcazde Miranda, Rosario. Unpublished and untitled dissertation for the degree of Doctor of Philosophy and Letters, University of Valencia. February, 1949.

Archivo de la Corona de Aragón, *Real Audiencia* [cited as ACA]
> *Acordadas*, nos. 382, 383, 384, 385, 387, 390, 558, 559, 561, 563, 565, 566, 568, 569, 570, 571, 572, 573, 574, 577, 586, 587; *Diversorium*, nos. 492, 868, 869, 870, 871, 872, 873, 874, 875, 876, 878, 879, 880, 881, 882, 883, 884, 885, 886, 887, 888, 889, 890, 901, 902,

903, 904, 1183, 1184, 1185, 1186, 1187, 1188, 1189, 1190, 1191, 1192, 1193, 1194, 1195, 1196, 1197, 1198, 1199, 1208; *Consultas,* nos. 464, 466, 467, 814.

Archivo General de Simancas [cited as AGS]

Secretaría de Hacienda, legs. 632, 633, 634, 635, 636, 755, 756, 757, 758, 759, 760, 761, 762, 763, 764, 765, 766, 767, 768, 769, 770, 771, 772, 773, 774, 775, 776, 777, 778, 779, 780, 781, 782, 783, 784, 785, 786, 787, 788, 789, 790, 791, 792, 793, 802, 852, 853, 855, 856, 857, 1115; *Intendencia de Ejército:* legs. 539–582; *Intendencia de Provincias:* legs. 583–599; *Dirección General de Rentas: Circulares:* nos. 1, 2, 3; *Correspondencias,* nos. 6, 7, 11, 12, 13; *Informes,* nos. 29–223. *Superintendencia de Hacienda: Rentas Generales, Sección 22:* legs. 1062, 1063, 1064, 1065, 1066, 1067, 1068, 1069, 1070, 1115, 1358; *Rentas Provinciales:* legs. 1391, 1410, 1411–1415, 1416–1418, 1419–1428, 1429–1434, 1435–1445, 1446–1456, 1457–1477, 1478–1518, 1519–1524, 1525–1537, 1538–1546, 1547–1552, 1553–1565, 1566, 1567–1575, 1576–1586, 1587–1592, 1593–1598, 1599–1604, 1605–1668, 1669–1673, 1674–1677, 1678–1700, 1701–1709, 1710–1723, 1724–1736, 1737–1738.

Archivo Histórico Muncipal de Barcelona [cited as AHMB]

Catastro, Gremio de Texedores de Velos de Seda: 1750, 1752, 1754, 1756, 1758, 1760, 1762, 1764, 1766, 1768, 1770, 1772, 1774, 1776, 1778, 1780, 1782, 1784, 1786, 1788, 1790, 1792, 1794, 1796, 1798, 1800; *Gremio de Terciopeleros:* 1750, 1752, 1754, 1756, 1758, 1760, 1762, 1764, 1766, 1768, 1770, 1772, 1774, 1776, 1778, 1780, 1782, 1784, 1786, 1788, 1790, 1792, 1794, 1796, 1798, 1800; *Gremio de Barreteros Fabricantes de Medias, y démas Maniobras de Aguja:* 1750, 1752, 1754, 1756, 1758, 1760, 1762, 1766, 1768, 1770, 1772, 1774, 1776, 1778, 1780, 1782, 1784, 1786, 1788, 1790, 1792, 1794, 1796, 1798, 1800; *Gremio de Galoneros:* 1750, 1752, 1754, 1756, 1758, 1760, 1762, 1764, 1766, 1768, 1770, 1772, 1774, 1776, 1778, 1780, 1782, 1784, 1786, 1788, 1790, 1792, 1794, 1796, 1798, 1800; *Gremio de Torcedores de Seda:* 1750, 1752, 1754, 1756, 1758, 1760, 1762, 1764, 1766, 1768, 1770, 1772, 1774, 1776, 1778, 1780, 1782, 1784, 1786, 1790, 1792, 1794, 1796, 1798, 1800; *Gremio de Texedores de Lino:* 1750, 1752, 1754, 1756, 1758, 1760, 1762, 1764, 1766, 1768, 1770, 1772, 1774, 1776, 1778, 1780, 1782, 1784, 1786, 1788, 1790, 1792, 1794, 1796, 1798, 1800; *Gremio de Pelayres:* 1750, 1752, 1754, 1756, 1758, 1760, 1762, 1764, 1766, 1768, 1770, 1772, 1774, 1776, 1778, 1780, 1782, 1784, 1786, 1788, 1790, 1792, 1794, 1796, 1798, 1800; *Gremio de Texedores de Lana:* 1750, 1752, 1754, 1756, 1758, 1760, 1762, 1764, 1766, 1768, 1770, 1772, 1774, 1776, 1778, 1780, 1782, 1784, 1786, 1788, 1790, 1792, 1794, 1796, 1798, 1800. *Junta General de Comercio:* Vols. I–LXXX.

Archivo Histórico Municipal de Barcelona, *Depósito Santa Cruz* [cited as AHMB, Santa Cruz]

Comercial: Cota B, nos. 35, 36, 64, 116–146, 228–286. *Judicial Corregidor.*

Archivo Histórico Nacional [cited as AHN]

> *Consejo:* legs. 41066, 41067, 50134, 50135, 51501, 51522, 51523, 51524, 51525, 51527, 53176, 53179; *Consejo, Libros de Sala de Alcalde de Casa y Corte [Libros de Govierno]:* 1675, fol. 1; 1682, fol. 309; 1714–1715, Tomo 3, fol. 293; 1725; fol. 178; 1739, fols. 297–304; 1752, fols. 270–274; 1757, fol. 347; 1759, fols. 231–232; 1760, fols. 127–129; 1761, fols. 600–602; 1766, Tomo I, fols. 388–396; 1768, fols. 391–399; 1770, fols. 331–334, 582–583; 1771, fols. 68–73, 74–82, 329–340, 412–420, 498–505, 582–583; 1772, fols. 414–426; 1773, fols. 297–317; 1774, fols. 616–619; 1776, fols. 467–483; 1779, fols. 292, 794–798; 1782, fols. 567–569; 1783, fols. 521–524, 748–752; 1784, Tomo II, fols. 332–337, 338–343, 590–594; 1785, Tomo II, fols. 382, 391, 480, 491; 1786, fols. 1340–1344; 1787, Tomo II, fols. 827–832, 1114–1117; 1789, fols. 682–695, 976–981; 1791, fols. 31–36; 1793, fols. 801–805, 821–829; 1801, fols. 1214, 1216; 1802, fols. 1892–1901. *Documentos Curiosos:* 17808, no. 166. *Biblioteca: Colección de Reales Cédulas:* 1742, Vol. II–1801, Vol. XXVI.

Archivo del Ministerio de Hacienda [cited as AMH]

> *Colección de Órdenes Generales de Rentas:* III, 126–127; VII, 412–435; VIII, 95, 192, 222, 270; X, 23, 27, 28, 35–36, 86, 98, 106–107, 112, 114, 170–176, 194–201, 269–271, 279–280, 285, 289–292, 323, 358–359, 369, 380, 381, 418–419; XI, 19–26, 43, 99–100, 105–106, 182–183, 230, 240, 242, 285, 288–289, 293, 295–296, 297–298, 303–305, 307–310, 311–315, 319–320, 321, 348, 372–383, 406, 412–414, 416, 421, 423, 434–439, 442, 481, 484, 517; XII, 1–2, 19–20, 83–84, 159–177, 203–204, 205–212, 213, 237–250, 257, 273, 299–300, 326–327, 367–368, 452–457, 458–460, 479–484, 624–629; XIII, 6, 21–22, 58, 65–66, 67–68, 73–75, 78, 83–91, 109–112, 138–139, 148–149, 184–186, 272–274, 276–279, 326–334, 378, 416–417, 478–479; XIV, 90–97, 102, 110–111, 116–117, 124–127, 132–133, 164–173, 174–175, 216–217, 250, 333–334, 415–455; XV, 3–4, 29–33, 38–39, 95–96, 225, 332–333, 492–495, 628; XVI, 21, 101–102, 113, 115–118, 162, 180, 222, 248–249, 279–281; XVII, 172, 228, 288–289, 310–311, 318, 358–359; XVIII, 11–12, 25–28, 50–51, 77, 159–169, 194–197, 216–239, 241–242, 251–252, 292, 299–302, 313–317, 327, 342–356, 440–442, 444–445, 527–536; XIX, 67–71, 87–88, 97–104, 105–108, 337, 370, 376; XX, 84–86, 102–103, 150–153, 156–159, 214–215, 247, 252, 296–302, 304–309, 328–329, 340–349, 391–394, 395–399, 400, 429, 433, 479–481, 489–492, 529–530, 562–563, 615; XXI, 27–28, 29–33, 45–49, 116, 123–124, 157–158, 179, 191–196, 211–212, 291–294, 313–318, 329, 421–423, 437–440, 474–476; XXII, 45–47, 51–55, 109–110, 203–209, 215–216, 285–288, 293–295, 323–332, 349, 351–356, 371–375, 377–383, 501–512, 556, 568–

G, 7418; Galicia, G, 7421, 7425, 7427, 7429, 7434, 7437; Guada-laxara, G, 7449; Jaen, G, 7452; Leon, G, 7457; Madrid (province only), G, 7463; La Mancha, G, 7465; Murcia, G, 7469; Palencia, G, 7472; Salamanca, G, 7476; Segovia, G, 7482; Sevilla, G, 7493; Soria, G, 7489; Toro, G, 7503; Valladolid, G, 7505; Zamora, G. 7508.

LIBRARIES, MANUSCRIPT SECTIONS

Biblioteca Nacional, *Sección de Manuscritos* [cited as BN]
    MSS 2349, 2350, 6389, 9400, 10695, 13005, 13006, 14497, 18735.
Biblioteca Centra de Barcelona, *Sección de Manuscritos* [cited as BCB]
    Real Junta Particular de Comercio de Barcelona [cited as *Junta de Comercio*]: legs. 12, 23, 30, 32, 33, 39, 51, 52, 53, 57, 65, 68, 104, 133. Jaime Caresmar. *Discurso sobre la Agricultura, Comercio y Industria, con Inclusión de la Consistencia y Estado en que se Halla cada Partido ó Veguería de los que Componen el Princi-pado de Cataluña. 1780.* (Handwritten)

INDEX

Index

Abancino, Antonio, 43
Abbeville, 31
Abrantes, Duke of, 116n
Academia de Agricultura at Lerida, 158
Academy of Fine Arts of Saint Ferdinand, 160n
Academy of History, 160n
"Additions" (*agregados*), 134n
Africa, 64
Alava, 134n. *See also* Basque provinces
Alberoni, Cardinal, 31n
Alcabala and *cientos*, 37, 58, 152; origin of, 110; nature of, 110, 130; harshness of, 116, 119, 130, 132; abolition of, 120; reform of rates, 121–122, 128, 131; concessions of 1752, 123; concessions of 1753, 123–124; concessions of 1756, 125; concessions of 1779, 125–127; exemptions from, 130
Alcabala de alta mar, 110n
Alchian, A. A., 164n
Alcova de Medina, Pedro Thomas de, 63
Alcoy, production of woolens at, 21, 26
Alfonso XI, 110
Alicante, 134n, 137n, 139
Almarzo, Royal Factory for Serges at, 30, 36, 39, 44, 46n
Almojarifazgo, 134n
Alsace-Lorraine, production of cottons in, 7
Ambassadors as recruiters of foreign artisans, 69, 70, 73
America, 23, 148; linens exported to, 24
American colonies: rise in population of, 165; as market for Spanish products, 166; control of trade with, 166
American commerce: limitations on, 3, 136–137; liberalization of, 137, 139, 140, 181
American market during wars, 177
American ports, 52

Andalusia, 111n, 134n, 164n, 166, 171, 172, 173, 175
Andujar, 116n
Apprentices: at Valencia, 13; in province of Segovia, 24, at Leon, 25; and masters, 89; regulation of, 89; admittance to guild as, 92; removal of restrictions from, 99–100, 107. *See also* Craft guilds; Guilds
Apprenticeship, 77
Aragon, 86, 134n, 166, 167, 171, 174, 175, 176; silk production in, 8, 26; cotton production in, 18n; woolen production in, 21, 26; linen production in, 24; Royal Company of Commerce and Factories of, 54, 55n, 61, 64, 65, 104; taxes in, 114, 116; autonomy of, 167, 178; Imperial Canal of, 174, 175
Aranda, Count of, 170n
Aranjuez, 173
Arbitrio, 116
Archduke Charles of Austria, 167
Argumosa, Bentura, 74n
Arkwright, Richard, 85
Asia, 142
Asturias, 134n, 175; linen production in, 24; nobility in, 168
Atlantic Ocean, 175
Avila, city of: cotton production at, 18, 26; Royal Factory for Woolens at, 30, 36, 39, 44, 46n, 47, 82; Royal Factory for Cottons at, 30, 34, 35, 36, 37, 40, 44, 46, 47, 49; woolen production at, 39
Avila, province of: woolen production in, 21, 26; linen production in, 24
Azeca, Castle of, 31n

Baeza, 158
Balance of trade, 2
Bank of Spain, 162